NATIONAL LIBRARY SERVICE FOR THE BLIND AND PHYSICALLY HANDICAPPED

LIBRARY OF CONGRESS

AN INTRODUCTION TO BRAILLE MATHEMATICS

by

HELEN ROBERTS

BERNARD M. KREBS

BARBARA TAFFET

Based on
the Nemeth Braille Code for Mathematics
and Science Notation, 1972

LIBRARY OF CONGRESS

WASHINGTON

1978

Library of Congress Cataloging in Publication Data

Roberts, Helen.

    An introduction to Braille mathematics.

At head of title: National Library Service for the Blind and Physically Handicapped, Library of Congress.

    Includes index.
    Supt. of Docs. no.: LC 19.2:M42

    1. Blind—Printing and writing systems. 2. Mathematical notation. I. Krebs, Bernard Marvin, 1911—joint author. II. Taffet, Barbara, joint author. III. Nemeth, Abraham. The Nemeth Braille code for mathematics and science notation. IV. National Library Service for the Blind and Physically Handicapped. V. Title.

[HV1672.R53]   510'.1'48   76-608128

ISBN 0-8444-0190-0

TABLE OF CONTENTS

FOREWORD

An Introduction to Braille Mathematics has been designed as an easily assimilated presentation of the special symbols and complex rules and procedures laid down in the **Nemeth Code for Mathematics and Science Notation.** Lessons and exercises have been arranged in a smooth, step-by-step progression; wherever possible, rules and guidelines have been couched in familiar terms rather than the highly technical vocabulary of the mathematics expert. This style of presentation should enable the braille transcriber with a general knowledge of mathematical notation to become fully conversant with the provisions of the code and to make a meaningful contribution in this vital area of specialized service.

The opportunity for blind persons to achieve their educational and professional goals depends to a great extent on the availability of basic texts and reference material in a suitable medium. A well-trained braille transcriber is the prime resource in the production of textbook material. The National Library Service for the Blind and Physically Handicapped, formerly the Division for the Blind and Physically Handicapped, Library of Congress, has lent its support and encouragement in the development and publication of this comprehensive manual as an expression of its gratitude to the volunteers for their indispensable services in helping blind individuals reach their highest potential.

Work on this manual was begun under the inspired leadership of Helen Roberts, whose thorough expertise was gained through firsthand experience in the development of the Nemeth code. Helen's warmth and dedication as a volunteer transcriber and exceptional teacher touched everyone she met. Her untimely death halfway through this project was, and still is, felt as a cruel loss by all who knew her. We dedicate this book to her memory, which will live on in the work of those who serve and in the lives of those who are being served by her endeavors.

By good fortune, Barbara Taffet, a friend, associate, and student of Helen's, stepped forward to fill the void. Her understanding of the Nemeth code and her painstaking efforts have carried this work to completion; her service to transcribers and blind people is worthy of the highest praise.

For their invaluable assistance, we gratefully acknowledge:

The late Robert S. Bray, former Chief of the Division for the Blind and Physically Handicapped, and Frank Kurt Cylke, Director of the National Library Service for the Blind and Physically Handicapped, for their devotion to expanding the horizons of blind people through the written word and for their active support of this publication;

Donna Pastore, for contributing her knowledge and expertise while working closely with the authors;

Maxine B. Dorf and Alice Mann, for their suggestions and evaluation on the work in progress;

Virginia Brooks Scharoff, for her generous and far-reaching support, cooperation, and encouragement;

Kay Hollander, Deborah Gordon, Nancy Schattner, and Beatrice Scheps, for their competent and rigorous service in preparing working drafts of the manuscript for publication;

The Pinellas Braille Group of St. Petersburg, Fla., Volunteer Braille Services of Washington, D.C., the Industrial Home for the Blind, and the Jewish Guild for the Blind, for lending their staff, equipment, and facilities to aid in preparation of this manuscript.

Bernard M. Krebs, Librarian
Jewish Guild for the Blind

CERTIFICATION

The Course

The homework exercises in this manual are designed to prepare certified literary braillists for the Library of Congress examination leading to certification in braille mathematics transcribing. Students may study independently, train under the supervision of a qualified braille mathematics instructor, or enroll in the Library of Congress free correspondence course.

Students enrolled in this correspondence course complete the homework exercises and return them for review and evaluation by an instructor at the Library of Congress. After the exercises have been reviewed, the instructor returns a detailed report pointing out errors, making helpful comments, and giving a new assignment.

The Application

Candidates may use the application on page **vii** of this manual to enroll in the free correspondence course or to apply directly for the examination and certification in braille mathematics. Students wishing to enroll should complete the homework exercises for **Lesson 1** and return them with the application form to the Library of Congress.

Mailing

Please pack exercises and test materials between sheets of cardboard and return them in a large envelope. Do not fold pages, and be sure that test pages are packed in proper order and securely tied. Send all materials to Volunteer Training Section, National Library Service for the Blind and Physically Handicapped, Library of Congress, Washington, D.C. 20542. The instructor will return reports and materials submitted with an addressed postage-free mailing label.

APPLICATION

Date_____

I hereby request that (check appropriate box):

☐ I be enrolled in the Library of Congress correspondence course in the transcription of braille mathematics.

☐ My test in the transcription of braille mathematics be examined for certification.

Name in full_____
(Indicate whether Mr., Miss, or Mrs.   If married, give husband's initials)

Address_____

_____
ZIP

Telephone number (give area code)_____

Name as it should appear on certificate (please print)

_____

Date of certification in literary braille at the Library of Congress_____

Approximate number of braille pages you have transcribed:

    Literary braille_____

    Mathematics braille_____

Are you familiar with textbook format?   Yes_____   No_____

Group affiliated with_____
(If enrolling in correspondence course, put Library of Congress)

    Address of group_____

    _____

    Name of group chairman_____

    Signed_____

LESSON 1

ORIENTATION

§1. Philosophy: The braille code for mathematics is especially designed for the representation and transcription of mathematical and scientific notation. Its purpose is to convey, as accurately as possible, a clear conception of the printed text to the braille reader. Using braille indicators in conjunction with the 63 braille characters, this code is capable of providing equivalent symbols for the hundreds of mathematical and scientific ink-print signs now in use and yet to be devised. The one-to-one correspondence between braille and ink-print symbols makes it possible to produce an accurate transference from ink-print to braille or from braille to ink-print.

§2. Nontechnical and Technical Texts:

a. Nontechnical Texts: For the purposes of the Nemeth code, a nontechnical text is any work in which no mathematical or scientific notation appears. Such texts must be transcribed in accordance with the rules of English braille.

b. Partially Technical Texts: A partially technical text is a science book or a work which utilizes a small number of mathematical symbols. Such texts must be transcribed according to the rules of English braille. However, when the replacement of symbols by words is not practical or possible, or when the mathematical display is used for solving equations or performing computations, the symbols and rules of the Nemeth code must be used, and the braille reader must be so advised. A list of the special symbols being used must be placed at the beginning of each braille volume in which they occur.

c. Technical Texts: A technical text is a work in the field of mathematics, statistics, physics, or chemistry. Such texts must be transcribed entirely according to the rules of the Nemeth code. The symbols and rules of the Nemeth code must also be used in works in other fields which make substantial use of mathematical or scientific notation. Since several revisions of the Nemeth code are in use, a transcriber's note stating that the text is transcribed in Nemeth code and giving the year the code was adopted must be included at the beginning of each volume.

NUMERALS AND THE NUMERIC INDICATOR

§3. Representation of Arabic Numerals: In the transcription of a technical text, digits are represented in two ways:

a. English Braille Numerals: English braille numerals represented by the letters "a" through "j" must be used for all Arabic numerals appearing on title pages, except those used in conjunction with mathematical symbols. English braille numerals must also be used for page numbers at the corners of pages and at the ends of page-separation lines.

b. Nemeth Code Numerals: In the Nemeth code, the 10 Arabic digits are represented by the letters "a" through "j" dropped to the lower part of the braille cell. Except as stated in **a** above, Nemeth code numerals must be used to represent all Arabic numerals in the body of the print text, forewords, contents pages, introductions, bibliographies, and indexes. They must also be used for all chapter, theorem, exercise, problem, and page-reference numbers.

1	2	3	4	5	6	7	8	9	0

§4. **Numeric Indicator:**

In a technical text, the numeric indicator must be used before a numeral following a space or occurring at the beginning of a braille line. However, the numeric indicator must not be used after a space intentionally inserted to divide a numeral into short regular groups of digits.

(1) 7

(2) 32

(3) 5980

(4) 9 inches and 15 inches are 2 feet.

(5) 931684572 can be divided into groups of three digits each: 931 684 572

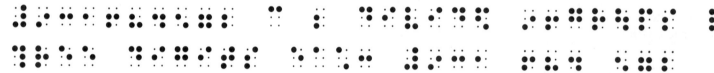

PUNCTUATION MARKS AND THE PUNCTUATION INDICATOR

§5. **Punctuation:** Unless otherwise stated, words and English braille numerals must be punctuated according to the rules of English braille. Mathematical expressions such as Nemeth code numerals, mathematical symbols, etc. must be punctuated in accordance with the rules of Nemeth code.

§6. **Punctuation Marks and Use of the Punctuation Indicator:** Since numerals and punctuation marks are represented by identical lower-cell braille symbols, the punctuation indicator ⠰ must be used before one or before a sequence of two or more of the punctuation marks listed below when they *follow* a numeral or any other mathematical expression.

Punctuation Indicator

Punctuation Marks

    Apostrophe   '

    Colon   :

    Exclamation Point   !

    Period   .

Question Mark	?	⠦

Quotation Marks

Outer (opening and closing)	" "	⠦ ⠴
Inner (opening and closing)	' '	⠠⠦ ⠴⠄

Semicolon	;	⠆

(1) 5 and 3 are 8; 5 and 13 are 18.

(2) "Do 6 and 4 equal 10?"

§7. **Punctuation Marks and Nonuse of the Punctuation Indicator:**

Punctuation Marks

Hyphen	-	⠤
Dash (short)	—	⠤⠤
Comma		
Literary	,	⠂
Mathematical		
American*	,	⠠
Continental*	.	⠠

*Although the symbols for the American and Continental commas differ in print, the difference is not shown in braille. A transcriber's note must be included at the beginning of the braille text to inform the reader of the Continental usage in the ink-print edition.

a. **Hyphen and Dash:** The punctuation indicator must not be used before the hyphen or the dash. Unless otherwise stated, a word or part of a word joined to a numeral by the hyphen or the dash must be contracted and punctuated according to the rules of English braille. A space must be left between a hyphen and an adjoining dash.

(1) He bought a 6-cent stamp.

(2) An octagon is 8-sided.

(3) 1-ary is the same as unary.

(4) 12—one dozen—costs 48 cents.

(5) It is 5- —as shown—not 6-sided.

b. Mathematical Comma: The mathematical comma  must be used for a comma occurring in a long numeral or following a numeral or other mathematical expression.   The punctuation indicator must not be used before the mathematical comma.

(1) In 1,234,567, 1, 3, 5, and 7 are odd numbers.

(2) Add: 10, 20, and 30.

(3) Chapter 5, Exercise 2, Page 23.

(4) 1·935

(the Continental comma is shown in print)

Note: In a sequence of punctuation marks, the punctuation indicator must precede the first punctuation mark following a mathematical expression.   However, it is omitted before the mathematical comma, the hyphen, or the dash.

(5) 6-, 7-, and 8-sided figures.

(6) It is "plus 3," not "minus 3."

(7) In "Figure 4", find the area.

(8) "The answer is 10—," he paused.

⠦⠠⠮ ⠁⠝⠎⠺⠻ ⠊⠎ ⠼⠁⠚⠤⠂⠴ ⠓⠑ ⠏⠁⠥⠎⠂

c. Literary Comma: The literary comma ⠂ must be used when a comma follows a word, an English braille numeral, or any other literary expression. The punctuation indicator must not be used before the literary comma.

(1) The polygon is 5-sided, not 6-sided.

(2) The sum, 4,426, is correct.

(3) Six-, seven-, and eight-sided figures.

(4) "We paused—," he said.

(5) Copyright 1958, 1962, and 1970.

(numerals on a title page)

INTRODUCTION TO SIGNS OF OPERATION

§8. **Signs of Operation:** A few signs of operation and their braille equivalents are listed below. Since the minus sign and the hyphen are represented by the same symbol in both print and braille, the student must determine the meaning of the symbols from their context.

Plus	$+$	⠬
Minus	$-$	⠤
Multiplication (times)		
Cross (Cartesian product)	$\times$	⠈⠡
Dot	$\cdot$	⠡
Division (divided by)	$\div$	⠨⠌
Plus or Minus	$\pm$	⠬⠤

Minus or Plus	$\mp$	⠲⠖
Plus Followed by Minus	$+\,-$	⠖⠤
Minus Followed by Plus	$-\,+$	⠤⠖
Minus Followed by Minus	$-\,-$	⠤⠤

§9. Spacing and Punctuation With Signs of Operation: Unless otherwise stated, a sign of operation must be unspaced from its related mathematical terms. A sign of operation is a mathematical symbol and must be punctuated accordingly.

(1) What does $16 + 4 + 100$ equal?

(2) Add: $6 + 4$, $5 + 3$, and $10 + 2$.

(3) $9 - 3 - 2$

(4) $5 \times 6 \times 10$

(5) $5 \cdot 6 \cdot 10$

(6) $24 \div 3 + 2$

(7) 38 ± 7

(8) 38 ∓ 7

(9) $10 + - 5$

(10) $10 - + 5$

(11) What is the meaning of $+, -, \times$?

(12) The symbol for "plus" is "$+$."

§10. Signs of Comparison: A few signs of comparison and their braille equivalents are listed below.

Equals	$=$	
Greater Than (is greater than)		
With Straight Sides	$>$	
With Curved Sides	$\succ$	
Less Than (is less than)		
With Straight Sides	$<$	
With Curved Sides	$\prec$	
Proportion (as)	$::$	
Ratio (is to)	$:$	

§11. Spacing and Punctuation With Signs of Comparison: A space must be left between a sign of comparison and a sign of operation or any other expression which precedes or follows it. A sign of comparison is a mathematical symbol and must be punctuated accordingly. A space must not be left between a sign of comparison and a punctuation mark which applies to it.

(1) Can $3 \pm 1 = +4$ and $+2$?

(2) $19 + 6 = 25$

(3) $7 > 4 > 3$

(4) $7 \succ 4 \succ 3$

(5) $8 + 10 < 19$

(6) $5 \prec 9 \prec 11$

(7) $2 : 4 :: 6 : 12$

(8) Use =, >, or <.

⠿⠿⠿ (braille)

(9) What is the meaning of the sign "="?

⠿⠿⠿ (braille)

<h1 style="text-align:center">FORMAT</h1>

§12. General Rules for Format: The principles provided in the *Code of Braille Textbook Formats and Techniques* should be followed unless specific format provisions are given in the braille code for mathematics. In the transcription of technical texts, a 41-cell braille line is recommended.

§13. Margins for Itemized Material With No Subdivisions:

a. When unsubdivided itemized material, including exercises or outlines, is numbered or lettered, the number or letter must begin in cell 1, and all runovers must begin in cell 3. If the material contains more than one paragraph, each new paragraph must begin in cell 5, and any runovers must begin in cell 3.

(1)

> 9
>
> 1.   If gasoline costs 42 cents a gallon, what will 1,425 gallons cost?
>
> 2.   At 60 cents a dozen, how much should 7 eggs cost?
>
>   Think: "What is 60 ÷ 12?" Is the answer 5? Then what is 7×5?

b. When unsubdivided itemized material is arranged side by side across the page in print, the braille format must be changed so that all numbers or letters start in cell 1.

(1)

1. 30×90	2. 71×300	3. $90 \div 2$
4. $382 + 802$	5. $568 - 392$	6. $147 - 26$

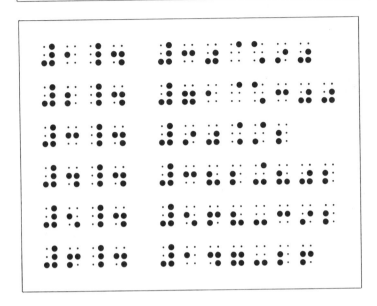

§14. Division of Mathematical Expressions Between Braille Lines:

a. A mathematical expression, such as a long numeral or an equation, must not be divided between braille lines or braille pages. If there is insufficient space on a line to accommodate the expression, this space must be left blank, and the entire expression must be brought down to the next line.

b. A hyphenated expression, such as "6-sided," containing one or more mathematical components must not be divided between braille lines or braille pages.

HOMEWORK

Prepare the homework for each lesson in the following way:

(1) Use 11 by $11\frac{1}{2}$-inch paper, and braille across the $11\frac{1}{2}$-inch width of the page.

(2) Use 41 cells and 25 lines.

(3) Treat the word EXERCISE and the appropriate exercise number as a heading. Center it on the first line of the first page of the homework. Skip a line after the heading and start the first problem on line 3. The work on all succeeding pages should begin on line 1.

(4) Write your name and address in print and in braille on the final page of each exercise. If space does not permit, attach a separate page with this information.

(5) Page numbers at the upper right-hand corners and at the ends of new page separation lines should correspond to the print page numbers on which the homework exercises appear. If more than one braille page is required to complete one print page, the page number should be preceded by the letters "a," "b," etc. The running braille page numbers appearing in the lower right-hand corners of the braille pages should be numbered consecutively, starting with number 1 in each lesson. When there is room to start a new ink-print page in the middle of a braille page, this should be done. **Note:** The upper-cell numerals of English braille must be used for page number designations in accordance with §3a.

1. I paid 90 cents for 12 oranges and found that 3 of them were spoiled. How much did each good orange cost?

2. He came to see us for 10 minutes, and left at 3 o'clock.

3. Round 374 and 962 to the nearest ten.

4. Use figures to write the following number: 5 billion, 703 million, 5 thousand.

5. 24 is a common multiple of 4 and 6. What is the least common multiple of 4 and 6?
    What is a common multiple of 3, 5, and 6? What is the least common multiple?

6. If 72813654 is written as 72 81 36 54, explain why it is easy to tell that this number is divisible by the digit 9.

7. Read Chapter 10, Section 15, Examples 4 through 10, Page 136.

8. Read the numbers: 48,530,000; 39,037,602,385; 9,402,061.

9. Write these numbers: 12, 379, 500, 333, 2,000, 1,250,794.

10. Find the average of 150, 245, 410, and 1,296.

11. Arrange the numbers in descending order: 12, 10, 2, 1, 3, 6, 9, 4, 11, 5, 7, 8.

12. What is 6,671,873 rounded to the nearest hundred thousand: 6,600,000 or 6,700,000?

13. John said, "If 13 and 4 are 17, then 14 and 3 are 17." Is he correct?

14. To solve the problem, do we "add 300," or do we "take away 300"?

15. How much less than 63 is 42? Mary first said, "The answer is 11", and then she said "No, it is 21." Which is correct?

16. How many minutes are there in a 24-hour day?

17. If 1-ary and unary are the same, are 2-ary and binary the same? What is the same as 3-ary?

18. Is the answer 36—or 37—cents a dozen?

19. Is 1971 a 2-, 3-, or 4-place number?

20. Write the largest 3-digit, 4-digit, and 5-digit numbers you know.

21. Name six-, seven-, and eight-sided figures.

22. Tell the meaning of each of the following signs: $+$, $-$, $\times$, $\cdot$, $\div$, $\pm$, $\mp$, $+-$, $-+$.

23. Add: $1943 + 462 + 92 + 233 + 4 + 78$.

24. If $5 + 10$ equals 15, what does $10 + 5$ equal?

25. Does $5 - 2$ name a whole number? $9 - 6$?

26. Add or subtract as the signs tell you: $6942 + 3819$; $294,107 + 365,904$; $10,259 - 7386$; $362 - 41$.

27. If 100×4 equals 400, what does 100×5 equal? 100×6? 100×7?

28. Instead of using the symbol "$\times$" to indicate multiplication, we can use a dot "$\cdot$". For example, 37×52 can be expressed as $37 \cdot 52$.

   Use the dot to write 19×17.

29. What is $21 \div 7$?

30. What is $115 \div 7$?

31. What is $100 \div 10$?

32. What is $1000 \div 10$?

33. Do as the signs tell you: 948×67; 348×521; $1750 \div 15$; $4321 \div 1000$.

34. What are the least and greatest values of 4 ± 1, 400 ± 10, 6 ∓ 1, 600 ∓ 10?

35. Does $20 + - 5$ have meaning?

36. What does $50 - + 5$ mean?

37. Tell the meaning of each of the following: $=$, $>$, $\succ$, $<$, $\prec$, $\therefore$, $\because$

38. If $5 + 10 = 15$, then does $15 - 10 = 5$?

39. If $10 \times 10 \times 10 = 1000$, what does $10 \times 10 \times 10 \times 10$ equal?

40. Is $16 > 9$?

42. Is $6 + 3 < 7$?

41. Is $3 > 8$?

43. Is $14 - 12 < 1$?

44. Are $5 : 2$, $10 : 4$, and $15 : 16$ equivalent ratios?

45. Are the following sentences true or false:
   $8 : 5 :: 40 : 25$; $4 : 9 :: 10 : 50$; $260 : 52 :: 10 : 2$?

LESSON 2

NUMERALS AND THE NUMERIC INDICATOR (CONTINUED)

§15. Numeric Indicator and Punctuation Marks:

a. The numeric indicator must be used after a hyphen connecting a numeral to a preceding word or punctuation mark.

   (1) hydrogen-3

   (2) 1-to-1 correspondence

   (3) He lived from 1885?-1946.

b. The numeric indicator must not be used after a hyphen connecting a numeral to a preceding numeral or other mathematical expression, or after the mathematical comma in a long numeral. The numeric indicator must be used in all other instances when a numeral follows a punctuation mark.

   (1) Do exercises 1-9 and 35-45.

   (2) The marks ranged from 65-100.

   (3) 1,674,932

   (4) "12 dozen"

   (5) "4 + 4" is another name for '8'.

   (6) '71

   (7) He arrived at 7:45.

   (8) 7:45-8:45

(9) The answer—25—is correct.

⠀⠀⠀⠀⠀⠀⠀⠀⠀⠀⠀⠀⠀⠀⠀⠀

(10) 50—60

⠀⠀⠀⠀⠀⠀⠀⠀⠀⠀

§16. Numeric Indicator With the Minus Sign: The numeric indicator must be used before a numeral following a minus sign when the minus sign follows a space or a punctuation mark, or begins a braille line.

(1) Is —5 a negative number?

⠀⠀⠀⠀⠀⠀⠀⠀⠀⠀⠀⠀⠀⠀⠀⠀⠀⠀⠀⠀

(2) Is —6 < —1?

⠀⠀⠀⠀⠀⠀⠀⠀⠀⠀⠀⠀

(3) ±5 means +5 and —5.

⠀⠀⠀⠀⠀⠀⠀⠀⠀⠀⠀⠀⠀⠀

(4) "—3 is a negative number."

⠀⠀⠀⠀⠀⠀⠀⠀⠀⠀⠀⠀⠀⠀⠀⠀⠀⠀⠀⠀

(5) —4 is the opposite of +4.

⠀⠀⠀⠀⠀⠀⠀⠀⠀⠀⠀⠀⠀⠀⠀⠀

(6) —50 + 9 — 2 = —43

⠀⠀⠀⠀⠀⠀⠀⠀⠀⠀⠀⠀⠀⠀

DECIMAL POINT

Decimal Point

American	·	⠠
Continental	,	⠠

§17. Use of the Decimal Point: Although the symbols for the American and Continental decimal points differ in print, the difference is not shown in braille. A transcriber's note should be included at the beginning of the braille text to inform the reader of the Continental usage in the ink-print edition.

In a numeral, no space should be left between the decimal point and the digits to which it applies.

(1) Is 1.306 less than 1.31?

⠀⠀⠀⠀⠀⠀⠀⠀⠀⠀⠀⠀⠀⠀⠀⠀⠀⠀

13

(2) $3.05 \times 3.7 = 11.285$

(3) 3,14

(the Continental decimal point is shown in print)

§18. The Decimal Point and the Numeric Indicator:

a. The numeric indicator must be used before a decimal point preceding a numeral when the decimal point follows a space or begins a braille line. The numeric indicator must also be used before a decimal point which follows any punctuation mark other than a hyphen connecting two mathematical expressions.

(1) .6 is the square root of .36.

(2) $.7 > .1$

(3) $5 \times .03 = .15$

(4) $.50 + .17 + 1.50 = 2.17$

(5) ".8 is a decimal fraction."

(6) .01-to-.25

(7) List the numerals from .01-.25.

b. The numeric indicator must be placed between a minus sign and a decimal point preceding a numeral when the minus sign begins a braille line, or follows a space or punctuation mark.

(1) $-.32 + .98 = +.66$

(2) Add —.75 and —.18.

(3) $.69 - .73 = -.04$

(4) The tolerance is ±.005, not —.005.

(5) Is "—.55" the correct answer?

MONETARY, PERCENT, AND PRIME SIGNS

§19. Monetary and Percent Signs:

Monetary Signs

Cent	¢	
Dollar	$	
Pound Sterling	£	
Percent Sign	%	

Monetary and percent signs must be placed in the same position as in ink-print. No space should be left between monetary or percent signs and their related quantities or symbols. Monetary and percent signs are mathematical symbols and must be punctuated accordingly.

(1) $25¢ — 5¢ = 20¢$

(2) .05¢ is what part of a quarter?

(3) $\$2.50 + \$2.50 = \$5.00$

(4) $.07

(5) £4

(6) $60\% \text{ of } 6 = 3.6$

(7) 35 is what % of 75?

(8) $80\% + 20\% = 100\%$

⠠⠎ (braille follows)

(9) $10\not{c}$, $20\not{c}$, and $30\not{c}$.

(10) "\$.25" is the same as "25$\not{c}$."

(11) 5%, 10%, and 15%.

§20. **Prime Sign:**

a. The prime sign may be used to denote feet, inches, minutes, or seconds. The braille symbol for the prime sign must be used wherever the print symbol appears, regardless of its meaning.

b. The prime sign must be placed in the same order as in ink-print. When more than one prime sign is used in print, the equivalent number of signs must be used in braille. Prime signs must be unspaced from each other and from the quantity to which they apply. The prime sign is a mathematical symbol and must be punctuated accordingly.

(1) $5'$ is the same as $60''$

(2) The box is $2'4''$ high.

(3) $12' + 15'' = 13'3''$

(4) Which is greater than $24''$: $1'$, $1'5''$, or $2'5''$?

SIGNS OF OMISSION

§21. **General Use of Signs of Omission:** In print, omission of mathematical or literary material may be shown by a blank space, a dash, a question mark, dots, or a combination of these or other signs devised by the author. Unless otherwise stated, the omission symbol to be used in braille should correspond to the print sign. If the omission sign used in print has no braille equivalent in the code, the sign may be represented by a devised braille symbol or by a drawing. A transcriber's note must be included to explain any devised braille symbol.

§22. Ellipsis ⠄⠄ ⠒⠒ ⠂⠂ and Long Dash ⸺

Any dot or series of dots in print representing an omitted term, entry, or line is an ellipsis. In braille, the ellipsis must be represented by a minimum of three dots.

When a dash is used to denote an omission in print, the long dash must be used.

§23. **Spacing With Ellipsis and Long Dash:**

a. The ellipsis and the long dash should generally be preceded and followed by a space. However, no space should be left between an ellipsis or long dash and a related decimal point, dollar, cent, pound sterling, percent, or prime sign.

(1) Sally, Ann, and . . . are coming.

(2) John said . .

(3) Two and —— are ten.

(4) $14.9 - 12.3 = \text{——}.6$

(5) $7¢ + 9¢ = \ldots ¢$

(6) $\ldots ¢ + 16¢ = 30¢$

(7) $\$25.00 + \$25.00 = \$\text{——}$

(8) $.004 = \text{——}\%$

(9) $\$7.35 = £\text{——}$

(10) $24'' = \text{——}'$

b. A space must be left between a sign of operation and an ellipsis or long dash.

(1) $5 \times \ldots = 15$

17

(2) $2 + 4 + 16 + 32 + \ldots + 712$

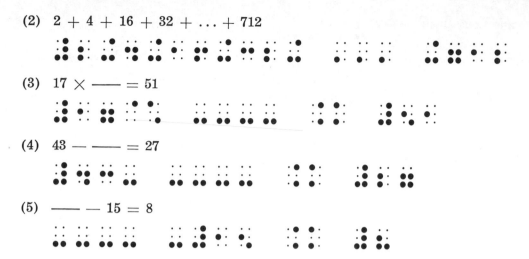

(3) $17 \times \underline{\quad} = 51$

(4) $43 - \underline{\quad} = 27$

(5) $\underline{\quad} - 15 = 8$

§24. **Punctuation With the Ellipsis and Long Dash:** The ellipsis and the long dash must be punctuated in accordance with their context—literary punctuation in literary context and mathematical punctuation in mathematical context. When the nature of the text is in doubt, the ellipsis and the long dash must be punctuated mathematically. Except for the hyphen, no space should be left between an ellipsis or a long dash and a related punctuation mark.

(1) Sally, Mary, ..., and ....

(2) 2, 4, 6, ..., 10.

(3) $100 \times 10 = \ldots.$

(4) The fundamental operations are ——, ——, ——, and ——.

(5) 1, 3, 5, ——, 15.

(6) $9 \times 12 = \underline{\quad}.$

(7) It is a ——-sided figure.

§25. **General Omission Symbol:**

a. The general omission symbol must be used to replace an omission in print represented by a blank space or by a question mark standing alone or in combination with hyphens or a dash. The general omission symbol must be spaced as the material which it replaces, and punctuated mathematically.

(1) $50 \div 10 =$

(2) $20 - \quad = 40$

(3) $6 + ? = 15$

(4) $? - 10 = 30$

(5) $24\ ?\ 12 = 2$

(the question mark represents a sign of operation)

(6) $8 \times 7 \ \underline{?}\ 56$

(the question mark over a dash represents a sign of comparison)

(7) $42 \times 3 = -?-$

(8) 10 is $?\%$ of 100

(9) $27¢ + 19¢ = -?-¢$

(10) $5, 10, ?, 20, ?.$

b. The number of general omission symbols to be used in braille must correspond to the number of omission signs used in print.

(1) $150 \times 10 = ????$

(2) $150 \times 10 = 1???$

(3) $150 \times ?? = 1500$

19

§26. Apostrophe-s: 's

a. When apostrophe-s is used to form the plural or possessive of a mathematical expression, the punctuation indicator must be used before the apostrophe. If the apostrophe is omitted in print, it must be omitted in braille.

(1) 1's and 2's

(2) How many 10's are there in 50?

(3) Insert +'s or ='s to make true sentences.

(4) 1s and 2s

(5) There are four 4s in 16.

(6) +s or =s

b. When apostrophe-s or "s" is attached to a mathematical expression, it becomes part of that expression and must be punctuated mathematically.

(1) 1's, 2's, and 3's.

(2) 1s, 2s, and 3s.

ORDINAL ENDINGS

§27. Ordinal Endings With Mathematical Expressions: Ordinal endings are formed by attaching "st," "nd," "rd," or "th" to a numeral or other mathematical expression. If the "n" or the "r" is omitted from an ordinal ending in print, it must be omitted in braille. The contractions for "st" and "th" must not be used. Ordinal endings are part of a mathematical expression and must be punctuated mathematically.

(1) 1st, 2nd, 3rd, and 4th.

(2) 1st, 2d, and 3d.

⠼⠂⠎⠞⠠ ⠼⠆⠙⠠ ⠯ ⠼⠒⠙⠸⠲

FORMAT (CONTINUED)

§28. **Margins for Instructions Preceding Itemized Material:** When itemized material is preceded by instructions, the instructions must begin in cell 5, and runovers must begin in cell 3. One line must be left blank above such instructions unless they begin a braille page or follow a new page-separation line. A line must not be left blank below the instructions. The last line of an instruction and the first line of the related problem must be on the same braille page.

(1)

53

Tell whether the following ratios are equivalent.

1. $3 : 2 = 75 : 50$
2. $6 : 4 = 15 : 30$

Which of the following sentences are true? Which are false?

3. $328 \div 4 = 41 \times 2$
4. $672 - 415 < 312 \div 3$

54

Multiply.

5. $11{,}251.54 \times 1436$
6. $1000 \times 476{,}792$

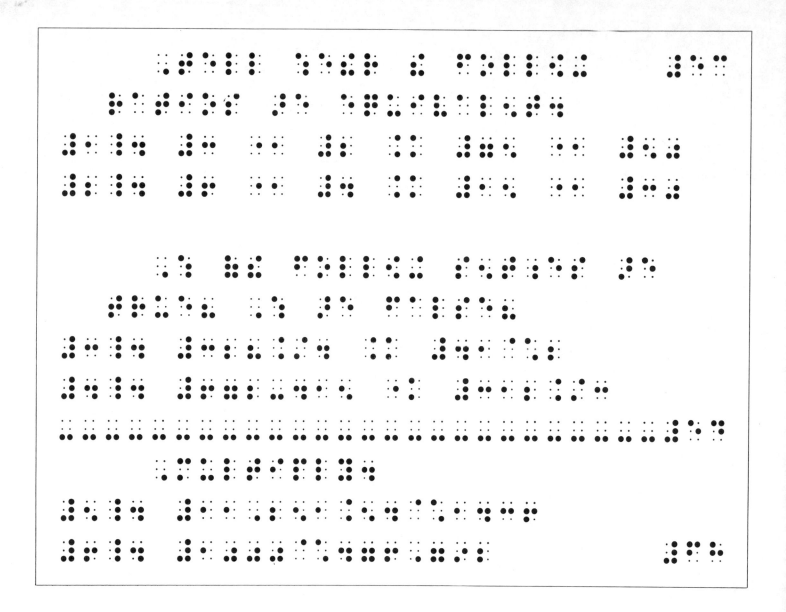

§29. **Margins for Unitemized Explanatory Portions of Text:** As in English braille, paragraphs in explanatory portions of text must begin in cell 3, and all runovers must begin in cell 1.

(1)

> Multiplication is a short way of adding quantities of the same size. For example, $6 + 6$ becomes 2 sixes or 2×6 and $7 + 7 + 7$ becomes 3 sevens or 3×7.
>
> Use the facts explained above to answer the following:
>
> 1. What would $10 + 10 + 10$ become?
>
> 2. How is 5×5 obtained?

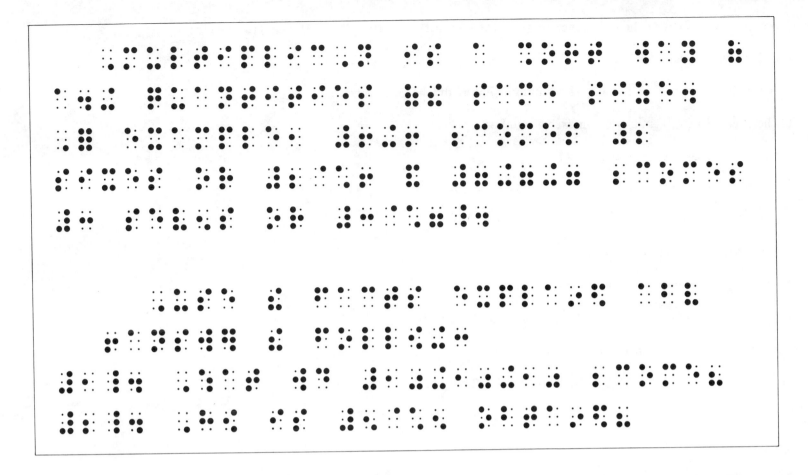

HOMEWORK

Prepare the following homework for submission to your teacher. Proofread carefully.

EXERCISE 2

1. Is there a 1-to-1 correspondence between the members of the sets in Exercise 2?

2. The odds are 10-to-1 against winning. What does this mean in terms of dollars?

3. Did Plato live from 427?-347 or from 428?-348?

4. From the table, tell which scores are included in the intervals 0-9, 15-19, and 40-49.

5. Find the total precipitation for the years 1954-56 and 1957-58.

6. Think: "9 and 9 are 18," and "2 more are 20."

7. In 7,462, does the "7" mean 7, or does it mean 7000? What does the "4" mean? the "6"? the "2"?

8. Is "30 + 5" another name for 35?

9. Are '7 · 8' and '8 · 7' names for the same number?

10. In 1948, '49, and '50, the average rainfall was 24.0, 23.1, and 64.0. What was the total rainfall for the 3 years?

11. Find the number of minutes between 10:55 and 11:10; 10:55 and 11:45.

12. From the data, what is the difference in growth between the 5—10 and the 15—20-year groups?

13. Which is the average—62 or 63?

14. Bob practiced from 9:45-11:30. How many minutes did he practice?

15. Is the product of —1 and —3 a negative number?

16. What is the sum of —119 and —67?

17. Find the integer named by: —24—0; —5—0; —40—0.

18. Does —45 ÷ 9 = —5?

19. What is the sum of —10 and +8?

20. A proper divisor of —42 is ±2. Is ∓2 a proper divisor?

21. Which arrows represent "—5" and "—10" on the number line?

22. What is the value of 0.02? of 0.002? of 0.0025?

23. Round to the nearest tenth: 9.45, 3.86, 423.55, 2.981, 9.815.

24. Round .469 to the nearest hundredth. Is your answer .46, or is it .47?

25. Add: .236 + 1.49 + .01 + 7.6.

26. Are the following sentences true or false: .04 > .039; .305 < .34?

27. Does .092 + .171 + .355 = .618?

28. What is ".6 × 7.25"? Would you have to multiply again to find "7.25 × .6"?
    Does 4.350 ÷ .6 = 7.25? Does 4.350 ÷ 7.25 = .6?

29. List the tenths from .1-to-.10.

30. Name the hundredths from .01-.25.

31. Find the sum of —.38 and —.42.

32. Which point is farther from zero: —.5 or —5?

33. The maximum error is ±.05, not —.05.

34. Find the point labeled "—.75."

35. In one week Beth earned $2.75, 60¢, and 85¢. She spent 25¢, 58¢, and $1.32. How much did she have left?

36. The sign read "Candy bars—6 for 29¢." Jim bought 12 candy bars. How much change did he receive from $1.00?

37. Find: $9.86 + $.07 + $468.57.

38. What does $.75 — $.52 equal?

39. Does 41¢ — 32¢ = 9¢? Can 9¢ also be written $.09?

40. What is 50% of $120?

41. Does 5% + 62% = 67%, or .67%?

42. 55 is what % of 100?

43. Is 6′ the same as 72″?

44. Does 5′7″ + 2′9″ = 8′4″?

45. If the total length of a rectangle is 4″, 23% of it is .23 × 4″, or .9″, and 40% of it is .40 × 4″, or 1.6″.

46. Carl, Carol, and ... are part of the set. Bob and ... are not.

47. Explain the meaning of the dots in 1.141222 ... 2 ...

Write the missing information that will make each sentence true.

48. 16 + 420 = ...

49. 12 × ... = 144

50. 1 + 3 + ... + ... + 81 + 243 = 364

51. Ten and —— are twenty.

52. 100 times —— is 3400.

53. 146 − _____ = 32

54. 25¢ + 50¢ = ...¢

55. 73¢ − ...¢ = 24¢

56. $1.28 + 4.39 + 6.75 = $_____

57. 40.23 ÷ 23 = _____.75

58. 25 = _____% of 100

59. 36″ = _____′

60. The opposite of multiplication is ..., and the opposite of addition is ... .

61. Fifteen plus twelve are _____, and six more are _____.

62. 1, 3, 5, ..., 9, ...

63. 2, 4, _____, 8, _____.

64. .432 − .0087 =

65. 8 : 15 :: 24 : ?

66. 51,858 ÷ ? = 402

67. ? + 64 + 58 + 97 = 265

68. 36,000,000 = 3.6 × -?-

69. 25 is ? % of 50

70. 1435 × 6 = 86??

71. .42, .43, .44, ?, ?, ?.

Use +, —, ×, or ÷ to make true sentences.

72. 100 ? 35 = 3500

73. 650 ? 274 = 376

74. 1,354 ? 52 = 1,406

75. 70.45 ? 14.09 = 5

76. .006 ? .002 = .003

Replace each ? by the correct sign: =, <, or >.

77. 8174 + 9698 ? 18,872

78. —10 ? —8

79. 12,589 ? 589 + 11,000

In our work so far we have learned about numbers, equalities, inequalities, monetary computation, and omissions. We will now study plural, possessive, and ordinal forms of numbers. Remember, these forms can also be used with other mathematical symbols or expressions.

80. Mathematical sentences use signs such as +'s or ='s.

81. Which is more: two 3's, or three 2's?

82. What is 10 ÷ 2? Are there 5 2s in 10? Are there 2 5s in 10?

83. Find the 9th term of 1 + 4 + 7 + 10 + ...

84. Find the sum of the 1st seven terms of the sequence 3, —6, 12, ...

85. Beginning with 5, find the 23d odd integer.

86. Which terms in the sequence above are 1st, 2nd, and 3rd?

ALPHABETS

Specific provision is made for the transcription of the letters of the English (Roman), German, Greek, Hebrew, and Russian (Cyrillic) alphabets. The letters of each alphabet and their braille equivalents are listed on the following pages. Note that the letters of the Hebrew alphabet have no capitalized form.

English (Roman) Alphabet

Regular uncapitalized	Regular capitalized	Script uncapitalized	Script capitalized	Sanserif capitalized	Braille equivalent	Regular uncapitalized	Regular capitalized	Script uncapitalized	Script capitalized	Sanserif capitalized	Braille equivalent
a	A	*a*	𝒜	A	⠁	n	N	*n*	𝒩	N	⠝
b	B	*b*	ℬ	B	⠃	o	O	*o*	𝒪	O	⠕
c	C	*c*	𝒞	C	⠉	p	P	*p*	𝒫	P	⠏
d	D	*d*	𝒟	D	⠙	q	Q	*q*	𝒬	Q	⠟
e	E	*e*	ℰ	E	⠑	r	R	*r*	ℛ	R	⠗
f	F	*f*	ℱ	F	⠋	s	S	*s*	𝒮	S	⠎
g	G	*g*	𝒢	G	⠛	t	T	*t*	𝒯	T	⠞
h	H	*h*	ℋ	H	⠓	u	U	*u*	𝒰	U	⠥
i	I	*i*	ℐ	I	⠊	v	V	*v*	𝒱	V	⠧
j	J	*j*	𝒥	J	⠚	w	W	*w*	𝒲	W	⠺
k	K	*k*	𝒦	K	⠅	x	X	*x*	𝒳	X	⠭
l	L	*l*	ℒ	L	⠇	y	Y	*y*	𝒴	Y	⠽
m	M	*m*	ℳ	M	⠍	z	Z	*z*	𝒵	Z	⠵

German Alphabet

Name of letter	Regular uncapitalized	Regular capitalized	Script uncapitalized	Script capitalized	Braille equivalent
ah	a	A	*(script)*	*(script)*	⠁
beh	b	B	*(script)*	*(script)*	⠃
tseh	c	C	*(script)*	*(script)*	⠉
deh	d	D	*(script)*	*(script)*	⠙
eh	e	E	*(script)*	*(script)*	⠑
eff	f	F	*(script)*	*(script)*	⠋
gheh	g	G	*(script)*	*(script)*	⠛
hah	h	H	*(script)*	*(script)* or *(script)*	⠓
ee	i	I	*(script)*	*(script)*	⠊
yaht	j	J	*(script)*	*(script)* or *(script)*	⠚
kah	k	K	*(script)*	*(script)*	⠅
ell	l	L	*(script)*	*(script)*	⠇
em	m	M	*(script)*	*(script)*	⠍
en	n	N	*(script)*	*(script)*	⠝
oh	o	O	*(script)*	*(script)*	⠕
peh	p	P	*(script)*	*(script)*	⠏
koo	q	Q	*(script)*	*(script)*	⠟
err	r	R	*(script)*	*(script)*	⠗
ess	s	S	*(script)* or *(script)*	*(script)*	⠎
teh	t	T	*(script)*	*(script)*	⠞
oo	u	U	*(script)*	*(script)*	⠥
fao	v	V	*(script)*	*(script)*	⠧
veh	w	W	*(script)*	*(script)*	⠺
iks	x	X	*(script)*	*(script)*	⠭
ypsilon	y	Y	*(script)*	*(script)* or *(script)*	⠽
tset	z	Z	*(script)*	*(script)*	⠵

Greek Alphabet (Standard)

Name of letter	Regular uncapitalized	Regular capitalized	Script uncapitalized	Script capitalized	Braille equivalent
alpha	α	A	𝑎	𝒜	⠁
beta	β	B	𝒷	ℬ	⠃
gamma	γ	Γ	𝓇	𝒯	⠛
delta	δ	Δ	𝒹	𝒟	⠙
epsilon	ε	E	ℰ	ℰ	⠑
zeta	ζ	Z	ℐ	𝒵	⠵
eta	η	H	𝓃	ℋ	⠱
theta	θ	Θ	𝒹	𝒩	⠹
iota	ι	I	𝒾	𝒥	⠊
kappa	κ	K	𝓊	𝒦	⠅
lambda	λ	Λ	𝒶	ℒ	⠇
mu	μ	M	𝓂	ℳ	⠍
nu	ν	N	𝓃	𝒩	⠝
xi	ξ	Ξ	ℐ	𝒳	⠭
omicron	o	O	𝑜	𝒪	⠕
pi	π	Π	𝓈	𝒫	⠏
rho	ρ	P	𝓅	𝒫	⠗
sigma	σ	Σ	𝜎	ℒ	⠎
tau	τ	T	𝓆	𝒯	⠞
upsilon	υ	Υ	𝓋	𝒱	⠥
phi	φ	Φ	𝒻	𝒫	⠋
chi	χ	X	𝓍	𝒳	⠡
psi	ψ	Ψ	𝓎	𝒴	⠽
omega	ω	Ω	𝓌	𝒲	⠺
sampi	ϡ				⠖
stigma	ϛ				⠯
vau	Ϝ				⠶
koph (goph)	Ϟ or Ϙ				⠿

Hebrew Alphabet

Hebrew letters do not possess a capitalized form.

Name of letter	Regular	Script	Braille equivalent	Name of letter	Regular	Script	Braille equivalent
aleph	א			lamed	ל		
veth	ב			mem	מ		
gimel	ג			nun	נ		
daleth	ד			samekh	ס		
heh	ה			ayin	ע		
vav	ו			feh	פ		
zayin	ז			tsadi	צ		
cheth	ח			koph	ק		
teth	ט			resh	ר		
yod	׳			sin	ש		
chaph	כ			thav	ת		

Russian (Cyrillic) Alphabet

Name of letter	Regular uncapitalized	Regular capitalized	Script uncapitalized	Script capitalized	Braille equivalent	Name of letter	Regular uncapitalized	Regular capitalized	Script uncapitalized	Script capitalized	Braille equivalent
ah	а	А	*a*	*A*		zeh	з	З	*з* or *ʒ*	*Ʒ*	
beh	б	Б	*б*	*Б*		ee	и	И	*u*	*И*	
veh	в	В	*ƅ*	*В*		kah	к	К	*x* or *к*	*К*	
gheh	г	Г	*v*	*Г*		ell	л	Л	*л*	*Л*	
deh	д	Д	*g* or *э*	*D*		em	м	М	*м*	*М*	
yeh	е	Е	*e*	*Е*		en	н	Н	*н*	*Н*	
zheh	ж	Ж	*ж* or *ж*	*Ж*		oh	о	О	*o*	*О*	

Russian (Cyrillic) Alphabet (continued)

Name of letter	Regular uncapitalized	Regular capitalized	Script uncapitalized	Script capitalized	Braille equivalent	Name of letter	Regular uncapitalized	Regular capitalized	Script uncapitalized	Script capitalized	Braille equivalent
peh	п	П	*n*	*П*	⠏	cheh	ч	Ч	*ч*	*Ч*	⠟
err	р	Р	*р*	*Р*	⠗	shah	ш	Ш	*ш* or *ш̲*	*Ш*	⠱
ess	с	С	*с*	*С*	⠎	shchah	щ	Щ	*щ*	*Щ*	⠭
teh	т	Т	*m* or *m̄*	*Т*	⠞	yerih	ы	Ы	*ы*		⠮
oo	у	У	*у*	*У*	⠥	eh	э	Э	*э*	*Э*	⠪
eff	ф	Ф	*ф*	*Ф*	⠋	yu	ю	Ю	*ю*	*Ю*	⠳
khah	х	Х	*х*	*Х*	⠓	yah	я	Я	*я*	*Я*	⠫
tseh	ц	Ц	*ц*	*Ц*	⠉						

GERMAN, GREEK, HEBREW, AND RUSSIAN ALPHABETS AND ALPHABETIC INDICATORS

Alphabetic Indicators

German Letter Indicator

Greek Letter Indicator

   For Standard Letters

     For Alternative Forms of Letters

Hebrew Letter Indicator

Russian (Cyrillic) Letter Indicator

Capitalization Indicator (single)

§30. Use of German, Greek, Hebrew, and Russian Alphabetic Indicators:

a. The appropriate alphabetic indicator for German, Greek, Hebrew, and Russian letters *must always be* used to identify the alphabet to which the letter belongs. The effect of an alphabetic indicator extends only to the letter which follows it. Thus, in a sequence of unspaced letters, the appropriate alphabetic indicator must be used before each letter.

(1) 𝖆

⠨⠁

(German uncapitalized ah)

(2) α

⠈⠁

(Greek uncapitalized alpha)

(3) א

⠠⠠⠁

(Hebrew alef)

(4) а

⠈⠈⠁

(Russian uncapitalized ah)

(5) $\alpha\beta\gamma$

⠨⠁⠨⠃⠨⠛

(Greek uncapitalized alpha, beta, gamma)

(6) α 𝖇 א б

⠈⠁ ⠸⠃ ⠠⠠⠁ ⠈⠈⠃

(Greek uncapitalized alpha, German uncapitalized beh, Hebrew alef, Russian uncapitalized beh)

(7) $\alpha + \beta = \pi - \theta$

⠨⠁ ⠲ ⠨⠃ ⠨⠅ ⠨⠏ ⠤ ⠨⠹

(8) $\mu \pm 1.645\ \sigma$

⠨⠍ ⠲⠤ ⠼⠁⠲⠋⠙⠑ ⠨⠎

(9) $\pi < 0 < 2\pi$

⠨⠏ ⠪ �b ⠪ ⠼⠃⠨⠏

(10) 𝖆 α + 𝖇 β

⠨⠁ ⠨⠁ ⠲ ⠸⠃ ⠨⠃

b. When a letter is capitalized, the capitalization indicator must be placed between the alphabetic indicator and the letter. The effect of the capitalization indicator extends only to the letter which follows it. Thus, in a sequence of unspaced letters, the capitalization indicator must be placed before each capitalized letter.

(1) $\mathfrak{A}$

(German capitalized ah)

(2) Σ

(Greek capitalized sigma)

(3) A

(Russian capitalized ah)

(4) Δ Ω

(Greek capitalized delta and omega)

(5) $\mathfrak{A}\ \alpha + \mathfrak{B}\ \beta$

(German capitalized ah, Greek uncapitalized alpha plus German capitalized beh, Greek uncapitalized beta)

c. The letters of the German, Greek, Hebrew, and Russian alphabets are mathematical expressions and must be punctuated accordingly.

(1) α , $\mathfrak{a}$, $\aleph$, a .

(2) θ is a multiple of π.

(3) α's and ω's.

(4) The set of $\mathfrak{T}$ -sentences.

§31. Alternative Forms of Greek Letters: The following Greek letters possess an alternative uncapitalized print form. The difference is shown in braille by placing the Greek letter alternative form indicator ⠨⠈ in front of these letters. If a Greek letter is represented by its alternative form *instead of* its standard form throughout the print text, the symbol for the standard form must be used in braille. However, a transcriber's note must be included at the beginning of the text to inform the reader of such changes in braille usage. The alternative form should be used in braille only when both forms—standard and alternative—appear in the same print text.

Name of letter	Alternative print form	Braille equivalent
alpha	α	⠨⠈⠁
beta	β	⠨⠈⠃
theta	ϑ	⠨⠈⠹
sigma	ς	⠨⠈⠎
phi	φ	⠨⠈⠋

(1) φ and ϕ have separate identities.

(2) φ ϑ and ϕ Θ are the least elements of each set.

ENGLISH ALPHABET AND THE ENGLISH LETTER INDICATOR

English Letter Indicator ⠰

Capitalization Indicator (single) ⠠

§32. Use of the English Letter Indicator With English Letters in Regular Type:

a. The English letter indicator must be used with a single capitalized or uncapitalized English letter or with an uncapitalized combination of letters corresponding to a short-form word of English braille *if, in braille, the letter or short-form combination is preceded by a space or by one or more punctuation marks and is followed by a space or by one or more punctuation marks.*

When the English letter indicator is used, its effect extends to the letter or to the entire short-form combination following it. If a letter is capitalized, the capitalization indicator must be placed between the English letter indicator and the letter.

Single letters and short-form combinations which are not words or abbreviations are mathematical expressions and must be punctuated accordingly.

(1) Set R contains x elements.

(2) Vitamins A and D.

(3) p is larger than q.

(4) cd is more than ac.

(5) l, m, n are in Set S.

(6) a, b, c, ... , z.

(7) Find A, B, and C.

(8) ab, cd, and gd are equal.

(9) n:v means "the mapping n of v."

(10) "v varies as x."

(11) "a" is less than "B".

(12) The hypothesis about "ab" is not true.

(13) A.   12 + 6 — 8 = ?
     B.   4 × 6 × 1000 = ?

b. Unless otherwise stated, the English letter indicator must be used with a single English letter or a short-form letter combination joined to a word, to part of a word, to a numeral, to a letter, or to any other material by a hyphen or a dash. Unless otherwise stated, a word or part of a word joined to a letter by the hyphen or the dash must be contracted and punctuated according to the rules of English braille.

(1)   not-p

(2)   x-intercept

(3)   Label the X- and Y-axes.

(4)   Find the r-, s-, and t-planes.

(5)   Find the ab-plane.

(6)   n-tuple

(7)   unary, binary, ... , m-ary.

(8)   Which is larger—A or B?

(9)   A—not B—has a greater area.

(10)   Sections 1-a and a-1.

(11)   Use a-f to find the solution.

(12)   Read exercises A—D.

§33. Nonuse of the English Letter Indicator With English Letters in Regular Type:

a. The English letter indicator must not be used with a single English letter or short-form combination in regular type immediately preceding or following a sign of comparison. However, the English letter indicator must be used with a single letter or a short-form combination which is separated from a sign of comparison by a mark of punctuation.

(1) If a = c = d, then ac = cd.

(2) p < q and R > S.

(3) a : b :: c : d

(4) j = 1, 2, ..., n

(5) 40% of N = 120

(6) r = rate

(7) x, y, z = 100

(8) In "x = y", x and y are unknowns.

(9) n:v = m:p

(10) "x" = "y"

b. The English letter indicator must not be used with a combination of letters which corresponds to a short-form word if the short-form combination contains any capitalized letters.

(1) Ac means A times c.

(2) Let Dcv be "c divides v."

c. The English letter indicator must not be used with two or more unspaced capitalized or uncapitalized letters which do not correspond to a short-form word. English braille contractions must not be used where contractible letter combinations occur in a mathematical sequence of letters in which each letter has a separate identity.

Since the effect of the capitalization indicator extends only to the following letter, each capitalized letter in a mathematical sequence of letters must be capitalized individually. Such sequences of letters are mathematical expressions and must be punctuated accordingly.

(1) Is ca the same as ac?

(2) Measure line wh.

(3) "xy is the same as yx."

(4) Find the points on the xy- and st-axes.

(5) Prove PQRS is a rhombus.

(6) Find chords AC, AL, and EF.

(7) If th = ef, then lm = ch.

d. The English letter indicator must not be used with one or more English letters in regular type which occur in an unspaced sequence of terms consisting of a mixture of numerals, letters from other alphabets, signs of operation, or any other unspaced mathematical symbol.

(1) $3a \times 4b = 12ab$

(2) 2x means $2 \times x$.

(3) Δy is an increment in y.

(4) $C = 2\pi r + \pi\Delta r$

(5) $s = r\theta$

(6) a + b = c

(7) e × e × e = e-cubed

(8) Ax + By + Cz + D = 0

(9) CE + ED > DC

(10) ab × cd = ac × bd

(11) Substitute —y for +y.

(12) a + a + a + a + ... + a

(13) a + b + c + ... n

(14) Sides d′ and d are similar.

(15) R′S′T′

(16) 35 equals N% of 120

(17) x¢ = \$1.00

(18) 40 dimes equals \$x

e. When a single English letter or a combination of unspaced letters has a plural, possessive, or ordinal ending, the English letter indicator must be used or must not be used as though such endings were not present. The English letter indicator must not be used with the letter "s" when the "s" is part of the apostrophe-s combination.

(1) a's, b's, and c's.

(2) A's, B's, and C's.

(3) ps, qs, and rs.

(4) Ps, Qs, and Rs.

(5) The ab's, cd's, and ef's.

(6) The ABC's and XYZ's.

(7) Find the nth root of x.

(8) The abth and jkth columns.

(9) 2nth

ABBREVIATIONS

§34. Capitalization and Punctuation With Abbreviations: Abbreviations must be capitalized and punctuated in accordance with the rules of English braille. The single capitalization indicator ⠠ must be used before a single capitalized letter, and the double capitalization indicator ⠠⠠ must be used before a sequence of two or more unspaced capitalized letters when each letter represents an individual word. The effect of the double capitalization indicator is terminated by any symbol other than a letter.

§35. Definition of Abbreviations:

a. Abbreviations consist of the following items:

i. Universal literary abbreviations commonly listed in a dictionary.

(1) Mon.

(2) Sept.

(3) assoc.

(4) a.m.

ii. Abbreviations of measurement.

(1) lbs.

(2) ft

(3) Yd.

(4) Tell how many qts., pts., and oz. are in one gal.

(5) A unit of work is the ft-lb.

(6) The car traveled x-mi. per hr.

iii. Acronyms.

(1) Unesco

(2) ASCAP

iv. Personal, postal district, or geographic initials.

(1) H. G. Wells

(2) Washington, D.C.

⠀⠀

(3) U.S.A.

⠀⠀⠀⠀⠀⠀⠀⠀⠀⠀⠀⠀⠀⠀⠀⠀⠀⠀⠀⠀⠀⠀⠀⠀⠀⠀⠀⠀⠀⠀⠀⠀⠀⠀

v. Initials of agencies, organizations, business firms, etc.

(1) CIO

⠀⠀⠀⠀⠀⠀⠀⠀⠀⠀⠀⠀⠀⠀⠀⠀

(2) B.P.O.E.

⠀⠀⠀⠀⠀⠀⠀⠀⠀⠀⠀⠀⠀⠀⠀⠀⠀⠀⠀⠀⠀⠀⠀⠀⠀⠀⠀⠀⠀⠀⠀⠀⠀⠀

(3) IBM

⠀⠀⠀⠀⠀⠀⠀⠀⠀⠀⠀⠀⠀⠀⠀⠀

vi. Abbreviations formed from the principal letters of a word, phrase, or name.

(1) ans.

⠀⠀⠀⠀⠀⠀⠀⠀⠀⠀⠀⠀

(2) Atty. Gen.

⠀⠀⠀⠀⠀⠀⠀⠀⠀⠀⠀⠀⠀⠀⠀⠀⠀⠀⠀⠀⠀⠀⠀⠀⠀⠀⠀⠀

(3) Geo.

⠀⠀⠀⠀⠀⠀⠀⠀⠀⠀⠀⠀

vii. Special abbreviations confined to a special field or a particular book.

(1) SAS means "side angle side".

⠀⠀

(2) iff means "if and only if".

⠀⠀

b. A single letter or sequence of letters which does not represent a word or a phrase, as well as model numbers, serial numbers, etc., must not be considered abbreviations and must be transcribed according to other rules of the code. When there is doubt whether a particular item is an abbreviation, it must be treated as if it were not an abbreviation.

(1) Model number 1074FE.

⠀⠀

(2) Blood types are A, B, AB, and O.

⠠⠃⠇⠕⠕⠙ ⠞⠽⠏⠑⠎ ⠜⠑ ⠠⠁⠂ ⠠⠃⠂ ⠠⠁⠠⠃⠂ ⠯

⠠⠕ ⠲⠲⠲⠲⠲

§36. Spacing With Abbreviations:

a. An abbreviation consisting of two or more components must be written spaced or unspaced to conform with the print text. Abbreviations must be placed in the same position as in print. The English braille practice of placing abbreviations before the numeral or letter to which they refer must not be followed.

(1) mph

⠍⠏⠓

(2) m.p.h.

⠍⠲⠏⠲⠓⠲

(3) m. p. h.

⠍⠲ ⠏⠲ ⠓⠲

(4) i.e., 8 + 10 = 18

⠊⠲⠑⠂ ⠼⠓ ⠖ ⠼⠁⠚ ⠶ ⠼⠁⠓

(5) London, S.W.

⠠⠇⠕⠝⠙⠕⠝⠂ ⠠⠎⠲⠠⠺⠲

(6) H. R. Jones, Ph.D.

⠠⠓⠲ ⠠⠗⠲ ⠠⠚⠕⠝⠑⠎⠂ ⠠⠏⠓⠲⠠⠙⠲

(7) L.C.D. means "least common denominator."

⠠⠇⠲⠠⠉⠲⠠⠙⠲ ⠍⠑⠁⠝⠎ ⠦⠇⠑⠁⠌ ⠉⠕⠍⠍⠕⠝ ⠙⠑⠝⠕⠍⠊⠝⠁⠞⠕⠗⠲⠴

(8) Find the LCM.

⠠⠋⠊⠝⠙ ⠮ ⠠⠇⠠⠉⠠⠍⠲

(9) Sq. Yd.

⠠⠎⠟⠲ ⠠⠽⠙⠲

(10) sq. mi.

⠎⠟⠲ ⠍⠊⠲

(11) fl.oz.

(12) ClPA means "closure property for addition."

(13) Vol. 10, pp. 130-140

b. Unless otherwise stated in the rules, a space must be left between an abbreviation and a numeral, a letter, a sign of operation, a sign of comparison, a monetary sign, a percent sign, a sign of omission, or any other sign. If a sign of omission is used to represent an abbreviation, the sign of omission must be spaced as the abbreviation which it replaces. An abbreviation and a preceding or following numeral or letter to which it applies must be placed on the same braille line.

(1) 100 B.C.

(2) It is 10 a.m., EST.

(3) 4 gal 2 qt 1 pt

(4) 12 Sq. Yd.

(5) 60 m.p.h. = 88 ft. per sec.

(6) n ft.

(7) 170 ft = x yd y ft

(8) 300 mph × 3 hr = 900 mi

(9) 9 sq ft — 5 sq ft = 4 sq ft

44

(10) The buttons cost 36¢ doz.

⠀⠀⠀⠀⠀⠀⠀

(11) The bond pays 6% ann.

⠀⠀⠀⠀⠀⠀⠀

(12) ? bu = 12 pk

⠀⠀⠀⠀⠀⠀⠀

(13) There are ⎯?⎯ oz in 1 lb.

⠀⠀⠀⠀⠀⠀⠀

(14) 14 cm ? 12 cm = 2 cm

⠀⠀⠀⠀⠀⠀⠀

(15) 64 hrs. = _____ da. _____ hr.

⠀⠀⠀⠀⠀⠀⠀

(16) 1 da. = 24 ⎯?⎯

⠀⠀⠀⠀⠀⠀⠀

(17) 3 gal 5 qt = 4 _____ 1 qt

⠀⠀⠀⠀⠀⠀⠀

§37. Contractions in Abbreviations: Unless otherwise stated, contractions may be used in abbreviations in accordance with the rules of English braille. However, the abbreviations "in." or "in," usually meaning "inches," must never be contracted. If an abbreviation consists entirely of the letters **st**, the "st" contraction may only be used as an abbreviation for "street" or "saint." It must not be used for any other word, such as "straight."

(1) in. is the abbreviation for "inches."

⠀⠀⠀⠀⠀⠀⠀

(2) 5 in + 25 in = 30 in

⠀⠀⠀⠀⠀⠀⠀

(3) Use a 36-in ruler.

⠀⠀⠀⠀⠀⠀⠀

(4) He lives on 24th St.

⠀⠀⠀⠀⠀⠀⠀

(5) How many st. angles are there?

⠀⠀⠀⠀⠀⠀⠀

(6) How many min. are there in one hr.?

⠀⠩⠕⠺⠀⠍⠁⠝⠽⠀⠍⠊⠝⠲⠀⠜⠑⠀⠮⠗⠑⠀⠔⠀⠕⠝⠑⠀⠦⠗⠲⠦

(7) statamp-oersted

⠎⠞⠁⠞⠁⠍⠏⠤⠕⠑⠗⠌⠫

(8) FORTRAN is a computer language.

⠠⠠⠋⠕⠗⠞⠗⠁⠝⠀⠊⠎⠀⠁⠀⠉⠕⠍⠏⠥⠞⠻⠀⠇⠁⠝⠛⠥⠁⠛⠑⠲

(9) Wed., Thurs.

⠠⠺⠑⠙⠲⠀⠠⠹⠥⠗⠎⠲

(10) Ariz., Ark., and Conn.

⠠⠜⠊⠵⠲⠀⠠⠜⠅⠲⠀⠯⠀⠠⠉⠕⠝⠝⠲

(11) Read chap. 4.

⠠⠗⠑⠁⠙⠀⠡⠁⠏⠲⠀⠼⠙⠲

§38. **Abbreviations and the English Letter Indicator:**

a. The English letter indicator must be used with an abbreviation consisting of a single letter or a combination of letters corresponding to a short-form word when the abbreviation has no period in print, or, if there is a period, the period merely ends a sentence.

(1) F is the abbreviation for Fahrenheit; the abbreviation for Centigrade is C.

(2) N 30 degrees W.

⠠⠝⠀⠼⠉⠚⠀⠙⠑⠛⠗⠑⠑⠎⠀⠠⠺⠲

(3) 10 g + 10 g = 20 g.

⠼⠁⠚⠀⠛⠀⠖⠀⠼⠁⠚⠀⠛⠀⠶⠀⠼⠃⠚⠀⠛⠲

(4) 1 l = 1000 cubic centimeters

⠼⠁⠀⠇⠀⠶⠀⠼⠁⠚⠚⠚⠀⠉⠥⠃⠊⠉⠀⠉⠑⠝⠞⠊⠍⠑⠞⠻⠎

(5) Yr is the abbreviation for "year."

⠠⠽⠗⠀⠊⠎⠀⠮⠀⠁⠃⠃⠗⠑⠧⠊⠁⠰⠝⠀⠿⠀⠦⠽⠑⠜⠲⠴

(6) 1 yr = 12 months

⠼⠁⠀⠽⠗⠀⠶⠀⠼⠁⠃⠀⠍⠕⠝⠹⠎

(7) It is a 1-g weight.

(8) 1 g-mole

(9) I-O means "Input-Output".

(10) "d-c" stands for "direct current."

(11) 1 light-yr

b. The English letter indicator must not be used with an abbreviation consisting of a single letter or a combination of letters corresponding to a short-form word if the abbreviation is followed by its related period. When it is doubtful whether a period ends a sentence or applies to an abbreviation, the period must be considered as applying to the abbreviation, and the English letter indicator must not be used.

(1) C. is the abbreviation for Celsius.

(2) We met Mister P. and Mister Q.

(3) Cubic meters is abbreviated cu. m.

(4) N. 30 degrees W.

(5) 10 g. + 10 g. = 20 g.

(6) Use a 1-g. weight.

(7) He is 1 yr. old today.

(8) 1 yr. = 12 months

(9) The abbreviation for Centigrade is C.

(10) 1 light-yr.

c. The English letter indicator must not be used with an abbreviation that consists of two or more letters and does not correspond to a short-form word, whether or not it is followed by a period.

(1) He worked for 3 hrs.

(2) 62 cg 8 mg

(3) Does 1 km = 1000 m?

(4) 7 da = 1 wk

§39. Abbreviations and the Numeric Indicator: The numeric indicator must be used before a numeral or a decimal point and its numeral connected to a preceding abbreviation by a hyphen.

(1) The airplane is a DC-6.

(2) U-238 means Uranium-238.

(3) e.g. - .07

HOMEWORK

Prepare the following homework for submission to your teacher. Note that letters are used as main outline designations in the last group of itemized problems. Use the margin format principles as stated in §13. Proofread carefully.

EXERCISE 3

Practice writing these German letters:

1. 𝔞 , 𝔟 , 𝔡 , 𝔪 , 𝔯 , 𝔰 , 𝔱 .

2. 𝔄 , 𝔅 , 𝔇 , 𝔐 , 𝔑 , 𝔖 , 𝔗 .

3. Prove that a model of 𝔗 is a model of the set of theorems of 𝔗 .

4. Theorem 4.4 shows $\mathfrak{D}$ is an infinite model of $\mathfrak{M}$ and that $\mathfrak{D}'$ is a model of $\mathfrak{M}$ having a cardinality $\mathfrak{S}$.

Practice writing the standard and alternate forms of these Greek letters:

5. α, β, γ, δ, θ, μ, π, σ, ϕ, ω.

6. Γ, Δ, Π, Σ, Φ, Ω.

7. α δ ϑ s φ .

8. Π and Σ denote the product and sum of consecutive terms.

9. Prove that ϕ is the inverse of φ .

10. Construct a circle of radius 1 and obtain the functions of θ, given that: $\theta = 1$; $\theta = \pi$; $\theta = \pi + 0.3$.

11. Use the diagram to find the values of α, β, and γ. Does $\alpha + \beta = \gamma$?

12. Prove that for ordinal numbers α, β, and γ, $\gamma\alpha = \gamma\beta$ and $\gamma > 0$ imply $\alpha = \beta$.

Practice writing these Hebrew letters:

13. א, ב, ח, ת .

14. The א is equal to our digit 1.

15. Establish the relation א א = א .

Practice writing these Russian letters:

16. а, б, и, к, я .

17. А, Б, И, К, Я .

18. Explain why э′ and Д′ are equal.

Practice writing letters from the English alphabet.

19. There are n elements in Set R.

20. Use the data to prove that r is greater than s.

21. Is line ab equal to line cd?

22. Study the diagram. Are ac and al equal distances from td?

23. List the 24 permutations that can be made from the 4 letters a, b, c, and d—taken 3 at a time.

24. Is a, b, c, d, ..., z a finite sequence?

25. Study diagram a and list the coordinates of the points P, Q, R, and S.

26. The notation T:V means "T is a function whose domain is V."

27. Verify: If "p or q" is true and "p" is false, then "q" is true.

28. Use symbolism to represent the negation of a disjunction: p or q, is the conjunction of not-p and not-q.

29. If x, y, and z are used to denote the first, second, and third coordinates, we can speak of the x-, y-, and z-coordinates of a point as well as the x-, y-, and z-axes. Do we have to use the letters x, y, and z? Can we use other letters and have a-, b-, and c-coordinates and axes?

30. Label the ab- and cd-planes.

31. Can we say that a natural generalization of a binary relation is that of an n-ary relation as a set of ordered n-tuples?

32. Write the multiplication facts for table entries A—H.

33. Solve exercises a-d in Section 5-c. Then read Section D-2.

34. If d varies directly as t, and if d = 8 when t = 4, find d when t = 5.

35. N = 36% of 1200.

36. Prove: If x, y, and u are real numbers such that x < y and x = u, then u < y.

37. Express x in terms of r, s, and t: r : s = t : x.

38. Prove: If a < b and c < 0, then ac > bc.

39. Use Theorem 6.4 to explain why n:v = m:p.

40. From the data above, explain why "p" = "r".

41. In triangle ABC, D is a point on AB, E is a point on AC and DE is drawn. AD = 6, DB = 4, AC = 15. If DE is parallel to side BC, the length of EC is: 4, 6, 10.

42. Use numerals to prove that ab is the same as ba.

43. Locate the xy- and st- coordinate planes.

44. Solve: 3b — 3 = 37 — 2b; r + r + r — 30 = 180; 8x — 9 + x — 17 = 3x + 4 + 8x — 12; m = 5m — 30.

45. Draw the graphs of x — 3y = 14 and 3x + 2y = 20.

46. The expression x — y has 2 terms: x and —y. Name the terms in a + b — c.

47. What number does N stand for in N × 9 = 45? in 5 × N = 45?

48. ab + cd — ef is a trinomial. Which are its terms: ab, cd, ef, or ab, +cd, —ef?

49. If C in C = πd is 100, d = _____.

50. Write the logarithmic equation for S = 2πrh and C = πd.

51. What does the notation Δx and Δy stand for?

52. If triangles DEF and D′E′F′ are similar, is it true that each pair of angles D and D′, E and E′, C and C′ are equal?

53. Bob invested "d" dollars, part at x% and part at y%. If his annual income is "I" dollars, what amount did he invest at x%?

54. The total of the nine letters in the word "addressed" contains 3 d's, 2 e's, and 2 s's. How many permutations are possible with the letters taken all together?

55. Delineate the ab's, cd's, and xy's solutions.

56. Use symbols to write the nth root of a.

57. Write the expression which denotes the pth power of the non-negative qth root of b when b > 0.

58. What represents the cell corresponding to the abth row and jkth column?

Solve the following problems.

A. An object travels 88 ft. per sec. at 60 m.p.h. How far will it travel in 1 sec. when the speed is 750 m.p.h.?

B. What is the volume of a cylinder 9 in. long and 4 in. wide?

C. Find the volume of a rectangular prism with l = 2 ft, w = 4 ft, and h = 3 ft.

D. If 1 cm = .1 dm, then 67 cm × .1 dm = 6.7 dm. Express 14.0 cm and 104.0 cm as decimeters.

E. There are p mi. in 1 km. How many kilometers are in 100 mi.?

F. 3 lb 10 oz = 4 _____ 4 oz.

G. 9 min. + 12 hrs. = _____ min.

H. 10 sq.yd. + 10 sq.yd. = __?__ sq.yd.

I. 14 g. − 11 g. = __?__ g.

J. Light travels __?__ mi. in 1 light-yr.

K. A plane flies N 30 degrees E at 580 mph. How many miles north and how many miles east of its starting point will it be at the end of 3 hrs?

L. Water freezes at 32 degrees F. Is this the same as 0 degrees C?

M. A ray of light travels 9,468,000,000,000 km in 1 yr. Express this measurement in tetrameters.

N. 16 yr 15 mo = __?__ yr __?__ mo

O. What is the difference between a-c and d-c electricity?

P. The approximate weight of a hydrogen atom is .00000000000000000000000167 g. Express this number using scientific notation.

Q. Mrs. R. S. Smith worked from 1:50 p.m. until 3:20 p.m. at $1.60 per hr. How much did she earn?

R. An airplane left New York for Los Angeles at 10 a.m., EST. It arrived at 12:30 p.m., PST. What was the flight time?

S. What is the L.C.D. of 12 and 30?

T. What is the GPE for the measurement 4.7?

U. What are the basic differences between the DC-6 and the DC-7 airplanes?

V. Mrs. H. Olds bought a GE stove, Model number 23496ACS.

W. In what substances are vitamins A, B, and C found?

LESSON 4

BOLDFACE, ITALIC, SCRIPT, AND SANSERIF TYPE

§40. Type Forms and Type-Form Indicators: Specific provision is made by the use of type-form indicators for the transcription of boldface, italic, script, and sanserif print type forms. A type-form indicator is not required to show regular type. (See pages 27 - 31 for the various print type forms of the letters of the English, German, Greek, Hebrew, and Russian alphabets.)

Type-Form Indicators for Letters, Numerals, and Compound Expressions

Boldface Type Indicator	⠘
Italic Type Indicator	⠨
Sanserif Type Indicator	⠠⠴
Script Type Indicator	⠈

§41. Type-Form Indicators With Letters:

a. The appropriate type-form indicator must be used when it is necessary to show that a letter from any alphabet is printed in a type form other than regular type. A type-form indicator *must always* be followed by an alphabetic indicator.

(1) **A**

⠘⠠⠰⠁

(boldface English capitalized a)

(2) **a**

⠘⠰⠁

(boldface English uncapitalized a)

(3) *α*

⠘⠨⠁

(boldface Greek uncapitalized alpha)

(4) **a**

⠘⠈⠁

(boldface German uncapitalized ah)

(5) a

⠘⠈⠈⠁

(boldface Russian uncapitalized ah)

(6) *A*

⠨⠠⠰⠁

(italic English capitalized a)

(7) *a*

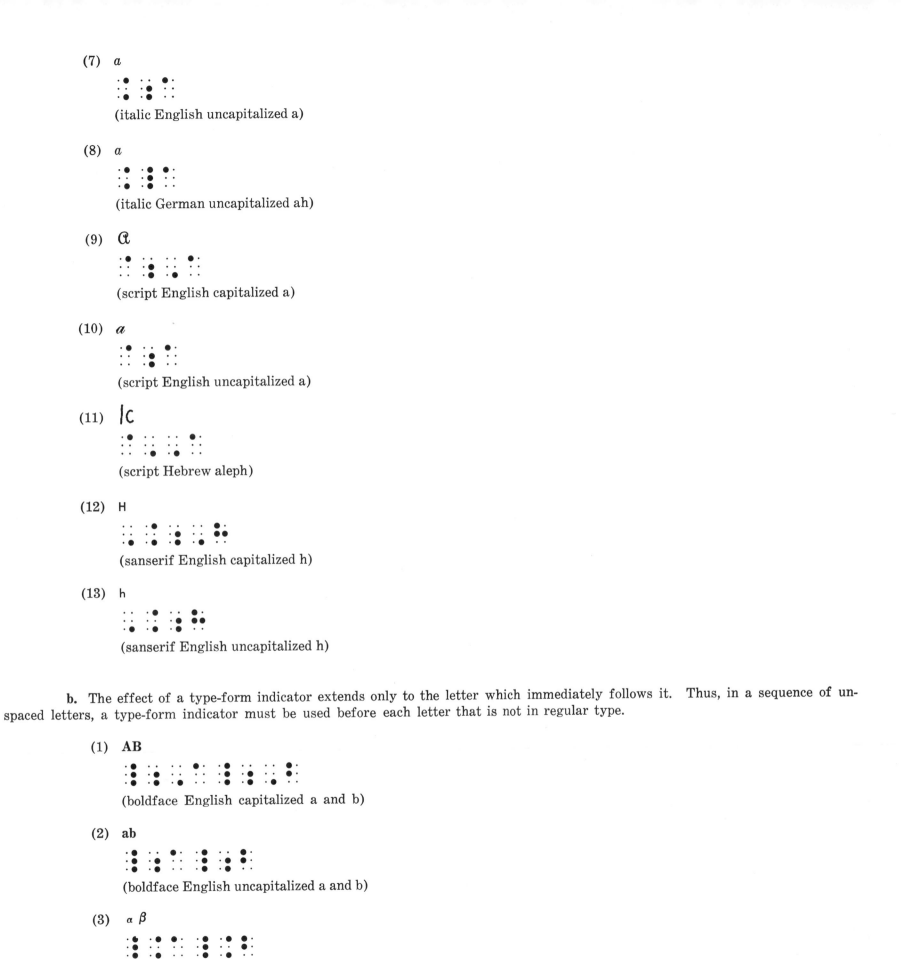

(italic English uncapitalized a)

(8) *a*

(italic German uncapitalized ah)

(9) 𝒶

(script English capitalized a)

(10) *a*

(script English uncapitalized a)

(11) ⏐c

(script Hebrew aleph)

(12) H

(sanserif English capitalized h)

(13) h

(sanserif English uncapitalized h)

b. The effect of a type-form indicator extends only to the letter which immediately follows it. Thus, in a sequence of un-spaced letters, a type-form indicator must be used before each letter that is not in regular type.

(1) **AB**

(boldface English capitalized a and b)

(2) **ab**

(boldface English uncapitalized a and b)

(3) **α β**

(boldface Greek uncapitalized alpha and beta)

(4) *ab*

⠀⠀ ⠀⠀ ⠀⠀ ⠀⠀ ⠀⠀ ⠀⠀

(italic English uncapitalized a and b)

(5) 𝒜 ℬ

⠀⠀ ⠀⠀ ⠀⠀ ⠀⠀ ⠀⠀ ⠀⠀

(script English capitalized a and b)

(6) *AbCd*

⠀⠀ ⠀⠀ ⠀⠀ ⠀⠀ ⠀⠀ ⠀⠀ ⠀⠀ ⠀⠀ ⠀⠀ ⠀⠀ ⠀⠀

(italic English capitalized a, boldface uncapitalized b, italic capitalized c, script uncapitalized d)

(7) pqrs

⠀⠀ ⠀⠀ ⠀⠀ ⠀⠀ ⠀⠀ ⠀⠀ ⠀⠀ ⠀⠀

(regular English uncapitalized p, boldface q, boldface r, regular s)

(8) xiyj

⠀⠀ ⠀⠀ ⠀⠀ ⠀⠀ ⠀⠀ ⠀⠀ ⠀⠀ ⠀⠀

(regular English uncapitalized x, boldface i, regular y, boldface j)

(9) αa

⠀⠀ ⠀⠀ ⠀⠀ ⠀⠀ ⠀⠀

(regular Greek uncapitalized alpha, boldface English uncapitalized a)

(10) ʜH

⠀⠀ ⠀⠀ ⠀⠀ ⠀⠀ ⠀⠀ ⠀⠀ ⠀⠀

(sanserif English capitalized h, regular English capitalized h)

(11) **p + q = r**

⠀⠀ ⠀⠀ ⠀⠀ ⠀⠀ ⠀⠀ ⠀⠀ ⠀⠀ ⠀⠀ ⠀⠀ ⠀⠀

(boldface English uncapitalized p, q, r)

§42. Type-Form Indicators With Numerals:

a. The appropriate type-form indicator must be used when it is necessary to show that numerals are printed in a type form other than regular type. The numeric indicator must always be used between a type-form indicator and a numeral or decimal point.

(1) **0**

⠀⠀ ⠀⠀ ⠀⠀

(boldface zero)

(2) *3*

(italic 3)

(3) *.3*

(italic .3)

(4)

(script 4)

(5) $+ 0$

(ordinary plus, boldface zero)

(6) $- 0$

(ordinary minus, boldface zero)

b. The effect of a type-form indicator with numerals extends until there is a change in type. Thus, when numerals contain digits in more than one type form, the appropriate type-form indicator and the numeric indicator must be used before each change in type. However, when the change is to regular type, only the numeric indicator is used.

(1) **123**

(boldface 1, 2, 3)

(2) 4*5*6

(boldface 4, italic 5, regular 6)

(3) 4567

(boldface 4 and 5, regular 6 and 7)

(4) 1234

(regular 1 and 2, boldface 3 and 4)

(5) **100** + **200** = **300**

(boldface 1, 2, and 3; all zeros in regular type)

(6) *28*-571

(italic 28, hyphen, boldface 571)

(7) *47*-653

(italic 47, hyphen, regular 653)

§43. **Type-Form Indicators With Compound Expressions:**

a. When it is necessary to show that a compound expression consisting of a numeral joined by a hyphen to a word or abbreviation is entirely printed in the same nonregular type, the appropriate type-form indicator must be used before the numeral. The effect of the type-form indicator extends throughout the compound expression.

(1) **35-ohm**

(the entire expression is in boldface type)

(2) *35-ft*

(the entire expression is in italic type)

b. If, in the compound expression, there is a change from nonregular to regular type after the hyphen, the hyphen must be preceded by the literary termination sign

(1) 35-ohm

(35 in boldface type, ohm in regular type)

c. If, in the compound expression, there is a change from regular to nonregular type after the hyphen, only the appropriate type-form indicator must be used after the hyphen.

(1) 35-**ohm**

(35 in regular type, ohm in boldface type)

d. If, in the compound expression, there is a change from one nonregular type to a different nonregular type after the hyphen, the appropriate type-form indicator must be used before each part of the expression.

(1) 35-*ohm*

(35 in boldface type, ohm in italic type)

56

§44. Use and Nonuse of Type-Form Indicators in Technical Texts:

a. When a uniform type form is used throughout a print text for letters, numerals, or other mathematical symbols, the type form must be considered regular type, and type-form indicators must not be used. For example, type-form indicators must not be used when the letters of all formulas throughout a text are uniformly printed in italic type. However, the specific type form must be shown when a different type form is introduced to convey a special mathematical distinction, as when the author uses different type forms to distinguish between two meanings of the same letter. A type form which has no mathematical significance, or which is used only to attract the reader's attention, must not be shown in braille.

(1) R denotes the set of rational numbers, and $\mathfrak{R}$ denotes the set of real numbers.

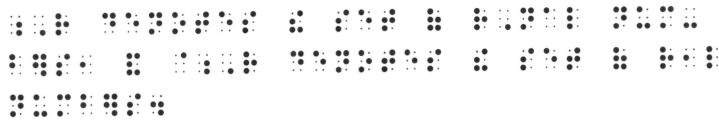

b. When boldface type is used in print to identify letters as vectors or to denote a zero as the null vector, the boldface type has mathematical significance and must be shown in braille.

(1) Is there a vector **s** such that $\mathbf{r} + \mathbf{s} = \mathbf{t}$?

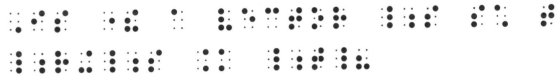

(2) In $\mathbf{pv} = \mathbf{0}$, **v** is a vector and **0** is the null vector.

(3) $\mathbf{a} + \mathbf{0} = \mathbf{a}$

(4) $\mathbf{B} = 2\mathbf{i} + 3\mathbf{j} + 2\mathbf{k}$

Type-Form Indicators for Labeled Mathematical Statements, Words, and Phrases

Opening Boldface Type Indicator

Closing Boldface Type Indicator

Opening Italic Type Indicator

Closing Italic Type Indicator

§45. Type-Form Indicators With Labeled Mathematical Statements:

a. When a labeled mathematical statement such as a theorem, definition, axiom, lemma, etc. is printed in nonregular type, the label must be transcribed as though it were entirely capitalized, and the statement must be preceded and followed by its appropriate opening and closing type-form indicators. The type-form indicators must be preceded and followed by a space.

    (1) **Theorem 4.** *The diagonals of a rectangle are equal.*

    (2) *Definition.* x + yi = a + bi, if and only if x = a and y = b.

b. In the body of a labeled mathematical statement, if a word or a phrase is printed in a different nonregular type for emphasis or special distinction, the word or phrase must be preceded and followed by its appropriate type-form indicators. When two type-form indicators must be used consecutively, they must be unspaced from each other.

    (1) **Definition.** A *hexagon* is a polygon which has 6 sides.

    (2) *Definition.* **Equal arcs** are arcs that can be made to coincide.

    (3) **Definition.** *A polygon that has 5 sides is a* **pentagon.**

§46. Type-Form Indicators With Unlabeled Statements:

    a. In an unlabeled statement, a word or a phrase printed in boldface type for emphasis or special distinction must be preceded and followed by the boldface type-form indicators in accordance with the rules of §45 above.

(1) Name the set of letters in **apple.**

(2) LCM stands for **least common multiple.**

b. In an unlabeled statement, an italicized phrase showing emphasis or special distinction and beginning or ending with a numeral, letter, or other mathematical symbol or expression must be preceded and followed by the italic type-form indicators in accordance with §45 above.

However, an italicized word or an italicized phrase both beginning and ending with a word must be transcribed according to the rules of English braille.

(1) *O is the vertex.*

(2) *The common internal tangent is PC.*

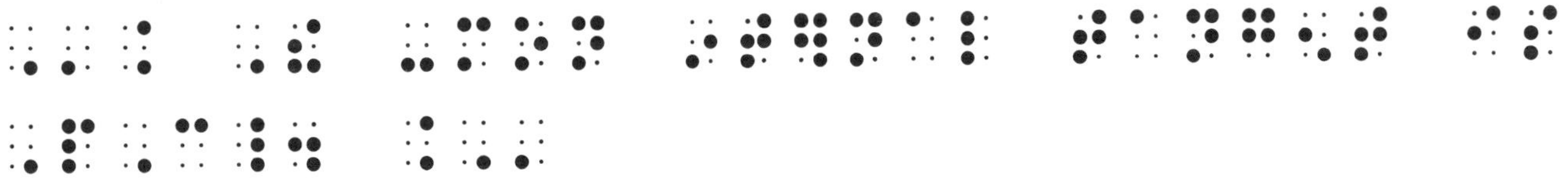

(3) LCD means *least common denominator.*

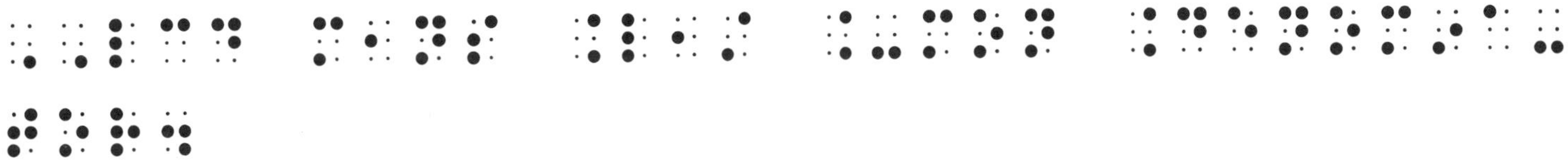

(4) *If* $a + b = b + a$*, then addition is commutative.*

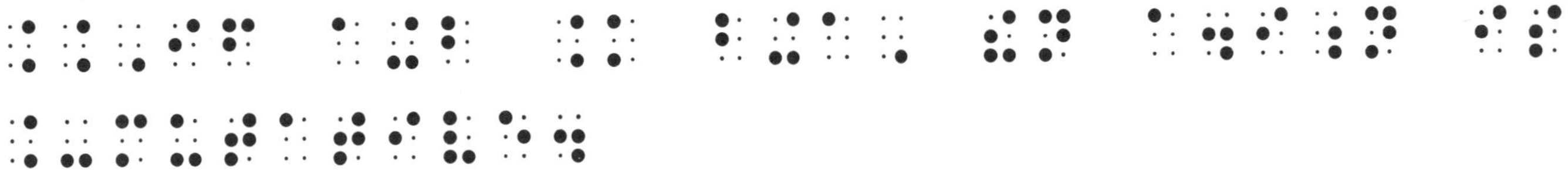

FORMAT (CONTINUED)

§47. Margins for Labeled Mathematical Statements and Formal Proofs:

a. A labeled mathematical statement or a formal proof, such as a theorem, definition, axiom, proposition, postulate, lemma, etc., should be transcribed in the following format:

i. A line must be left blank before the beginning and after the end of the entire labeled statement or formal proof. However, a line should not be left blank before or after a new page-separation line or at the beginning or end of a braille page.

ii. The labeled statement or formal proof must begin in cell 3, and its runovers must begin in cell 1.

iii. If the labeled statement or formal proof contains subheadings such as *Given, Prove,* or *Conclusion,* the subheadings must begin in cell 3, and their runovers must begin in cell 1. A line must not be skipped above a subheading. A subheading should be capitalized or italicized in accordance with the print text. If the subheading is in boldface type, it should be entirely capitalized in braille.

(1) **Theorem 1. If two angles of a triangle are equal, the sides opposite these angles are equal.**

    Given: Triangle ABC with angle A equal to angle C.

    Prove: BA = BC.

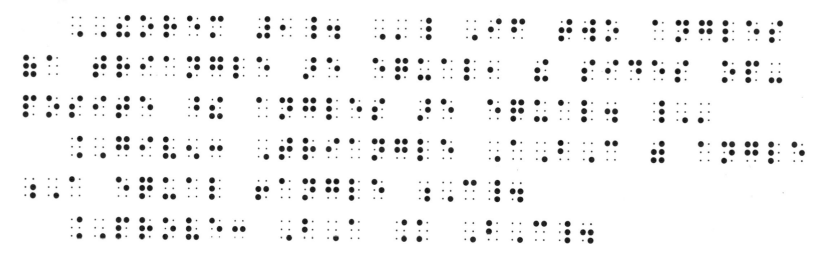

b. When a formal proof is presented in step-number form and divided into two columns, usually headed *Statements* and *Reasons*, the following format must be used:

    i. A line should be left blank before the beginning and after the end of the step-numbered items.

    ii. The print columnar form must not be followed in braille. Each item from the *Reason* column must be placed beneath its matching item from the *Statement* column.

    iii. The letters "S" for *Statement* and "R" for *Reason* must be placed immediately after the appropriate step number. Similarly, other column headings should be indicated by appropriate letters.

    iv. Each step number must begin in cell 1, and any runovers must begin in cell 3.

    v. A transcriber's note must be included to explain the change in format and to specify the meaning of the letters used to replace the headings. The note must be placed at the beginning of each volume in which a change of format occurs.

(1) **Theorem 2. All right angles are equal.**

    Given: Angle ABC and angle DEF are right angles.

    Prove: Angle ABC equals angle DEF.

    Proof:

Statements	Reasons
1. Angle ABC and angle DEF are right angles.	1. Given.
2. Angle ABC equals 90 degrees; angle DEF equals 90 degrees.	2. A right angle contains 90 degrees.
3. Angle ABC equals angle DEF.	3. Transitivity postulate.

HOMEWORK

Prepare the following homework for submission to your teacher. If a transcriber's note is required, it should be placed on a separate transcriber's note page in accordance with the rules of the *Code of Braille Textbook Formats and Techniques*. Proofread carefully.

EXERCISE 4

Write these German letters as indicated.

1. Boldface: **a**, **b**, **m**, **n**. **A**, **B**, **M**, **N**. **aA**.

2. Script: *a, b, m, n. A, L, M, N. a A.*

Write these Greek letters as indicated.

3. Boldface: a, β, γ, ϵ. A, B, Γ, E. aA.

4. Script: *a, b, Γ, ε. A, B, Γ, E. a A.*

Write these Hebrew letters as indicated.

5. Script: אָ, ב, ג, ו, ז. אָ ב.

Write these Russian letters as indicated.

6. Boldface: а, б, л, м. А, Б, Л, М. аА.

7. Script: *а, б, л, м. А, Б, Л, М. аА.*

Write these English letters as indicated.

8. Boldface: **a, b, r, s. A, B, R, S. aA.**

9. Italic: *a, b, r, s. A, B, R, S. aA.*

10. Script: *a, b, r, s.* ℛ, ℬ, ℛ, S. *a*ℛ.

11. Sanserif: b, c, h, m. B, C, H, M. bB.

12. In $\mathcal{R} \times \mathcal{R}$ the two perpendicular vectors **w** and **t** whose sum is **v** are perpendicular components of **v**.

13. Find the angle between the vectors **A** = —3**i** + 5**j** — **k** and **B** = —6**i** — 10**j** + 2**k**.

14. Prove that **A** $\times$ **B** = **B** $\times$ **A**.

Write these numerals as indicated.

15. Boldface: **0, 1, 2, 3, 456, 789.**

16. Italic: *0, 1, 2, 3, 456, 789.*

In each numeral below, give the number for which each black digit stands.

17. 893,**7**41

18. 999,**9**99

19. 5**2**2,489

20. 300 + **3**00 = 600

If the items in boldface or italic type are incorrect, replace them with the right answer.

21. Is it possible to generate a **10,000-volt** potential difference by rubbing a comb with wool?

22. A 36-in. ruler is the same as a *2*-yd. ruler.

23. The filament resistance is lower in a 500-watt light bulb than in a 100-**amp** bulb.

24. A 1000-gram weight equals a **5.2**-*oz.* weight.

As a result of your earlier work in mathematics you should be familiar with the properties of the consequences of the axioms discussed in the preceding sections. In order to have the most important consequences available for future reference, we shall review a few standard theorems and definitions.

Theorem 1. *The line is a connected set.*

Theorem 2. *Any convergent sequence is bounded.*

Theorem 3. **For all a, b, and c in the set of real numbers, a + b = c + b if and only if a = c.**

Corollary. **For all a, b, and c in the set of real numbers, b + a = b + c if and only if a = c.**

Definition. The *empty set* **is a set which contains no elements.**

Definition. *Equal angles* **are formed by the same amount of rotation.**

Definition. *A composite proposition that always has a truth value is called a* **tautology.**

Answer the following questions.

25. Name the set of letters in **football.**

26. Define **fractional number.**

27. Use Exercise 4 to show that *R divides QS.*

28. *Addition is commutative when a + b = b + a.* Explain why.

29. If A is the set of letters in *Alaska* and B is the set of letters in *Texas,* what is the intersection of A and B?

30. State the *commutative law for multiplication.*

Theorem 4. If two sides of a triangle are equal, the angles opposite these sides are equal.

Given: Triangle ABC with BA = BC.

Prove: Angle A equals angle C.

Proof:

Statements	*Reasons*
1. Draw BD bisecting angle ABC and meeting AC at D.	1. Every angle has one and only one bisector.
2. Angle 1 equals angle 2.	2. A bisector divides an angle into two equal parts.
3. BA = BC.	3. Given.
4. BD = BD.	4. Identity postulate.
5. Triangle ABC is congruent to triangle CBD.	5. s.a.s. = s.a.s.
6. Angle A equals angle C.	6. Corresponding angles of congruent triangles are equal.

LESSON 5

SIGNS OF GROUPING

§48. **Use of Signs of Grouping:** The signs of grouping listed below must be used throughout a technical text both for literary and for mathematical material. The parentheses, brackets, and braces of English braille must only be used to enclose literary material on title pages. Any sign of grouping not listed below must be devised using two or more braille symbols whose last cell is ⠶ for the opening sign and ⠶ for the closing sign. A transcriber's note must be included to explain the devised sign of grouping.

While signs of grouping most commonly occur in pairs, the text must be followed when only the opening or only the closing grouping sign is shown in print. No space should be left between an opening or a closing sign of grouping and the material which it encloses.

Parentheses

    Opening   (

    Closing   )

Brackets (square)

    Opening   [

    Closing   ]

    Boldface Opening   [

    Boldface Closing   ]

Barred Brackets

    Opening

    Closing

Angle Brackets

    Opening   ⟨

    Closing   ⟩

Braces (curly brackets)

    Opening   {

    Closing   }

Barred Braces

Opening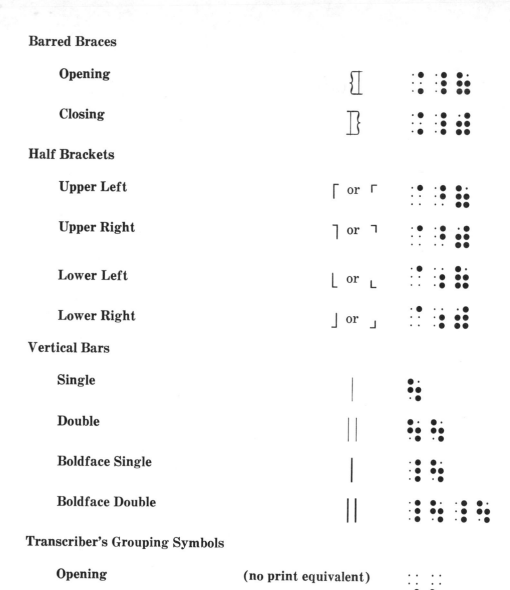

Closing

Half Brackets

Upper Left ⌈ or Γ

Upper Right ⌉ or ⌐

Lower Left ⌊ or L

Lower Right ⌋ or ⌙

Vertical Bars

Single |

Double ||

Boldface Single |

Boldface Double ||

Transcriber's Grouping Symbols

Opening (no print equivalent)

Closing (no print equivalent)

§49. **Punctuation With Signs of Grouping:** A sign of grouping must be punctuated mathematically and must not itself be considered a punctuation mark. Thus, except for the mathematical comma, hyphen, and dash, the punctuation indicator must be used before a punctuation mark following a sign of grouping.

(1) (α), (β).

(2) ("two").

(3) ("2")

(4) (—"two")

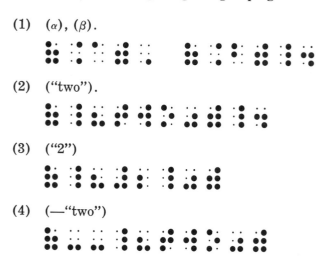

§50. Contractions With Signs of Grouping: Although contractions may generally be used in words, parts of words, and abbreviations, the contractions listed below must not be used, whether capitalized, uncapitalized, or italicized, when they come in direct contact with a sign of grouping or when they are separated from a sign of grouping by a punctuation mark. Except as noted in subsection **a, ii** below, if a contraction cannot be used in one part of a word, contractions must not be used in any part of the word. Words and abbreviations, whether contracted or uncontracted, must be punctuated according to the rules of English braille.

    a. The following categories restrict the use of contractions:

        i. The one-cell whole-word alphabet contractions for *but, can, do, ..., as.*

        (1)   (but not in division)

        (2)   (that is)

        (3)   (you can do it)

        (4)   (Not now.)

        (5)   (*you* cannot do so)

        (6)   ("Can you go?")

        (7)   (but, you must not)

        (8)   (More.   Not less.)

        ii. The whole-word lower-sign contractions for *be, enough, were, his, in, was, to, into, by.* Part-word contractions may be used in *enough, were,* and *into.*

        (1)   The x (in the example below) is the variable.

        (2)   (Be sure you are correct)

        (3)   (that is enough)

(4)   (were you sure of your answer)

(5)   (*his* answer is wrong)

(6)   ("in all cases it holds true")

(7)   (This cannot be.)

(8)   (into every dividend)

(9)   (this fact must be looked into)

(10) ("By your leave.")

(11) (to within a tolerance of 5 cm)

(12) (by your calculations)

iii. The whole- or part-word contractions for *and, for, of, the, with.*

(1)   Mary (and Sandra) can add.

(2)   (*and,* in addition)

(3)   {Andrea, Andrew, Sandra}

(4)   We are (for and with) you.

(5)   (For example.)

(6) (What did you come for?)

(7) Read (formula 4.6) p. 36.

(8) The y (of the example above) is negative.

(9) ["of course not"]

(10) (Find the proof.)

(11) {the months of the year}

(12) Add 4 + 3 (then divide).

(13) Do it (without dividing) mentally.

§51. Signs of Grouping With Numerals: The numeric indicator must not be used before a numeral in regular type, before a decimal point, or after a minus sign immediately following any of the print opening signs of grouping listed above. The numeric indicator is required with any numeral not in regular type.

(1) (1), (2), and (3).

(2) {10,000}

(3) | 3 |

(4) (1, 2, and 3)

(5) (1 + 2 = 3, 1 + 3 = 4)

(6) (1-to-1 correspondence)

(7) (.1 < .2)

(8) (—10 and +4 is —6)

(9) (2 is imaginary; ['2' is real])

(10) (2 and 3)

§52. Signs of Grouping With Letters:

a. The English letter indicator must not be used when a single English letter or an unspaced combination of letters in regular type is entirely enclosed within signs of grouping.

(1) (a), (b), and (c).

(2) [x], [x], {R}, | y |, ‖ f ‖

(3) (ab) and (cd) are not equal.

(4) (xy) and (XY)

b. When a single English letter or an unspaced combination of letters is in direct contact with only its opening or closing sign of grouping, the English letter indicator must be used or must not be used as though the grouping signs were not present. However, the English letter indicator must not be used when a grouping sign carries a prime or other modifying symbol.

(1) (a, b, and c)

(2) (p is less than q)

(3) ("M is greater than N")

(4) (x's and y's)

(5) (nth root of x)

(6) (x-intercept)

(7) (not-p)

(8) (ab is the same as ba)

(9) (side AB)

(10) (—r, +s, and —t)

(11) (b′ is read "b prime")

(12) (a = b, b = c, ab = cd)

(13) (j = 1, 2, 3, . . . , n)

(14) a) 3 × 4 = _?_

(15) t]′ and v]′ have unique meaning.

c. The English letter indicator must be used with any English letter printed in nonregular type even though it is enclosed within, or in contact with, signs of grouping.

(1) (j)

(2) (r, s, and T)

d. The appropriate alphabetic indicator must be used with any letter from the German, Greek, Hebrew, or Russian alphabets even when enclosed within, or in contact with, signs of grouping.

(1) (𝖆)

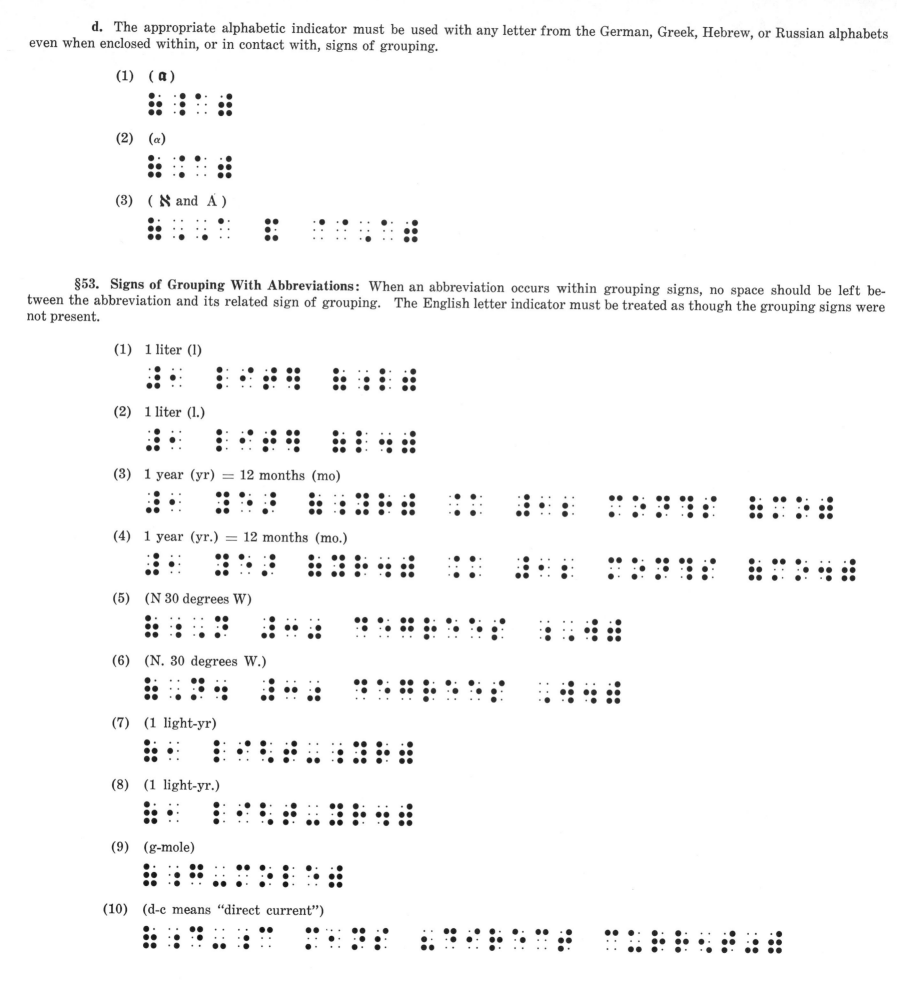

(2) (α)

(3) (א and א́)

§53. **Signs of Grouping With Abbreviations:** When an abbreviation occurs within grouping signs, no space should be left between the abbreviation and its related sign of grouping.   The English letter indicator must be treated as though the grouping signs were not present.

(1) 1 liter (l)

(2) 1 liter (l.)

(3) 1 year (yr) = 12 months (mo)

(4) 1 year (yr.) = 12 months (mo.)

(5) (N 30 degrees W)

(6) (N. 30 degrees W.)

(7) (1 light-yr)

(8) (1 light-yr.)

(9) (g-mole)

(10) (d-c means "direct current")

(11) 1 foot (ft) = 12 inches (in)

(12) (i.e.)

(13) (L.C.M. means *least common multiple*)

(14) (EST)

(15) {Wed., Thurs., Fri.}

§54. Enclosed Lists:

a. Definition: To save time and space, special provision is made for the transcription of a sequence of mathematical items enclosed in signs of grouping. Such an *enclosed list* must begin and end with an ink-print sign of grouping. The items of the list can only be numerals, letters, or other mathematical expressions, the ellipsis, the long dash, or any sign of omission. The items of the list must be separated by commas.

An enclosed list must not contain a word, an abbreviation, an ordinal ending, a plural ending, a sign of comparison, or any punctuation mark except the commas which separate items.

b. Nonuse of the Numeric and English Letter Indicators With Enclosed Lists: In an enclosed list, the English letter indicator must not be used with any English letter or combination of letters in regular type. In addition, the numeric indicator must not be used before a numeral or decimal point in regular type which begins an item in an enclosed list. However, the English letter and numeric indicators must be used with any letter or numeral in a nonregular type form.

(1) {a, b, c, d}

(2) (0, a, 1, b, 2)

(3) (A, A′, B, B′, C)

(4) (a, 2x, b)

(5) (α, a, β, b)

(6) (ab, cd, ef)

⠿⠀⠿⠀⠿⠀⠀⠀⠿⠿⠀⠀⠀⠿⠿⠀⠿

(7) <—1, 0]

⠀⠀⠀⠿⠀⠀⠀⠀⠀⠀⠀⠿⠀⠿

(8) (—1, —2, —3)

⠿⠀⠀⠀⠀⠿⠀⠀⠀⠀⠿⠀⠀⠿⠀⠿

(9) [.1, .02, .003]

⠀⠿⠀⠀⠀⠀⠀⠀⠿⠀⠀⠀⠀⠀⠀⠿⠀⠿⠀⠿

(10) (0, —1, ±2)

⠿⠀⠀⠿⠀⠀⠀⠿⠀⠀⠀⠀⠿⠀⠀⠿

(11) (1 + h, 2 + k, 0)

⠿⠀⠿⠀⠀⠿⠀⠀⠀⠀⠿⠀⠀⠿⠀⠀⠀⠿⠿

(12) (5 + 5, 10 + 10)

⠿⠀⠿⠀⠀⠿⠀⠀⠀⠀⠿⠀⠀⠿⠀⠀⠀⠿⠿

(13) (a, b, c, . . . , z)

⠿⠀⠀⠀⠀⠀⠿⠀⠀⠀⠀⠿⠀⠀⠀⠀⠀⠀⠀⠀⠀⠀⠿⠿

(14) (2, 4, 6, ——, 10)

⠿⠀⠀⠀⠀⠿⠀⠀⠀⠀⠿⠀⠀⠀⠀⠀⠀⠀⠀⠀⠀⠀⠀⠿⠿

(15) (1, 3, ?, ?, 9)

⠿⠀⠀⠀⠀⠿⠀⠀⠀⠿⠀⠀⠀⠿⠀⠀⠀⠀⠿⠿

(16) (x, 7, y, 8)

⠿⠀⠿⠀⠀⠀⠀⠀⠀⠿⠀⠀⠀⠀⠀⠀⠿⠀⠀⠀⠿⠿

(17) (j, k)

⠿⠀⠀⠿⠀⠿⠀⠀⠀⠀⠿⠀⠿⠀⠿

c. Items in an enclosed list must not be divided between braille lines or braille pages. If there is insufficient space on a line to accommodate the expression, this space must be left blank, and the entire enclosed list must be brought down to the next line.

(1) The replacement set is {0, 1, 2, 3, 4, 5, 6, 7, 8, 9}.

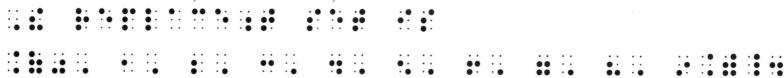

§55. Signs of Grouping With Plural Endings and Parts of Words: In accordance with the ink-print text, the appropriate grouping symbols must be used to enclose plural endings and parts of words.

    (1) Which problem(s) are correct?

    (2) Notice the prefix in (bi)nomial.

§56. Spacing With Signs of Grouping:

    a. In an enclosed expression, no space should be left between a dash, an ellipsis, a sign of comparison, or any other symbol and its sign of grouping.

    (1) (——, 3, 5, 7, ——)

    (2) (..., 2, 4, 6, ...)

    (3) The symbol (=) denotes equality.

    (4) Use (> or <) to make a true statement.

    (5) $(+, -, \times)$

    (6) ($) and (¢) denote dollars and cents.

    b. The spacing before and after an enclosed expression is subject to the spacing rules for the signs which precede or follow the enclosure. In addition, no space should be left between an enclosed expression and a letter, a numeral, or another sign of grouping when these items are unspaced in print and are part of the same expression.

    (1) $(4 \times 30) + (4 \times 2) = 128$

    (2) $8 \times (40 + 3) = (8 + 40) \times (8 + 3)$

    (3) $\|\,a\,| - |\,b\,\| < |\,a - b\,|$

(4)   (rate) $\times$ (time) $=$ (distance)

(5) $(2 \times 3)\$ = 6\$$

(6)   Do examples (1)-(10).

(7)   (1) ... (10)

(8) $(2x - 3y)$ mi.

(9)   Solve for x $(x > 0)$.

(10) $f(x) = |x|$

(11) $P(x, y) = \phi(\theta)$

(12) $A(2) + B(1) + C(2) + D = 0$

(13) $3(x - 1)(x + 4) < 0$

(14) $[-4 - (-1)] + [-1 - (-3)]$

(15) $\{(1, 0), (1, 1)\}$

c. A space must be left between an opening and a closing sign of grouping when the blank space between them in print does not represent an omission.

(1)   Parentheses ( ) are symbols of grouping.

§57. Transcriber's Notes:

a. The transcriber's grouping symbols  must be used to enclose a transcriber's note which has been inserted in the text. They must not be used to enclose transcriber's notes on preliminary pages at the beginning of a braille volume.

b. A transcriber's note of seven words or less may be inserted directly into the text where it applies, leaving one space before and after the note. Longer notes must be inserted at a convenient point nearest the material referred to and must be placed, indented, and run over in accordance with the rules of the *Code of Braille Textbook Formats and Techniques*.

c. The same rules governing the punctuation and contraction of expressions with signs of grouping also apply to transcriber's grouping symbols. The numeric indicator must be used after the opening transcriber's grouping symbol, and the English letter indicator must be used or must not be used as though the grouping signs were absent.

(1) What place value does the red 2 have in 22?

(2) In 4 + 5, 4 is an even number.

(3) An F denotes negation.

(4) Which number is greater 2 or 3?

§58. Representation of Numerals in Nondecimal Bases:

a. A nondecimal numeration system may use letters to supplement the 10 Arabic numerals and to represent the additional digits required. In such instances, uncapitalized letters must be used in braille. If capitalized letters are used in print, a transcriber's note must be included to explain the change to uncapitalized letters.

The letters used to represent digits in a nondecimal numeration system must be treated as numerals, and the numeric indicator must be used where required. Such numerals are mathematical symbols and must be punctuated accordingly.

(1) 13T8 and T1E5 are base 12 numerals. T represents 10 and E represents 11.

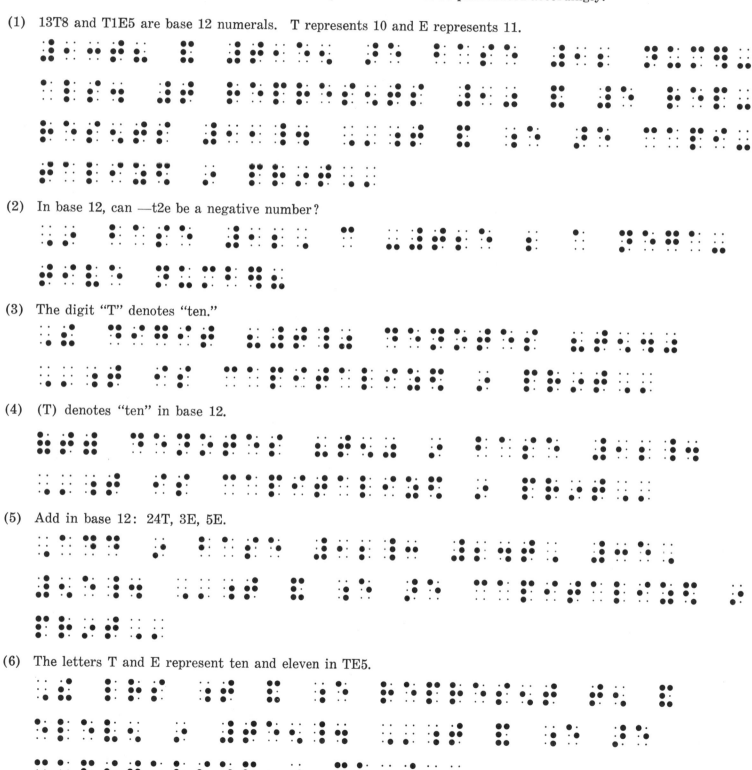

(2) In base 12, can —t2e be a negative number?

(3) The digit "T" denotes "ten."

(4) (T) denotes "ten" in base 12.

(5) Add in base 12: 24T, 3E, 5E.

(6) The letters T and E represent ten and eleven in TE5.

b. A nondecimal numeration system may use special signs, such as χ (dek) and ε (el), in conjunction with the 10 Arabic digits; or it may use an arbitrary set of signs, such as \$ ¢ %, which contains no Arabic digits. In such cases, one-cell symbols preferably chosen from the letters of the English alphabet must be selected to represent these special signs. A transcriber's note must be inserted to specify the meanings assigned to these symbols, and must also include a drawing of any print sign lacking an equivalent symbol in the code.

The symbols for these special signs in nondecimal numeration systems must be treated as numerals, and the numeric indicator must be used where required. Such signs are mathematical symbols and must be punctuated accordingly.

(1) Some base 12 numerals are $\chi\,\varepsilon\,5$, $\varepsilon\,5\,\chi$, and $2\,\varepsilon\,6\,\chi$.

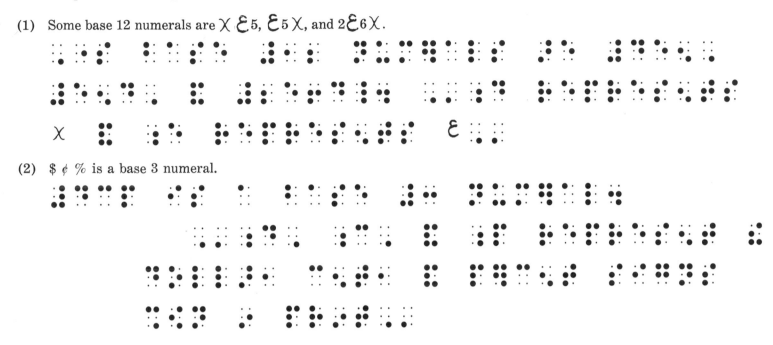

(2) \$ ¢ % is a base 3 numeral.

HOMEWORK

Prepare the following homework for submission to your teacher. If a transcriber's note is required, be sure to include it in its proper place. Proofread carefully.

EXERCISE 5

1. ("20%"), ("25%"), and ("50%") are the same as what fractions?

2. Find the volume of a sphere having a radius of 6 inches. (Use $\pi = 3.14$)

3. Draw a regular hexagon (a figure with 6 equal sides and 6 equal angles) inside a circle.

4. What is the least common denominator (L.C.D.) of 8 and 16?

5. Define a geometric progression (GP).

6. Prove: In logic, the result of each value of x (from an appropriate domain) behaves as a "statement function."

7. Multiplication (not addition) is the inverse of division.

8. For every sequence (in exercise 19) determine the difference.

9. Illustrate the way in which each member of X is a member of some (and, hence exactly one) member of A.

10. Is {Andrew, Albert, Andrea} a true set?

11. Use numerals to prove $a + b = b + a$ (for example, if $a = 2$ and $b = 3$, then $2 + 3 = 3 + 2$).

12. Complete: A (formal) proof is a finite column of formulas .... .

13. Find the sum (of the first seven terms) of the series 12, 9, 6, ...

14. How do we derive a (proof) schema of a (theorem) schema?

15. Write a numeral for the cardinal number of {the set of eggs in a dozen}.

16. Can you find the answer (without using pencil and paper) to problem 4?

17. Solve examples (1), (2), and (3). Is (.5) and (.6) an accurate estimate?

18. A conical pile of sand 6 ft. high has a base of 27 sq. ft. How many loads of sand are in the pile? (1 load = 1 cu. yd.)

19. Estimate the sizes of angles (d) and (e) using the measurements of the angles in (A), (B), and (C). Check, using (ab and de).

20. If $x > y$ (x is greater than y) and $x = 10$, what is the relationship when $y = 4$?

21. For vectors (a, b, c) and real numbers (p and q) can we say that $a + (b + c) = (a + b) + c$?

22. (γ, θ, ϕ) denotes what kind of coordinates?

23. What meaning does u]′ and w]′ have?

24. State the axiom for the inequality $a + c < b + c$, $(a < b)$.

25. 1 liter (l) is equal to how many cubic centimeters (cc)?

26. How many days are there in 1 year (yr)?

27. Write a description of the following set: {Pa., O., Ky., Va., Md.}.

28. In how many ways is it possible to set up a 1-to-1 correspondence between {a, b, c, d} and {w, x, y, z}?

29. Can we say (a, b, c, ...) is infinite?

30. (100, 200, _____, 400)

31. Picture the set of points on a real number line that are in the following intervals: $\langle -3, 2 \rangle$; $[0, 1)$; $[2, \pi]$.

32. Consider $x > 4$. If {0, 1, 2, 3, 4, 5, 6, 7, 8, 9} is the replacement set for the variable, what is the solution set?

33. Mark points corresponding to the ordered pairs (4 and 2), (5 and 0) on a set of axes. What does each point represent?

Graph.

34. $|x + y| = |x| + |y|$

35. $g(x) = (x - 1)(x - 2)(x - 3)$ and $G(t) = t(t - 1)(t - 2)(t - 3)$

Simplify.

36. $(y + 6) - (6 - y)$

37. $10a + [3a - (5a - 4)]$

38. $[(a + b) - 2c]\ [(a + b) + 3c]$

39. $|3 - 5| \cdot (x - 5)$

Answer the following questions.

40. Show that $M = \{(4, 2) + s(1, -1)\}$.

41. Does $x = 0$ when $\phi(\theta) = P$ is a point on the y-axis?

42. Tell what each of the following signs mean: $(+, -, \times, \div)$ and $(=, <, >)$.

43. Explain why brackets [ ] and braces { } are called symbols of aggregation.

44. For what value(s) of v will $v - 2$, $2v - 6$, and $4v - 8$ form an A.P.?

45. Which numeral is greater: 3 or 3 ?

46. What value has the digit t in e5t7?

47. Express each base 12 numeral as a decimal numeral: 4TEE; T1E5; E5T.

LESSON 6

SUPERSCRIPTS, SUBSCRIPTS, AND LEVEL INDICATORS

A mathematical expression can contain symbols placed above or below the normal baseline of writing. Superscripts appear above the baseline; subscripts appear below the baseline. Since it is not practical to write on different levels in braille, level indicators are used to identify the level of a superscript or subscript in relation to the baseline of writing.

Level Indicators

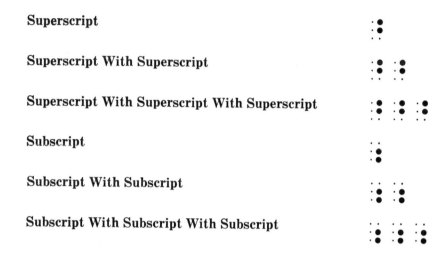

Superscript	⠔
Superscript With Superscript	⠔ ⠔
Superscript With Superscript With Superscript	⠔ ⠔ ⠔
Subscript	⠢
Subscript With Subscript	⠢ ⠢
Subscript With Subscript With Subscript	⠢ ⠢ ⠢

§59. Superscript Level Indicators: The superscript level indicator ⠔ must be used to show that the symbols immediately following it appear on the first level above the baseline of writing. Superscripts may carry superscripts of their own. In such cases, the superscript indicator must be doubled, tripled, etc. to indicate superscripts on the second, third, or higher levels of writing.

(1) x^2

(2) π^2

(3) n^m

(4) 24^7

(5) $3^{-0.05T}$

(6) $(y - k)^3$

(7) $A^{(k + 1) + m}$

(8) n^{ab}

⠰⠝⠰⠔⠁⠰⠔⠃

(9) $n^{a+1}b+1^{c+1}$

(8) n^{ab}

(9) $n^{a+1b+1c+1}$

§60. Subscript Level Indicators:

a. Except as stated in **b** below, the subscript level indicator ⠢ must be used to show that the symbols immediately following it appear on the first level below the baseline of writing. Subscripts may carry subscripts of their own. In such cases, the subscript level indicator must be doubled, tripled, etc. to indicate subscripts on the second, third, or lower levels of writing.

(1) f_n

(2) 3_k

(3) $a_{(k+1)}$

(4) $A_{n \rceil i}$

(5) $10_?$

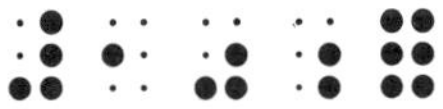

(6) δ_{ij}

(7) 10_8

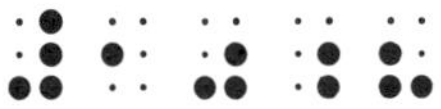

(8) $?_3$

(9) $(CO)_2$

(10) n_{x_y}

(11) $P_{x+1_{y}+1_{z}+1}$

83

b. The subscript level indicator must not be used before a *numeric* subscript on the *first* level below the baseline of writing if the numeral is a right-subscript to a *letter*. The numeric subscript may contain a comma, a decimal point, or one or more prime signs. The letter may be taken from any alphabet in any type form and may be part of a 2-letter chemical abbreviation. However, the letter must not be used as a numeral in a nondecimal numeration system or as part of a word or abbreviation.

The subscript level indicator must be used with a numeral on the first level below the baseline if a subscript contains any symbol other than a numeral with its comma or decimal point, or if the subscript carries a superscript or subscript of its own. Subscripts on the second or lower levels of writing always require their appropriate subscript level indicators.

(1) x_1

(2) ax_2

(3) A_{56}

(4) $x_{1,000}$

(5) $x_{5.3}$

(6) $x_{.7}$

(7) α_2

(8) Σ_0

(9) i_1

(10) CO_3

(11) Na_3

(12) TE_{12}

(13) five$_3$

(14) x_{2k}

(15) y_{-2}

(16) x_{2+k}

(17) a_{m1}

(18) x_{3_n}

(19) x_{y_2}

§61. Baseline Indicator:

a. In an unspaced expression the baseline indicator must be used after a superscript or subscript to indicate a return to the baseline of writing. However, the baseline indicator must not be used to return to the baseline after a numeric subscript not requiring a subscript indicator.

(1) $a^2 + b^2 + c^2$

(2) $4(x - y)^3 - 2(x - y)^3$

(3) $3a^3b + 6a^6b^2 + 9a^9b^3$

(4) $V = 2\pi^2Rr^2$

(5) x^n-dimensional system

(6) 6^2 — or 6×6 — is 36.

(7) $7_8 - 4_8$

(8) $\pm\, a_i b_j c_k d_l$

(9) $\text{five}_3 + \text{five}_3$

(10) $a_1 a_2 + b_1 b_2 + c_1 c_2$

(11) $\mathbf{v} = v_1 \mathbf{i}_1 + v_2 \mathbf{i}_2 + \ldots$

(12) $a_0 b_k + a_1 b_{k-1} + \ldots + a_k b_0$

b. The baseline indicator must be placed before a sign of grouping when a level indicator is in effect and the grouping symbol appears on the baseline of writing. However, the baseline indicator must not be placed after a numeric subscript not requiring a subscript indicator.

(1) $(x^2 + y^2) - (x^2 + y^2)$

(2) $(a^2)^8 (+2b)^3$

(3) $\{f_n\}$

(4) $|\, a_m - a_n\, |$

(5) $(x_1 y_1 + x_2 y_2)$

(6) $([CH_3]_2\, CH)$

(7) $f_1(x) = g(x) \cdot q_2(x) + f_2(x)$

c. No space should be left between an abbreviation and a related indicator. When it is necessary to return to the baseline, no space should be left before the baseline indicator.

(1) 144 ft² + 144 ft²

(2) 2 m³ + 2 m³

(3) 2 m.³ + 2 m.³

§62. Effect of Level Indicators:

a. The effect of one level indicator is terminated by another level indicator.

(1) $8x^5 - 6x^3y^2$

(2) $(r_a + s^2)$

(3) n^{x^y}

(4) $a^{(m^n)}$

(5) 10^{-4}

(6) $P_{x_{y_z}}$

b. The effect of a level indicator is terminated by the punctuation indicator. Thus, the punctuation indicator must be used after a word or an abbreviation in a superscript or subscript if the punctuation following it is on the baseline of writing. If the punctuation indicator is required in a superscript or subscript, the appropriate level indicator must be used before the punctuation indicator to show continuation of the level in effect.

(1) Multiply: $2^{10} \times 2^3$.

(2) e_i.

(3) The x^2's and x^3's.

(4) y_1's ... y_n's

(5) S_{angle}.

(6) $A^{m + m + m}$'s.

c. The effect of a level indicator is terminated by a comma unless the comma occurs in a long numeral. If a comma comes between two separate items in a superscript or subscript, the symbol ⠰ must be used to replace the comma or the comma and a space.

In such cases, the comma represented by this symbol does not terminate the superscript or subscript level already in effect. The symbol ⠰ must not be used to replace the comma on the baseline of writing.

(1) x^2, y^2, z^2

(2) (a_1, a_{1i}, a_{2i})

(3) Add: $2_{five}, 3_{five}, 4_{five}$.

(4) $e^{1,000}$

(5) $x^{1, 2}$

(6) $x^{i, j}$

(7) $x_{1, 2}$

(8) $x_{i, j, k}$

(9) $x_{n-1, n-1}, x_{n-1, n}, x_{n, n-1}$

(10) $x_{(a, b)} + y_a$

⠿ (braille)

(11) $P_{q_r, s}$

⠿ (braille)

(12) P_{n_1, n_2, n_3}

⠿ (braille)

d. The effect of a level indicator is terminated by a space or by a transition to a new braille line followed by literary text or by separate mathematical text. If a space separates the parts of an abbreviation or phrase in a superscript or subscript, the appropriate level indicator must be used before each part to show continuation of the level in effect.

(1) $2q^2$ is an even integer, and $3q^3$ is an odd integer.

⠿ (braille)

(2) A_k is the coefficient of x^k.

⠿ (braille)

(3) A_1 and A_2 are constants.

⠿ (braille)

(4) 6.696×10^8 miles per hour

⠿ (braille)

(5) 6.696×10^8 mph

⠿ (braille)

(6) $10^2 \ 10^3 \ 10^4$

⠿ (braille)

(7) $n_{\text{st. angles}}$

⠿ (braille)

(8) $n_{\text{obtuse angles}}$

⠿ (braille)

(9) $A^{n + n + n \text{ all } n\text{'s}}$ are equal.

⠿ (braille)

89

e. The effect of a level indicator is terminated by a space followed by a sign of comparison. If a sign of comparison occurs in a superscript or subscript, the appropriate level indicator must be used before the sign of comparison to indicate its level. The effect of a level indicator placed before the sign of comparison extends through the space following it. No space should be left between a sign of comparison and a related braille indicator.

(1) $a^2 + b^2 + c^2 = d^6$

(2) $a^{m+k} \div a^m = a^k$

(3) $4^x > 3^x$ when $x > 0$.

(4) $46_8 + 23_8 + 35_8 = 126_8$

(5) $s]_{t=a}$

(6) $S_{u=a}$

f. The effect of a level indicator extends through the space preceding and following an ellipsis or long dash. However, if the space is followed by literary text, by separate mathematical text, or by a sign of comparison, it terminates the effect of the level indicator and indicates a return to the baseline of writing.

(1) $x^{1+3+5+\ldots+(2n-1)}$

(2) $P_{n_1, n_2, \ldots}$

(3) $10^7 + \text{---}$ equals 10^{10}

(4) $10^7 + \cdots = 10^{10}$

(5) $10\_\_ = 6_8$

The appropriate level indicator must be used before an ellipsis or long dash located at a different level from the material preceding it. However, it is not necessary to indicate a return to the baseline after a numeric subscript not requiring the subscript indicator. No space should be left between an ellipsis or long dash and a related braille indicator.

(6) $a^1 b^2 c^3 d^4 \ldots z^n$

(7) $\pm\, a_{1i_1}\, a_{2i_2} \ldots a_{m_n}$

(8) $P_{s_1} \ldots s_n$

(9) $r_1 \ldots r_n$

(10) $n^{x^{y^{z^{\cdots}}}}$

(11) $n_{x_{y_z \cdots}}$

g. The effect of a level indicator extends through the space inserted in a numeral for the purpose of dividing it into short regular groups of digits.

(1) $e^{3.14159\ 26535}$

§63. Left-Superscripts and Subscripts:

a. The appropriate level indicator must be used before a superscript or subscript to the left of its related sign.

(1) ^3x

(2) $^n x$

(3) $^-2 + {}^-4 = {}^-6$

(4) $^+m - {}^-n = {}^+(m + n)$

(5) $(^-2, {}^-1, 0, {}^+1, {}^+2)$

91

(6) $(-3)^{-2} + {}^{+2}$

(7) ${}_3P_2$

(8) ${}_{48}C_9 \times {}_4C_4$

(9) ${}_nP_r = K({}_{n-1}P_{r-1})$

(10) ${}_y^x n$

(11) ${}_x^y n$

b. The appropriate superscript indicator must be repeated before a left-superscript when two superscripts are consecutive, but one applies to the expression preceding it and the other to the expression following it.

(1) $p^b {}^c q$

c. The subscript indicator must be used before a left-subscript when two subscripts are consecutive, but one applies to the expression preceding it and the other to the expression following it.

(1) $P_b {}_c Q$

(2) $P_1 {}_2 Q$

d. When a left-superscript is shown with a single-letter abbreviation, the English letter indicator is not used.

(1) $19{,}872{,}369 \ {}^\circ C$

(2) $10^{-23}{}^\circ F$

§64. Simultaneous Superscripts and Subscripts: When a mathematical expression carries a superscript and a subscript printed directly above and below each other, the subscript must be shown first, even if the subscript is numeric and requires no subscript level indicator.

(1) x_a^n

(2) 10_8^3

(3) x_1^2

(4) $\Sigma_0^n \, a_k$

(5) $a_1^2 + b_1^2 + c_1^2$

(6) $a_i^2 + b_i^2 + c_i^2 + \cdots$

(7) $[t]_0^4$

(8) $s]\, {t\,=\,b \atop t\,=\,a} = b - a$

(9) $n_{a_{b_c}}^{x^{y^z}}$

(10) ${}_m^n X$

§65. **Nonsimultaneous Superscripts and Subscripts:** When a mathematical expression carries a superscript and a subscript not printed directly above and below each other, the superscript and subscript must be transcribed in the same order as in print, and the baseline indicator must be inserted between them.

(1) $a^k{}_m$

(2) $10_8{}^3$

(3) $2 \times 10_6{}^2 + 3 \times 10_6{}^1 + 2$

(4) $x_1{}^2$

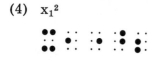

(5) $_y{}^x n$

(6) $^b{}_a n$

§66. **Prime Signs and Superscripts or Subscripts:** When a mathematical expression carries prime signs in addition to superscripts or subscripts, the prime signs must be shown first. However, if the prime signs do not occur at the beginning of the superscript or subscript, they must be placed in the same position as in print. A superscript level indicator must never be used before a prime sign.

(1) x'^2

(2) x''^3

(3) $A''x''^2 + B''y''^2 + I''z''$

(4) x'_a

(5) x'_2

(6) x'^b_a

(7) x'^2_1

(8) x''^3_1

(9) $A+'$

(10) $A^{2''}$

(11) $P_{x'}$

⠀⠀⠀(braille)

(12) $x_{2'}$

⠀⠀⠀(braille)

(13) $I^{2''}_{ue} = (H'_{44}\ x'_{ve})^{+'}$

⠀⠀⠀(braille)

(14) I'^2_{ue}

⠀⠀⠀(braille)

§67. Detached Superscripts and Subscripts: When an entire superscript or subscript stands alone, it should be written without a level indicator in braille, and a transcriber's note must be inserted to explain its print position.

(1) In x^2, the ^{2} is the exponent.

⠀⠀⠀(braille)

⠀⠀⠀(braille)

(2) In x_n, n denotes the base.

⠀⠀⠀(braille)

⠀⠀⠀(braille)

§68. Superscript and Subscript Combinations: Combinations of subscripts to superscripts or of superscripts to subscripts require level indicators composed of two or more braille symbols.

a. Such level indicators are used in the following way:

i. The first indicator shows the upward or downward position of the superscript or subscript in relation to the baseline of writing.

ii. The second indicator shows the upward or downward position of the superscript or subscript from the first position indicated.

iii. The third indicator shows the upward or downward position of the superscript or subscript from the second position indicated, etc.

b. Superscript With Subscript: ⠀⠀(braille)

(1) x^{n_a}

⠀⠀⠀(braille)

(2) $e^{x_1} \cdot e^{x_2} = e^{x_1 + x_2}$

⠀⠀⠀(braille)

(3) $p_1^{\alpha_1} \ldots p_r^{\alpha_n}$

(4) $A_{i_k+1}^{r_k+1}$

(5) ^{n_a}X

(6) $^{a^n}X$

c. Superscript With Subscript With Subscript:

(1) $x^{n_{r_j}}$

d. Superscript With Subscript With Superscript:

(1) $x^{y_{r^n}}$

e. Superscript With Superscript With Subscript:

(1) $x^{y^{z_n}}$

f. Subscript With Superscript:

(1) x_{y^r}

(2) x_{2^n}

(3) $_{y^a}X$

(4) $_{a_n}X$

g. Subscript With Superscript With Superscript:

  (1) $x_{y^{r^n}}$

h. Subscript With Superscript With Subscript:

  (1) $x_{y^{r_n}}$

i. Subscript With Subscript With Superscript:

  (1) $x_{y_{r^n}}$

FORMAT (CONTINUED)

§69. Margins for Itemized Material With Subdivisions:

    a. In transcribing itemized material with lettered or numbered subdivisions, the main item designation must begin in cell 1, and its runovers must begin in cell 5. Each lettered or numbered subdivision must begin in cell 3, and its runovers in cell 5. If any item has more than one paragraph, each new paragraph must begin in cell 7, and its runovers in cell 5.

    (1) **1.** Use numerals to write the following number sentences.

        a. Fifteen thousand six hundred thirty-two.

        b. Nine million four hundred six thousand.

        Now add the numerals you wrote in **a** and **b**. What is the sum?

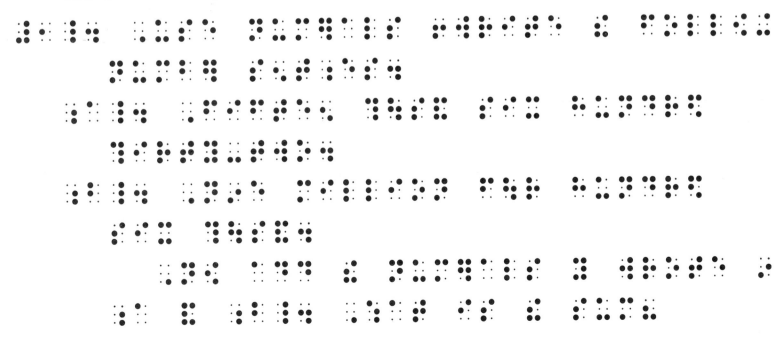

(2) **2. a.** Write each of the following as a fraction: .12; .78.

  b. Tell what digit is in tenth's place.

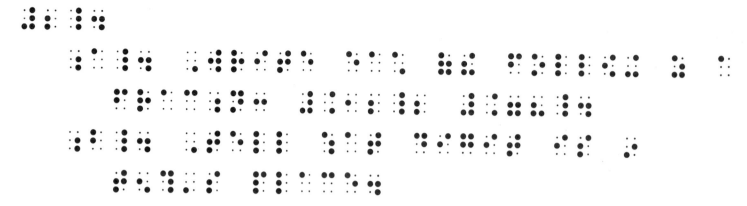

(3) **3.** Consider the theory with primitive notions and operations as stated above. The axioms are the following:

a. $\times$ is an associative operation.

b. $(x \times y)' = y' \times x'$.

c. If $x \times y = z \times z'$ for some z, then $x = y'$.

  (1) Show that the theory is consistent.

  (2) Show that this set of axioms is dependent.

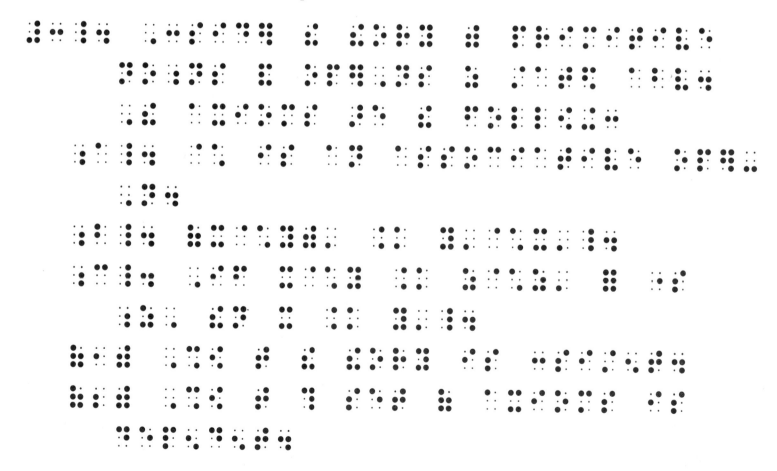

b. It is permissible to place the subdivisions of itemized material side by side across a page if all the subdivisions can be accommodated on one braille line. Otherwise, the format in **a** above must be used.

(1) **1.** Copy and multiply.

    a. 170×71 **b.** 1.25×12

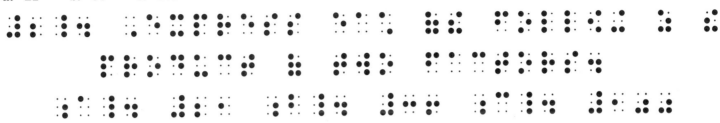

(2) **2.** Express each of the following as the product of two factors.

    a. 21   **b.** 36   **c.** 100

(3) Solve and check.

    3. a. $4x = 96$ **b.** $n + 2 = 8$

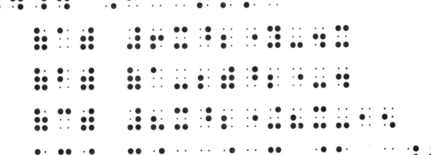

(4) **4.** Factor:

    (a) $6x^2y - 4x$ **(b)** $(a - 2)^2 - 4$

    (c) $8x^2 + 8x - 15$ **(d)** $x^2 + 3x = -2$

c. When itemized material is arranged in tabular form so that items are numbered at the margin and subdivisions are aligned beneath lettered column headings, the material should be transcribed in one of the following ways:

    i. If all the columns can be accommodated across the braille page, the print columnar arrangement must be followed. Each problem number must begin in cell 1. The letter identifying each column must be aligned with the first cell of the related column. A blank line must be left above and below the lettered column headings. At least two blank cells must be left between columns.

(1) Find the answers mentally.

	a	b	c
1.	16 + 9	17 + 4	14 + 23
2.	46 + 15	87 + 12	95 + 54
3.	157 + 452	134 + 63	458 + 12

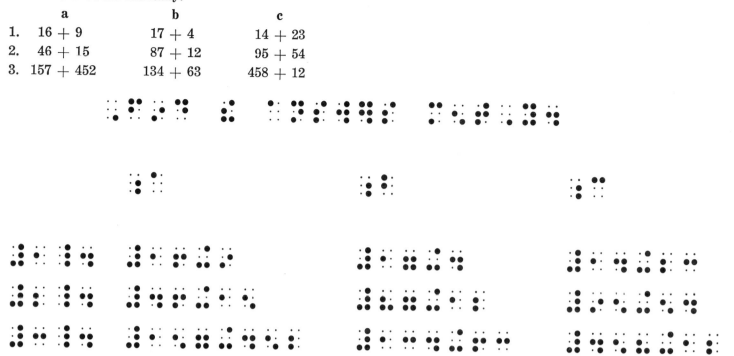

ii. If all the columns cannot be accommodated across the braille page, each subdivision in each problem must be lettered individually, and the format in **a** above must be followed.

(1) Mixed practice.

	a	b
1.	17 + 24 + 13 + 26 = ?	72 + 19 + 11 + 18 = ?
2.	4 × 17 × 25 = ?	16 × 8 × 17 = ?
3.	8 = 5% of ?	120 = 300% of ?

Prepare the following homework for submission to your teacher. Proofread carefully.

EXERCISE 6

1. Tell what number each of the following names.

   a. 2^2 b. 10^3 c. $(3.15)^4$

2. Which term of $(a + b)^{12}$ has the factor b^5?

3. Find the rth term of $(x + y)^n$.

4. What number is named by each of the following: 6^2, 5^3, and 7^4?

5. Use table 5 to approximate $e^{0.27}$.

6. Show that these number sentences are true.

   a. $4^2 \times 4^3 = 4^5$ b. $15^3 \times 15^4 = 15^7$

   c. $e^{1,000} \times e^{2,000} = e^{3,000}$

7. Factor:

   (a) $4x^4 + 19x^2y^2 + 49y^2$ (b) $100a^2b^2c^2 - 1$

   (c) $x^{2a + 2} + x^{2a + 1} + x^{2a}$

8. Simplify: $10^{0.30} \div 10^{-0.66}$; $(x^3 - y^3)^2 - (x^3 + y^3)^2$.

9. $12 \text{ ft}^2 \times 12 \text{ ft}^2 = ? \text{ ft}^2$

10. $14 \text{ m}^3 + 6 \text{ m}^3 = ? \text{ m}^3$

11. $21 \text{ m.}^3 + 39 \text{ m.}^3 = ? \text{ m.}^3$

12. What is a 3^2-dimensional system?

13. Prove that $f^{(n)}(x)$ exists.

14. Substitute to find $A^{n + n's}$.

15. Use a computer to find 9^{9^9}.

16. Find the limit as x approaches 0.6 of $2^{25x^2 - 10x - 1}$.

17. When will $E[x^2] = e^{2(a + b^2)}$?

18. Name the numeral in base ten equal to:

    a. 47_8 b. 34_6 c. 1101_2

19. Add in base 12: $27TE_{12}$ and $E5T_{12}$.

20. If the sets V_k expand as k increases, what happens to the sets C_k?

21. Use 6_8, 5_8, 13_8 to write three examples in base 8.

22. If $u_i = x_i - 68$, $x_i - 68$ yields what values of u_i's?

23. Add: $3_{\text{five}}, 4_{\text{five}},$ and 2_{five}.

24. Simplify: $x_a + bx_a + cx_a$.

25. Show that $\{a_{2n}\}$ and $\{a_{2n+1}\}$ are monotonic.

26. Use the formula on page 372 to find $a_{\overline{32}|}$ and $s_{\overline{32}|}$ at 2%.

27. What do we know if $P_{n_r} = (x_{n_k}, y_{n_k})$?

28. Generalize Eq. 5 for the case of k samples of size $n_1, n_2, \ldots, n_k$.

29. Use $\alpha_1, \beta_1, \gamma_1$ and $\alpha_2, \beta_2, \gamma_2$ to denote the direction vectors v_1 and v_2.

30. Use Table 4 to find the values of $x_{.05}$ and $x_{1,000}$.

31. Prove that if $a_1 b_2 - a_2 b_1 = 0$, then the graphs of the equations $a_1 x + b_1 y = c_1$ and $a_2 x + b_2 y = c_2$ are either parallel or coincident lines.

32. Choose x_1's from $(x_1 t + x_2)^5$.

33. The notation $m_{k,\,a}$ means "the kth moment about the point a."

34. Find $m_{1,\,0}, m_{2,\,0},$ and $m_{3,\,0}$ for the given functions.

35. Graph: $\| f - F \|_{[a,\,b]} < e$.

36. $m_{(k_1,\,a_1)(k_2,\,a_2)}$ is defined in Theorem 4.

37. Evaluate $F_{.10\,;\,1}$.

38. Find the number of $n_{\text{reg. triangles}}$ in the problem.

39. Find $D_t h]_{h\,=\,6}$ in the given problems.

40. $E(x) = ae^{a(t-1)}]_{t\,=\,1} = a$ occurs in the Poisson distribution.

41. Explain the meaning of $x^{2\,+\,4\,+\,6\,+\,\ldots\,+\,n}$.

42. $8^6 + — = 8^{10}$.

43. What do the three dots mean in $R_{s_1,\,s_2,\,\ldots}$?

44. Substitute and use $a^1 b^2 c^3 \ldots m^n$.

45. Do many of the sets V_n correspond to the sets $U_{n_1} \ldots U_{n_k}$?

46. If P_n denotes the nth prime, show that $P_1 P_2 \ldots P_n + 1$ is not a perfect square.

47. Which is larger $e^{3.14159\,26535}$ or π^e?

48. Find the sums:

    a. $+1.9 + +12.6$

    b. $+10.3 + -20.6$

    c. $-7.12 + -8.13$

    d. $|-2| + |-3|$

49. What is $(-4)^{-6\,+\,+6}$?

50. The permutations of the letters a, b, and c taken two at a time are ab, ac, ba, bc, ca, cb. Thus, $_3P_2 = 6$.

51. If $_nP_5 = 42_nP_3$, find n.

52. $_nC_r + _nC_{r-1} = \underline{\;?\;}$

53. Write these notations:

    (a) $x^a{}^by$ (b) $X_a{}_bY$ (c) $X_1{}_2Y$

54. P^n_k is a notation used for permutations.

55. $3 \times 10^2_6 + 4 \times 10^1_6 + 7 = \underline{\;?\;}$

56. When will $r^2_{p_1} = .25\pi^2$?

57. Use the summation sign to express $x_1^2 + x_2^2 + x_3^2 + \ldots + x_n^2$.

58. $4 \times 10_8{}^2 + 2 \times 10_8{}^1 + 5 = \underline{\;?\;}$

59. $2 \times 10^2{}_6 + 3 \times 10^1{}_6 + 2 = \underline{\;?\;}$

60. The symbol m'_k denotes the kth moment about the origin.

61. $a'_1, a'_2, \ldots, a'_n$ are inverses of $\underline{\;?\;}$.

62. From the given information we can deduce that $y^{4'}(0) = 3^2 \cdot 4$.

63. In x^3, the ^{3} is the superscript.

64. Prove that $(ab)^x = a^xb^x$ if k_1 and k_2 denote any real numbers such that $a = 2^{k_1}$ and $b = 2^{k_2}$. (Use the laws of exponents for 2^x where $(ab)^x = 2^{k_1x} \cdot 2^{k_2x}$.)

65. From the given information prove that the product of $e^{i\theta_1}$ and $e^{i\theta_2}$ equals $e^{i(\theta_1 + \theta_2)}$.

66. Take the natural logarithm of $e^{x_1 + x_2 + x_3 + \ldots + x_n}$.

67. In what situations is the factorization $a = 2^{a_0} 3^{a_1} 5^{a_2} \ldots$ regarded as extending indefinitely?

68. Name the prime factors of n^2 if $n = p_1^{x_1} p_2^{x_2} \ldots p_k^{x_k}$.

69. Practice writing the following symbols: $x^{P_{q}r}$, $x^{P_q{}^r}$, $x^{p^{q}{}_r}$, x_{2^p}, X_{p_qr}, $X_{p_q{}_r}$, $X_{P_{q_r}}$.

70. We have learned patterns that are often called laws. For example

    (1) $a + b = b + a$ is the commutative law for addition.

    (2) $a \times b = b \times a$ is the commutative law for multiplication.

        a. Use symbols to express the associative laws for addition and multiplication.

        b. Use symbols to express the distributive law.

71. a. In the sequence 10, 5, 0, —5, ..., which term is —75?

    b. Find the 9th term of $(x - y)^9$.

    Factor.

a	b
72. $x^2 - x - 12$	$x^2 + 12x + 35$
73. $6x^2 + 11x - 35$	$6x^{2a} + 11x^a + 4$
74. $9x^2 - 16y^2$	$ax^3x^2 + a^2$

LESSON 7

FRACTIONS AND FRACTION INDICATORS

§70. General Principles: Although the numerator and denominator of a fraction may be separated by a horizontal or a diagonal fraction line, unless otherwise stated the fraction should be transcribed linearly so that the numerator, the fraction line, and the denominator are written horizontally across one braille line.

The spacing before and after a fraction is subject to the spacing rules for the signs preceding or following the fraction. In addition, no space should be left between a fraction and a letter, a numeral, a sign of grouping, a braille indicator, or another fraction when these items are unspaced in print and are part of the same expression.

§71. Simple Fractions: A simple fraction is one in which neither the numerator nor the denominator is a fraction. A fraction is also considered a simple fraction when its numerator or denominator contains fractions at the superscript or subscript level only.

$$\frac{3}{4} \qquad \frac{a+b}{c+d} \qquad \frac{x^{\frac{1}{2}}}{y^{\frac{1}{2}}} \qquad x/y \qquad a+b\Big/c+d$$

Simple Fraction Indicators

    Opening

    Closing

Fraction Lines Used With Simple Fractions

    Horizontal Simple Fraction Line ———

    Diagonal Simple Fraction Line /

§72. Use of Simple Fraction Indicators:

    a. The opening and closing simple fraction indicators must be used to enclose a simple fraction whose numerator and denominator are separated by a horizontal fraction line.

The horizontal fraction line must be shown by ⠌ .

(1) $\dfrac{3}{4}$

(2) $\dfrac{a+b}{c+d}$

(3) $\dfrac{\Delta y}{\Delta x}$

104

(4) $\quad x\dfrac{1}{8}$

(5) $\quad V = \dfrac{1}{3}\pi r^2 h$

(6) $\quad \dfrac{1}{4} + \dfrac{3}{4} - \dfrac{1}{2} = \dfrac{1}{2}$

(7) $\quad \dfrac{a}{b} \times \dfrac{c}{d} = \dfrac{ac}{bd}$

(8) $\quad \dfrac{-1}{2} + \dfrac{-3}{4}$

(9) $\quad x^{-\frac{1}{2}}$

(10) $\quad x^{\frac{1}{2}} \cdot y^{-\frac{1}{2}}$

(11) $\quad \dfrac{x^{\frac{1}{2}} + 1}{y^{\frac{1}{2}} - 1}$

(12) $\quad x - \dfrac{1}{4}(x - 2x)$

(13) $\quad \left(\dfrac{3}{2}a + \dfrac{1}{2}b\right)$

(14) $\quad \left|\dfrac{a}{b}\right| = \dfrac{|a|}{|b|}$

(15) $\dfrac{1}{2}\dfrac{n-1}{n}=\dfrac{n-1}{2n}$

(16) $\dfrac{\$15.25}{\$25.50}$

(17) $\$\dfrac{3}{5}\div\$\dfrac{1}{5}=\$3$

(18) $\tfrac{3}{4}\cent-\tfrac{1}{4}\cent=\tfrac{1}{2}\cent$

(19) $\tfrac{1}{4}\%+\tfrac{1}{2}\%=\tfrac{3}{4}\%$

(20) $\dfrac{5''}{8}+\dfrac{2''}{8}=\dfrac{7''}{8}$

(21) $\dfrac{6}{8}=\dfrac{}{4}$

(22) $\dfrac{1??}{1000}=\dfrac{1}{10}$

b. Simple fraction indicators must be used to enclose a simple fraction whose numerator and denominator are separated by a diagonal line when the numerator and denominator are printed at different levels of writing on either side of the diagonal line or in a different type size from that normally used for such fractions throughout the text. The diagonal fraction line must be shown by

(1) $\dfrac{a}{b}\cdot\dfrac{c}{d}=\dfrac{a\cdot c}{b\cdot d}$

(2) Reduce $\dfrac{18}{24}$ to lowest terms.

(3) $3\,x/y$

106

(4) 2 1/y

⠼⠃⠸⠌⠁⠌⠽⠸⠌

(5) y 1/5

⠽⠼⠁⠌⠑

§73. **Nonuse of Simple Fraction Indicators:** Simple fraction indicators must not be used to enclose a simple fraction whose numerator and denominator are separated by a diagonal line when the numerator and denominator are printed at the same level of writing on either side of the diagonal line and in the same type size as the rest of the mathematical expression.

(1) 1/2

⠼⠁⠌⠃

(2) 2a/3b

⠼⠃⠁⠌⠉⠃

(3) a + b/c + d

⠁⠀⠖⠀⠃⠌⠉⠀⠖⠀⠙

(4) 5/8 + 3/8 = 8/8 = 1

⠼⠑⠌⠓⠀⠖⠀⠼⠉⠌⠓⠀⠶⠀⠼⠓⠌⠓⠀⠶⠀⠼⠁

(5) $\phi = \pi/6$

⠨⠋⠀⠶⠀⠨⠏⠌⠼⠋

(6) (x + y)/(x — y)

⠷⠭⠀⠖⠀⠽⠾⠌⠷⠭⠀⠤⠀⠽⠾

(7) $x^{\frac{1}{2}} + 1/y^{\frac{1}{2}} + 1$

⠭⠘⠼⠁⠌⠃⠀⠖⠀⠼⠁⠌⠽⠘⠼⠁⠌⠃⠀⠖⠀⠼⠁

(8) $x^{1/2} — y^{1/2}$

⠭⠘⠼⠁⠌⠃⠀⠤⠀⠽⠘⠼⠁⠌⠃

(9) $1/4\phi + 1/2\phi = 3/4\phi$

⠼⠁⠌⠙⠨⠋⠀⠖⠀⠼⠁⠌⠃⠨⠋⠀⠶⠀⠼⠉⠌⠙⠨⠋

(10) 3/8″ — 2/8″ = 1/8″

⠼⠉⠌⠓⠐⠂⠀⠤⠀⠼⠃⠌⠓⠐⠂⠀⠶⠀⠼⠁⠌⠓⠐⠂

§74. **Mixed Numbers:** A mixed number is an expression composed of a whole number followed by a simple fraction whose numerator and denominator are both numerals. Numerals in a mixed number may be represented by omission signs. An expression is not a mixed number if it contains any letters, even though the expression appears to be in the form of a mixed number.

$$1\tfrac{1}{2} \qquad 1\tfrac{1}{2}$$

Mixed Number Fraction Indicators

Opening

Closing

Fraction Lines Used With the Fractional Part of a Mixed Number

Horizontal Simple Fraction Line ———

Diagonal Simple Fraction Line /

§75. **Use of Mixed Number Fraction Indicators:** The opening and closing mixed number fraction indicators must always be used to enclose the fractional part of a mixed number. The appropriate braille symbol must be used to represent the horizontal or diagonal fraction line shown in print.

(1) $1\tfrac{1}{2}$

(2) $1\tfrac{1}{2}$

(3) $64\dfrac{325}{1000}$

(4) $1\dfrac{1}{2} + 2\dfrac{2}{3} = 4\dfrac{1}{6}$

(5) $1\tfrac{1}{2} + 2\tfrac{2}{3} = 4\tfrac{1}{6}$

(6) $(3\tfrac{1}{2} \times 2) + (\tfrac{1}{2} \times 3\tfrac{1}{2})$

(7) $2(\tfrac{1}{4}) + 2\tfrac{3}{4} = 3\tfrac{1}{4}$

(8) $2\frac{1}{4}x + 4 = 14 + \frac{1}{2}x$

(9) $1\frac{3}{4}\% + 4\% = 5\frac{3}{4}\%$

(10) $8\frac{1''}{2} + 7\frac{5''}{6}$

(11) $1\frac{15}{25} = ?\frac{3}{5}$

(12) $7/4 = 1\ ?/4$

§76. Complex Fractions: A complex fraction is one whose numerator and/or denominator are, or contain, one or more simple fractions or mixed numbers. A fraction is not a complex fraction if the only fractions it contains are at the superscript or subscript level; such a fraction is a simple fraction.

$$\frac{\dfrac{1}{4}}{\dfrac{3}{4}} \qquad \frac{\dfrac{a}{b} - \dfrac{c}{d}}{\dfrac{a}{b} + \dfrac{c}{d}} \qquad \frac{1/4}{3/4} \qquad \frac{4\dfrac{3}{4}}{5} \qquad \frac{1}{2}\bigg/\frac{3}{4}$$

Complex Fraction Indicators

    Opening

    Closing

Fraction Lines Used With Complex Fractions

    Horizontal Complex Fraction Line   ——————

    Diagonal Complex Fraction Line   /

109

§77. Use of Complex Fraction Indicators:

a. The opening and closing complex fraction indicators must be used to enclose a complex fraction, and the main complex fraction line must be represented by its appropriate braille symbol.

(1) $\dfrac{\dfrac{1}{4}}{\dfrac{3}{4}}$

(2) $\dfrac{a}{\dfrac{b}{c}}$

(3) $\dfrac{\dfrac{\pi}{8}}{2\pi}$

(4) $\dfrac{\dfrac{3-1}{4+3}}{\dfrac{2-1}{3+5}}$

(5) $\dfrac{\dfrac{1}{2}+\dfrac{1}{3}}{\dfrac{3}{4}-\dfrac{7}{9}}$

(6) $\dfrac{\left(\dfrac{3}{2}\right)\left(\dfrac{1}{2}\right)}{1\cdot2\cdot3}$

(7) $\dfrac{\dfrac{1}{6}}{5}+\dfrac{5}{\dfrac{1}{6}}$

(8) $\dfrac{1/3+1/4}{4/5-1/2}$

(9) $\dfrac{1/4}{3/4} + \dfrac{1/7}{5/7}$

(10) $\dfrac{33\frac{1}{3}}{100}$

(11) $\dfrac{2\frac{1}{3}}{4\frac{1}{5}}$

(12) $\dfrac{1}{2} \bigg/ \dfrac{3}{4}$

b. When a simple fraction contains a complex fraction at the superscript or subscript level, simple fraction indicators must be used to enclose the simple fraction, and complex fraction indicators must be used to enclose the complex fraction.

(1) $\dfrac{a^{\frac{\frac{3}{4}}{5}} + 1}{b}$

§78. Fractions and the Baseline Indicator: When a level indicator is in effect, the baseline indicator ⠰ must be used before a fraction line or closing fraction indicator belonging to a fraction on the baseline of writing. However, the baseline indicator must not be used after a numeric subscript not requiring a subscript indicator.

(1) $\dfrac{a^2}{b^2}$

(2) $\dfrac{x^{\frac{1}{2}}}{y^{\frac{1}{4}}}$

(3) $\dfrac{x^{1/2}}{2}$

111

(4)
$$\frac{\dfrac{x}{x-1}-1^2}{\dfrac{x}{x+1}+1^2}$$

(5) $r^2/4 - s^2/9 + t^2$

(6) $x^{1/2}/2$

(7)
$$\frac{y_2 - y_1}{x_2 - x_1}$$

(8) $a_1/b + a_2/b^2 + a_3/b^3 + \ldots$

§79. Fractions and the Ellipsis and Long Dash: No space should be left between an opening or closing fraction indicator and an ellipsis or long dash in the numerator or denominator of a fraction. However, a space must be left between a fraction line and an ellipsis or long dash. A space must also be left between a fraction and an ellipsis or long dash preceding or following the fraction.

(1)
$$\frac{\ldots \times 5}{2 \times 10} = \frac{15}{20}$$

(2)
$$\frac{2 + 4 + 6 + \ldots}{1 + 3 + 5 + \ldots}$$

(3)
$$\frac{\underline{\quad} \times 3}{3 \times 4} = \frac{12}{12}$$

(4)
$$\frac{1}{10} \ldots \frac{10}{10}$$

(5)
$$\frac{1}{10} \underline{\quad\quad} \frac{10}{10}$$

112

§80. Fractions and Abbreviations: Abbreviations in the numerator or denominator of a fraction must be unspaced from the fraction indicators or fraction lines. However, a space must be left between a fraction and an abbreviation preceding or following the fraction.

(1) $\dfrac{60 \text{ mi}}{1 \text{ hr}}$

(2) $60\,\dfrac{\text{mi.}}{\text{hr.}}$

(3) $\dfrac{\text{m}}{\text{cm}} \times \dfrac{\text{cm}}{\text{m}}$

(4) $\dfrac{\text{w.}}{\text{v.}}$

(5) $60 \text{ mph} = 88 \text{ ft/sec}$

(6) m./cm.

(7) $\text{m/cm} \times \text{cm/m}$

(8) $\dfrac{1}{5}\text{ in} + \dfrac{4}{5}\text{ in} = 1\text{ in}$

(9) $9\tfrac{1}{2}\text{ yd} - 3\tfrac{3}{4}\text{ yd}$

(10) $\dfrac{5}{8}\text{ yd} \quad \dfrac{1}{2}\text{ ft} \quad \dfrac{3}{4}\text{ in}$

(11) $1/4 \text{ in.} + 1/4 \text{ in.} = 1/2 \text{ in.}$

§81. **Enclosed Lists and Punctuation With Fractions:** Fractions and mixed numbers may be part of an enclosed list. Fraction indicators are part of a mathematical expression and must be punctuated accordingly.

(1) $\{0, \frac{1}{2}, 1, 1\frac{1}{2}\}$

(2) (1, 1/4, 2, 2 1/4)

(3) Add $\frac{1}{4}$, $\frac{1}{2}$, and $\frac{3}{4}$.

(4) $\frac{3}{10}$'s and $\frac{5}{10}$'s.

(5) The fence is $\frac{1}{2}$-mile long.

(6) The sign reads "$\frac{1}{2}$-off".

(7) $\frac{1}{2}$——$\frac{3}{4}$

(8) What is the sum of $1/6 + 1/3$?

(9) 5/8-mi.

(10) "1/4——3/4"

(11) $12\frac{1}{8}$, $12\frac{2}{8}$.

(12) Use a $1\frac{1}{2}$-lb. weight.

(13) $\dfrac{3}{\frac{6}{7}}$, $\dfrac{\frac{1}{8}}{4}$.

114

§82. Radicals: The symbol $\sqrt{\ }$ is called a *radical sign*. A *vinculum*, or horizontal bar, is generally used with the radical sign $\sqrt{\ }$ to show the extent to which the radical sign applies. The expression under the radical sign is called the *radicand*. A figure placed to the left and slightly above the radical sign is called the *index* of the radical.

$$\sqrt{4} \qquad \sqrt[3]{x+y}$$

Radical Sign ⠠⠩

Radical Indicators

    Index-of-Radical Indicator ⠼⠣

    Order-of-Radical Indicators

        First Inner Radical ⠰

        Second Inner Radical ⠰⠰

        Third Inner Radical ⠰⠰⠰

    Termination Indicator ⠻

§83. Simple Radicals:

    a. When a radical has a *vinculum,* the radical sign ⠩ must be placed before the radicand, and the termination indicator ⠻ must be placed after the radicand. However, the termination indicator must not be used when the radical sign occurs without a radicand, or when the *vinculum* is not shown in print.

    (1) $\sqrt{64}$

    (2) $\sqrt{a}$

    (3) $\sqrt{s(s-a)(s-b)(s-c)}$

    (4) $\sqrt{\dfrac{a}{b}+\dfrac{b}{a}}$

    (5) $\sqrt{a/b}$

(6) The $\sqrt{}$ is called a "radical sign."

⠀⠀⠀⠀[braille]

(7) $\sqrt{(x-1)}$

⠀⠀⠀⠀[braille]

b. The spacing before and after a radical is subject to the spacing rules for the signs preceding or following the radical. In addition, no space should be left between a radical and a letter, a numeral, a fraction, a sign of grouping, a braille indicator, or another radical when these items are unspaced in print and belong to the same expression.

(1) $\sqrt{5}\,y$

⠀⠀⠀⠀[braille]

(2) $\sqrt{x}^{2}$

⠀⠀⠀⠀[braille]

(3) $2a\sqrt{4ab}$

⠀⠀⠀⠀[braille]

(4) $\frac{1}{2}\sqrt{\frac{1}{4}}$

⠀⠀⠀⠀[braille]

(5) $\sqrt{\dfrac{10}{9}} = \sqrt{10}/3$

⠀⠀⠀⠀[braille]

(6) $\sqrt{9} - \sqrt{4} = 1$

⠀⠀⠀⠀[braille]

(7) $(\sqrt{2} + \sqrt{3})\,(\sqrt{2} - \sqrt{3})$

⠀⠀⠀⠀[braille]

(8) $2\sqrt{2} + 5\sqrt{2} = (2 + 5)\sqrt{2}$

⠀⠀⠀⠀[braille]

(9) $\sqrt{4}\sqrt{87} = 2\sqrt{87}$

⠀⠀⠀⠀[braille]

(10) $\dfrac{\sqrt{3}}{\sqrt{2}} \times \dfrac{\sqrt{2}}{\sqrt{2}} = \dfrac{\sqrt{6}}{2}$

⠀⠀⠀⠀[braille]

(11)
$$\dfrac{\sqrt{2} - \sqrt{\dfrac{1}{3}}}{\sqrt{3} - \sqrt{\dfrac{1}{2}}}$$

(12) $\quad p^{\sqrt{q}} + r$

(13) $\quad \sqrt{(x-1)} + \sqrt{(2x)} = 1$

c. When a radical has an index, the index-of-radical indicator ⠩ and the index of the radical must precede the radical sign.

(1) $\quad \sqrt[3]{27}$

(2) $\quad \sqrt[n]{a}$

(3) $\quad \sqrt[a+b]{x-y}$

(4) $\quad \sqrt[4]{729} + \sqrt[6]{27}$

(5) $\quad 3\sqrt[3]{125} \cdot 3\sqrt[5]{2}$

(6) $\quad \sqrt[5]{c}\ \sqrt[5]{d} = \sqrt[5]{cd}$

(7) $\quad \sqrt[m]{\dfrac{a}{b}} = \dfrac{\sqrt[m]{a}}{\sqrt[m]{b}}$

§84. **Nested Radicals:** When radicals are nested one within the other, the appropriate number of order-of-radical indicators ⠠⠜ must be used to show the depth of each *inner* radical.

If an inner radical has no index, the appropriate order-of-radical indicator must be placed before its radical sign. If an inner radical has an index, the appropriate order-of-radical indicator must be placed before the index-of-radical indicator.

117

The order-of-radical indicator used before an inner radical must also be used before its corresponding termination indicator. When more than one radical is completed at the same point, the radicals are terminated, beginning with the innermost radical.

(1) $\sqrt{x + \sqrt{x + y} + z}$

(2) $\sqrt{-\dfrac{1}{2} - i\,\dfrac{\sqrt{3}}{2}}$

(3) $\sqrt{\sqrt{13} + \sqrt{15} + \sqrt{117}}$

(4) $\sqrt{1 - \sqrt{a - b}} \times \sqrt{1 + \sqrt{a - b}}$

(5) $\sqrt{x + \sqrt{y + \sqrt{z}}}$

(6) $\sqrt{\sqrt[3]{16}} = \sqrt[3]{\sqrt{16}}$

(7) $\sqrt{b}\ \sqrt[3]{b}\ \sqrt{b}$

(8) $\sqrt{\sqrt[3]{\sqrt[4]{10}}}$

(9) $\sqrt[a]{\sqrt[b]{\sqrt[c]{abc}}}$

§85. Radicals and the Baseline Indicator: When a level indicator is in effect, the baseline indicator ⠐ must be used before a radical sign or radical indicator belonging to a radical on the baseline of writing. However, the baseline indicator must not be used after a numeric subscript not requiring a subscript indicator.

(1) $(r^2\sqrt{r})^2$

(2) $\sqrt{x^2 + y^2}$

⠿ (braille)

(3) $\sqrt{a^2}\ \sqrt{b^4}\ \sqrt{c} = ab^2\sqrt{c}$

⠿ (braille)

(4) $(s^2\sqrt[3]{s^4})^2$

⠿ (braille)

(5) $\sqrt[3]{x^2\sqrt{64x^6}}$

⠿ (braille)

(6) $\sqrt{\sqrt[3]{\sqrt[4]{\sqrt[5]{b^{48}}}}}$

⠿ (braille)

(7) $\sqrt{x_1 + y_2}$

⠿ (braille)

(8) $\sqrt{x_1 + \sqrt{x_2}}$

⠿ (braille)

§86. Radicals and the Ellipsis and Long Dash: When an ellipsis or a long dash occurs within a radical, no space should be left between the ellipsis or long dash and the termination indicator or order-of-radical indicator. However, a space must be left between the radical sign and an ellipsis or long dash. A space must also be left between a radical and an ellipsis or long dash preceding or following the radical.

(1) $\sqrt{a + b + c + \ldots}$

⠿ (braille)

(2) $\sqrt{x + \sqrt{x + \sqrt{\ldots}}}$

⠿ (braille)

(3) $\sqrt{4} \ldots \sqrt{64}$

⠿ (braille)

§87. Radicals and Abbreviations: When an abbreviation occurs within a radical, no space should be left between the abbreviation and the termination or order-of-radical indicator following it. However, a space must be left between a radical sign and an abbrevia-

119

tion. A space must also be left between a radical and an abbreviation preceding or following the radical.

(1) $\sqrt{9 \text{ ft}}$

⠀⠀(braille)

(2) $\sqrt{\text{ft.}}$

⠀⠀(braille)

(3) $2\sqrt{12}$ sq. in.

⠀⠀(braille)

§88. Enclosed Lists and Punctuation With Radicals: Radicals may be part of an enclosed list. The radical sign and radical indicators must be punctuated mathematically.

(1) $(\sqrt{9},\ 3,\ \sqrt{4},\ 2\sqrt{6})$

⠀⠀(braille)

(2) Simplify: $\sqrt{2},\ \sqrt{18},\ \sqrt{24}.$

⠀⠀(braille)

(3) "$\sqrt{}$" means "square root."

⠀⠀(braille)

FORMAT (CONTINUED)

§89. Displayed Expressions: When a mathematical expression or other material is set apart from the body of the text by skipped lines, centering, special indentation, etc., such displayed expressions must be transcribed in the following format:

    a. A line must not be skipped above or below a displayed expression unless the expression precedes or follows a heading, or unless a blank line is required under other provisions of the code.

    b. When a displayed expression occurs in unitemized explanatory portions of the text, it must begin in cell 3, and its runovers must begin in cell 5.

(1)   The expression $a(b + c) - d(b + c)$ has the form $ax - dx$ where $x = b + c$. Thus

$$ax - dx = x(a - d)$$

and therefore

$$a(b + c) - d(b + c) = (b + c)(a - d).$$

⠀⠀(braille)

(2) A sequence a_1, a_2, a_3, ..., a_n is said to
converge if, for each h > 0, there exists
a positive number M such that
$| a_n - A | <$ h, for all n > M.

A sequence that does not converge is said
to diverge.

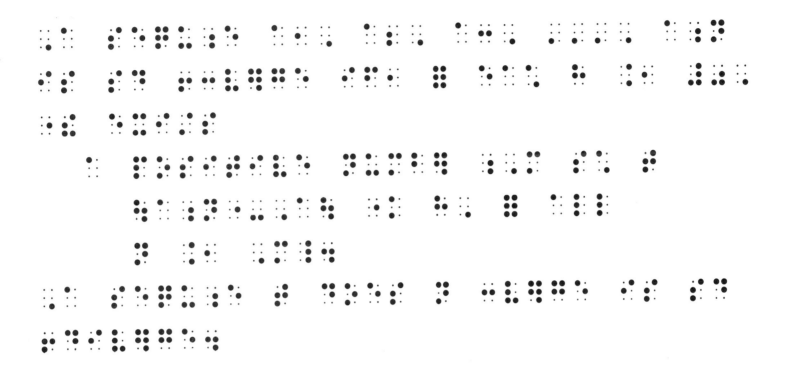

(3)   We use the number line to show

$$-6 < -5, 0 < +6, -8 < +2, -1 > -5, +1 > -1.$$

Is every positive integer greater than 0? Is
every negative integer less than 0?

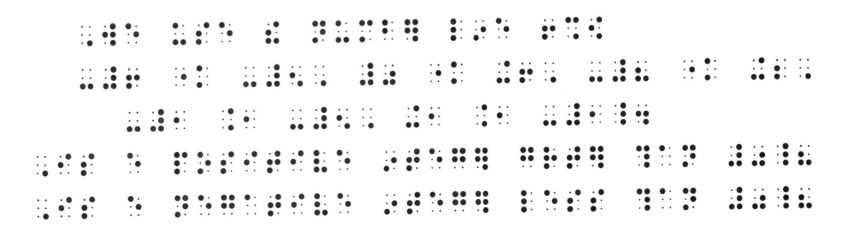

(4) The equation states that the product of 24 and some number is 264. How can you find the missing numeral?

$$24 \times N = 264$$

c. When a displayed expression occurs with an itemized text containing no subdivisions, it must begin in cell 5, and its runovers must begin in cell 7.

(1) 1. If A, B, C, C′ are constants, show that

$$Ax + By + C = 0$$
$$Ax + By + C' = 0$$

are parallel and the lines

$$Ax + By + C = 0$$
$$Bx + Ay + C' = 0$$

are perpendicular.

(2)   2. To find the product of 2 × 5.4

        First: multiply the tenths, 2 × .4 = .8,
        Second: multiply the ones, 2 × 5 = 10.

Then add: 10 + .8 = 10.8.

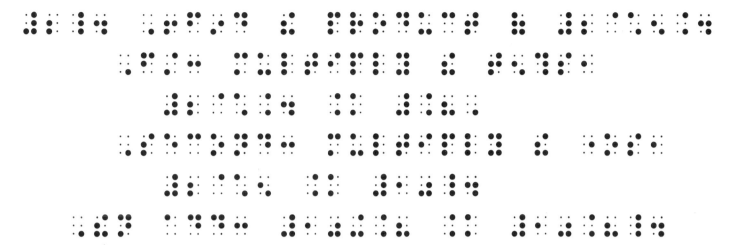

(3)   3. Use the number line to show

        −1 < +1, −5 < − 1, +12 > −8, +6 > +4.

If every negative integer is less than 0,
what is every positive integer?

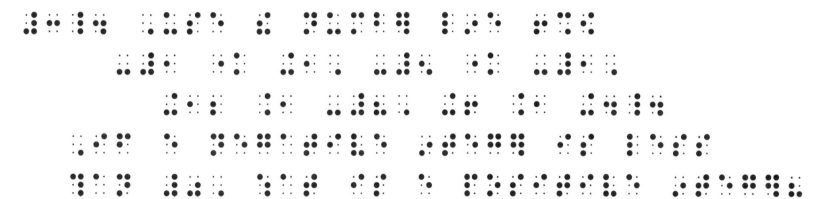

123

d. When a displayed expression occurs with an itemized text containing subdivisions, it must begin in cell 7, and its runovers must begin in cell 9.

(1)   1. Write each positive integer as a polynomial in 10.

    (a)   Compare
$$x^3 + 9x^2 + 7x + 1 \text{ and}$$
$$10^3 + 9(10)^2 + 7(10) + 1, \text{ that is } 1971.$$

    (b)   The number 185,000,000,000 can be written as
$$185 \times 10^9, \text{ or as } 1.85 \times 10^{11}.$$

    Use the principles in **a** and **b** to write
$$x^4 + 7x^3 + 5x^2 + 3x + 1 \text{ and } 125,000,000,000.$$

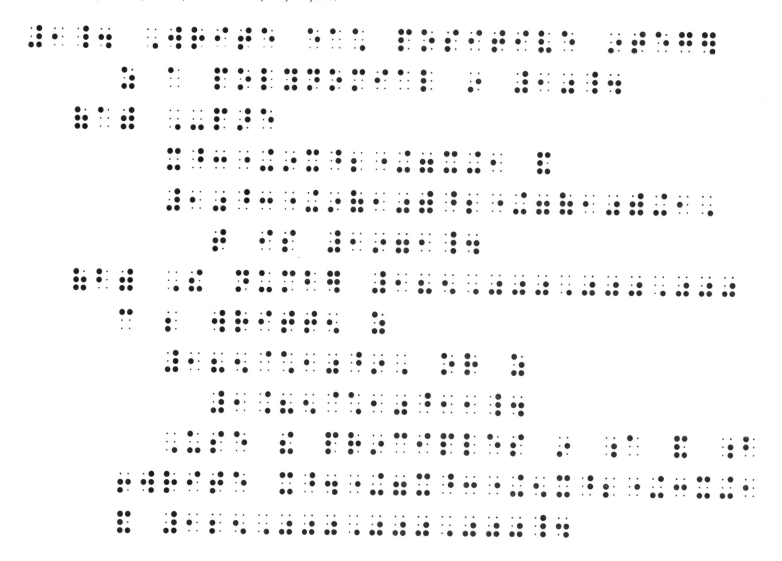

e. When a number or letter is used to identify a displayed expression, it must begin in the appropriate cell for displayed material in accordance with the rules of **a—d** above. If such numbers or letters occur to the right of the expression in print, they must be placed at the left of the expression in braille, and a transcriber's note concerning the change in position must be incorporated at the beginning of the first volume.

A page reference to a displayed expression must immediately follow that expression.

(1) Two basic laws of arithmetic are the
commutative law for addition
$$a + b = b + a, \qquad (1)$$
and the *commutative law for multiplication*
$$a \times b = b \times a. \qquad (2)$$

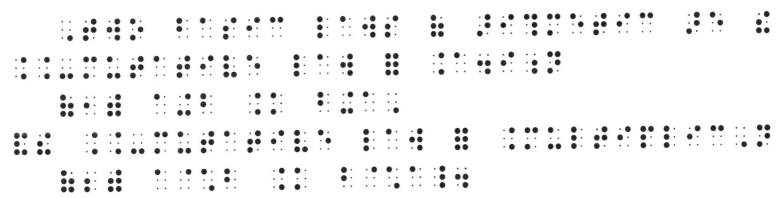

(2) 2. Use the formula
$$a_n = a_1 + (n - 1)d \qquad (12.3)$$
to find a_n and n when $a_1 = 1$, $d = 7$, $s_n = 204$.

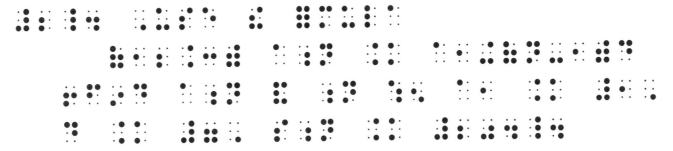

(3) 3. Give two examples illustrating
    (a) The associative law for addition
$$(a + b) + c = a + (b + c). \qquad (4)$$
    (b) The associative law for multiplication
$$(a \times b) \times c = a \times (b \times c). \qquad (5)$$

(4) The rules for subtraction depend upon those
for addition

$$a - b = a + (-b). \qquad (115\text{-}116)$$

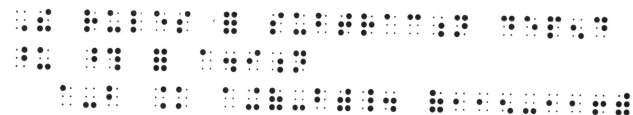

(5) 5. The distributive law can be stated in
the form

$$a \times (b + c) = ab + ac. \qquad (127\text{-}130)$$

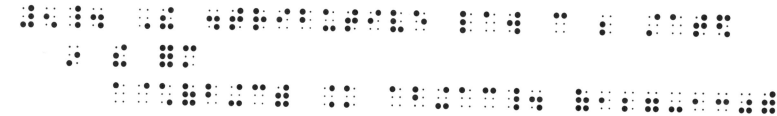

HOMEWORK

Prepare the following homework for submission to your teacher. Note: Page 130 contains material requiring a transcriber's note at the beginning of a braille volume. This note should be placed on a separate page at the beginning of the homework. Proofread carefully.

EXERCISE 7

1. Which fractions are unlike any other fraction: $\dfrac{3}{4}, \dfrac{1}{2}, \dfrac{1}{4}, \dfrac{4}{8}, \dfrac{7}{8}, \dfrac{15}{16}.$

2. Ted subtracted $\dfrac{1}{2}$ from $\dfrac{17}{18}$ and got $\dfrac{16}{16}$. Why isn't this a reasonable answer?

3. How many $\dfrac{2}{3}$'s are there in $\dfrac{5}{6}$?

4. Find the number of $\dfrac{1}{16}$'s there are in a $\dfrac{1}{2}$-foot line.

5. Find the value of $\dfrac{E}{r + R}$ when $E = \dfrac{5}{2}, r = \dfrac{3}{4}$, and $R = \dfrac{7}{8}$.

6. If $\dfrac{p}{q}$ and 0 are not equal, show that $a^{\frac{p}{q}} = b^{\frac{p}{q}}$ if and only if $a = b$.

7. What rule is illustrated by: $\left| \dfrac{c}{d} \right| = \dfrac{|c|}{|d|}$?

8. Estimate: $\dfrac{7987 \times 803 \times 0.061}{\pi}.$

9. Explain why the formula $A = \frac{1}{2}bh$ can be written as $A = \dfrac{bh}{2}.$

10. If $\dfrac{n}{\$90} = \dfrac{120}{100}$, what does n equal?

11. Does $\dfrac{1}{2}$ of \$ $\dfrac{4}{5}$ $= 40\cent$?

12. How many $\frac{1}{2}''$ are there in $1''$?

13. If $\dfrac{a}{b}$ and $\dfrac{c}{d}$ represent any two fractional numbers, then does

$$\dfrac{a}{b} \times \dfrac{c}{d} = \dfrac{a \times c}{b \times d}\,?$$

14. Solve and check:

   (a) $\dfrac{5}{8} + \dfrac{1}{2} + \dfrac{3}{4} = ?$

   (b) $\left(\dfrac{8}{7} \times \dfrac{6}{11}\right) \times \dfrac{7}{8} = ?$

   (c) $\dfrac{4}{8} = \dfrac{?}{2}$

   (d) $\dfrac{2}{3} \div \dfrac{5}{6} = \dfrac{2}{3} \times \dfrac{6}{5} = ?$

   (e) $\dfrac{^{+1}}{8} + \dfrac{^{+3}}{4} = ?$

   (f) $\dfrac{3}{4}\% + \dfrac{1}{4}\% + \dfrac{1}{2}\% = ?\%$

   (g) $\dfrac{\ldots \times 20}{\ldots \times 30} = \dfrac{60}{90}$

15. Simplify:

   (a) $5\dfrac{x}{y} + 3\dfrac{x}{y}$

   (b) $\dfrac{x+a}{ax} - \dfrac{1}{a} = \dfrac{a}{x+a}$

   (c) $\dfrac{1}{2}\left[\left(\dfrac{1}{2} - \dfrac{1}{3}\right) \div \dfrac{1}{6}\right]$

   (d) $(a^{\frac{1}{2}} - b^{\frac{1}{2}})^2$

16. Sketch the graph of $\dfrac{x^2}{9} + \dfrac{y^2}{36} = 1$.

17. What number does $5 \times \dfrac{1}{10^3}$ name?

18. Express $\dfrac{5a^{\frac{3}{4}}}{b^{\frac{5}{4}}}$ in radical form.

19. Use the formula $\dfrac{T_1}{T_2} = \dfrac{T_3}{T_4}$ to find the value of T_3 if $T_1 = 150$, $T_2 = 96$, and $T_4 = 144$.

20. Show $p\left(\dfrac{x_1 + x_2}{2}, \dfrac{y_1 + y_2}{2}\right)$ equidistant from $m(x_1, y_1)$ and $n(x_2, y_2)$.

21. Use $\dfrac{1 \text{ mi}}{1400 \text{ mi}}$ to find the relative error of the measurement 1 mi. in 1400 mi.

22. $\dfrac{5}{6}\text{lb} + \dfrac{7}{8}\text{lb} + \dfrac{1}{4}\text{lb} = \underline{\ ?\ }$

23. $\dfrac{4}{8}$ yd. $\dfrac{3}{4}$ ft. $= ?$ in.

24. Reduce $^{16}/_{32}$ and $^{14}/_{18}$ to lowest terms.

25. If $^a/_b$ and $^c/_d$ represent any two fractional numbers, then does $^a/_b \cdot {}^c/_d = {}^{a \cdot c}/_{b \cdot d}$?

26. In 3 a/b and r 1/4, the 3 and r are coefficients of the fraction. Explain.

27. Find the 7th term of 1/2, 1/4, 1/8, ...

28. Fractions may be expressed in many ways. For example, $2/3 = 8/12; 1/1 = 2/2 = 17/17 = x/x$.

29. Find the correct answer:

    (a) $7/15 \times 5/14 \times 1/8$ (d) $7/8' - 4/8'$

    (b) $5/6 \div 1/3$ (e) $(25)^{3/2} - (-343)^{2/3}$

    (c) $3/4\cent + 1/2\cent$

30. Express $\dfrac{6x^{5/6}}{x^{7/6}}$ in radical form.

31. Use Table 5.5 to compute $F_{1/4}$, $F_{2/4}$, and $F_{3/4}$.

32. Find $D_t\theta]_{\theta = \pi/2}$ in the given problem.

33. An object travels 88 ft./sec. at 60 mi./hr. How far will it travel in 1 sec. when the speed is 750 mi./hr.?

34. What is the sum of $4\frac{1}{4}$, $3\frac{3}{4}$, and $10\frac{1}{2}$?

35. Insert 6 arithmetic means between $7\frac{1}{2}a$ and $\frac{1}{2}a$.

36. Find the correct answer:

    (a) $2\dfrac{1}{3} \times 3\dfrac{1}{2} \times 1\dfrac{1}{6}$ (b) $3\dfrac{2}{3} + 1\dfrac{1}{2} + \dfrac{4}{5}$

    (c) $-1\dfrac{1}{7} \times (-2\dfrac{1}{3})$ (d) $(3\dfrac{1}{3})(43\dfrac{1}{6})$

    (e) $5\dfrac{4}{3} = 6\dfrac{?}{3}$ (f) $8\dfrac{4}{3} = ?\dfrac{1}{3}$

    (g) $3\dfrac{1}{3}y = 13\dfrac{1}{3}$ (h) $1\dfrac{7''}{8} + 2\dfrac{1''}{4}$

37. Find: $5\ 3/4 \div 2\ 2/3$; $14\ 7/8 \div 3\ 1/16$.

38. 1 cu. ft. holds about $7\frac{1}{2}$ gal. How many gal. are in a tank $1\dfrac{2}{3}$ ft $\times 1\dfrac{1}{2}$ ft $\times 1$ ft?

39. Find the premium for a $1\frac{1}{2}$-yr. policy at the yearly rate of 24$\cent$ per \$100.

40. Is there a 1-to-1 correspondence between the members of
        $\{\ 0, \frac{1}{2}, 1, 1\frac{1}{2}\}$ and
        $\{2 - 2, 1 \div \frac{1}{2}, 4 - 3, 1 + \frac{1}{2}\}$?

Simplify:

41. $\dfrac{\frac{1}{2}}{\frac{3}{4}}$ 42. $\dfrac{\frac{15}{22}}{\frac{47}{88}}$ 43. $\dfrac{\frac{4}{7}}{2}$

44. $\dfrac{\dfrac{55+42}{15}}{\dfrac{34+45}{18}}$

45. $\dfrac{\dfrac{x+y}{x-y}}{\dfrac{a}{b}}$

46. $\dfrac{19}{32\times\dfrac{1}{2}}$

47. $\dfrac{\dfrac{1}{8}+\dfrac{3}{4}}{7}$

48. $\dfrac{\dfrac{1}{2}+\dfrac{1}{3}}{\dfrac{3}{4}-\dfrac{7}{6}}$

49. $\dfrac{1+\dfrac{a}{b}}{1-\dfrac{a^2}{b^2}}$

50. $\dfrac{a+\dfrac{a}{b+c}}{c+\dfrac{c}{b+c}}$

51. $\dfrac{\dfrac{1}{a}}{b}\times\dfrac{b}{b}$

52. $\dfrac{3/5}{6}$

53. $\dfrac{11/3+14/5}{17/9+5/2}$

54. $\dfrac{33\dfrac{1}{3}}{100}$

55. $\dfrac{2\dfrac{1}{2}}{5\dfrac{1}{3}}$

56. $\dfrac{2\times12\dfrac{1}{2}}{2\times100}$

57. $\dfrac{x}{y^{\frac{1}{3}}}$

58. $\dfrac{3}{5}\Big/\dfrac{7}{9}$

59. Find the square units of the region in Fig. 5 whose area is $\dfrac{25^{\frac{3}{4}}-6^{\frac{3}{4}}}{\frac{3}{4}}$.

60. Simplify these radicals:

(a) $\sqrt{63}$
(b) $\sqrt{27}$
(c) $\sqrt{\dfrac{a+b}{a-b}}$

(d) $(r^2\sqrt{r^3})^3$
(e) $\sqrt{80a^6b^2}$
(f) $\sqrt{48x^3y^3}$

61. Find:

(a) $\sqrt{75}-\sqrt{48}$
(b) $2\sqrt{108}-3\sqrt{27}$

(c) $(7-2\sqrt{5})(7+2\sqrt{5})$
(d) $\sqrt{2}\sqrt{10}$

62. Simplify:

(a) $\dfrac{2+\sqrt{3}}{\sqrt{3}}$
(b) $\dfrac{4\sqrt{6}-3\sqrt{2}}{7\sqrt{3}+2\sqrt{5}}$
(c) $\dfrac{2-\sqrt{\frac{1}{4}}}{3-\sqrt{\frac{1}{2}}}$

63. Find the sum of 7 terms of $3\sqrt{2}$, 6, $6\sqrt{2}$, ...

64. Find equivalent numbers for the following:

$$(\sqrt{8},\ 4,\ \sqrt{16},\ 2\sqrt{2}).$$

65. The symbol $\sqrt{}$ means "square root."

66. Find: $\sqrt{(30)} \times \sqrt{(10)} \times \sqrt{(10)}$.

67. Simplify:

(a) $\sqrt[3]{72}$

(b) $\sqrt[3]{54}$

(c) $\sqrt[6]{(a+b)^3}$

(d) $\dfrac{\sqrt[3]{9}}{\sqrt[3]{18}}$

68. Find:

(a) $\sqrt[3]{16} + \sqrt[4]{162}$

(b) $\sqrt[5]{8} \cdot \sqrt[5]{2} \cdot \sqrt[5]{2}$

(c) $(3\sqrt[3]{a} + 2)^3$

(d) $\sqrt[3]{7} \ \sqrt[3]{7}$

(e) $\sqrt[4]{8r^2s^3t^5} \ \sqrt[4]{4r^6st^2}$

69. Express each of the following as an integer or as a single radical.

(a) $\sqrt{\sqrt{a}}$

(b) $\sqrt[3]{\sqrt{729}}$

(c) $\sqrt[3]{r\sqrt{r}}$

(d) $\sqrt{\sqrt{15} + \sqrt{17} + \sqrt{117}}$

(e) $\sqrt{\sqrt[3]{64}}$

(f) $\sqrt{\sqrt[3]{\sqrt[4]{b^{48}}}}$

(g) $\sqrt{s\sqrt[3]{s\sqrt{s}}}$

(h) $\sqrt{x^2\sqrt{x}}$

(i) $\sqrt{\sqrt{a^{12}}}$

70. Explain the meaning of $\sqrt{1 + 2 + 3 + \dots}$.

71. Find the radicand: $\sqrt{\dots} = 36$.

72. $\sqrt{12 \text{ ft.}} = ?$

73. $4\sqrt{24}$ sq. ft. $= ?$

Study the set of numbers below.

$$\{5, 8, 11, 14, 17, \dots\} \tag{1}$$

Each term after the first can be obtained by adding a fixed number (in this case, 3) to the preceding term. Such a set of numbers is called an *arithmetic sequence*. Is the set below an arithmetic sequence?

$$\{1, 5, 9, 13, \dots\} \tag{2}$$

What is the common difference?

Review the work on the indicated pages.

74. In our studies, we have used the symbols

$$+, -, \times, \div. \tag{20-21}$$

We have also used the symbols

$$=, >, <. \tag{22-23}$$

Use each symbol in a mathematical statement.

LESSON 8

ROMAN NUMERALS

§90. Capitalization and Punctuation of Roman Numerals: The single capitalization indicator ⠠ must be used before a Roman numeral consisting of one capitalized letter; the double capitalization indicator ⠠⠠ must be used before a Roman numeral consisting of two or more unspaced capitalized letters. The effect of the double capitalization indicator is terminated by any symbol other than a letter.

Roman numerals are mathematical expressions and must be punctuated accordingly.

§91. Roman Numerals and the English Letter Indicator: Generally, the English letter indicator with Roman numerals is treated in the same manner as when used with English letters. When the English letter indicator is used, its effect extends through the entire Roman numeral following it.

a. The English letter indicator must be used before a Roman numeral consisting of a single capitalized letter or before a Roman numeral consisting of one or more uncapitalized letters if the Roman numeral in braille is preceded by a space or by one or more punctuation marks and is followed by a space or by one or more punctuation marks.

The English letter indicator must not be used with a Roman numeral consisting of two or more capitalized letters in regular type.

(1) i, ii, iii, iv, v.

(2) I, II, III, IV, V.

(3) Solve problems i and ii.

(4) Read Volumes I and II.

(5) x denotes the number 10.

(6) V denotes the number 5.

(7) 1. Factor:
    i. $4ab + 4x^2 - a^2 - 4b^2$
    ii. $(m - n)^2 - (a + b)^2$

(8) Solve problems i-v and ix-xi.

(9) Read rule 3-i.

(10) quadrant-I

(11) Read chapters I-X and XV-XVI.

(12) Solve Exercises I-a and II-b.

(13) Figure V—not VI—is greater in area.

b. The English letter indicator must be used when it is necessary to show that a Roman numeral is printed in nonregular type.

(1) Name the number shown by the boldface numerals: **I, ii.**

c. The English letter indicator must not be used with a Roman numeral in regular type immediately preceded or followed by a sign of comparison. However, the English letter indicator must be used with a Roman numeral consisting of a single capitalized letter or one or more uncapitalized letters separated from a sign of comparison by a mark of punctuation.

(1) i = 1, v = 5, and x = 10.

(2) I = 1, V = 5, and X = 10.

(3) xi = 10 + 1

(4) LX = 50 + 10

(5) In Roman numerals, "C" = 100, "l" = 50, and "ix" = 9.

d. The English letter indicator must not be used with any Roman numeral in regular type in an expression consisting of a sequence of unspaced mathematical symbols.

(1) x — v = v

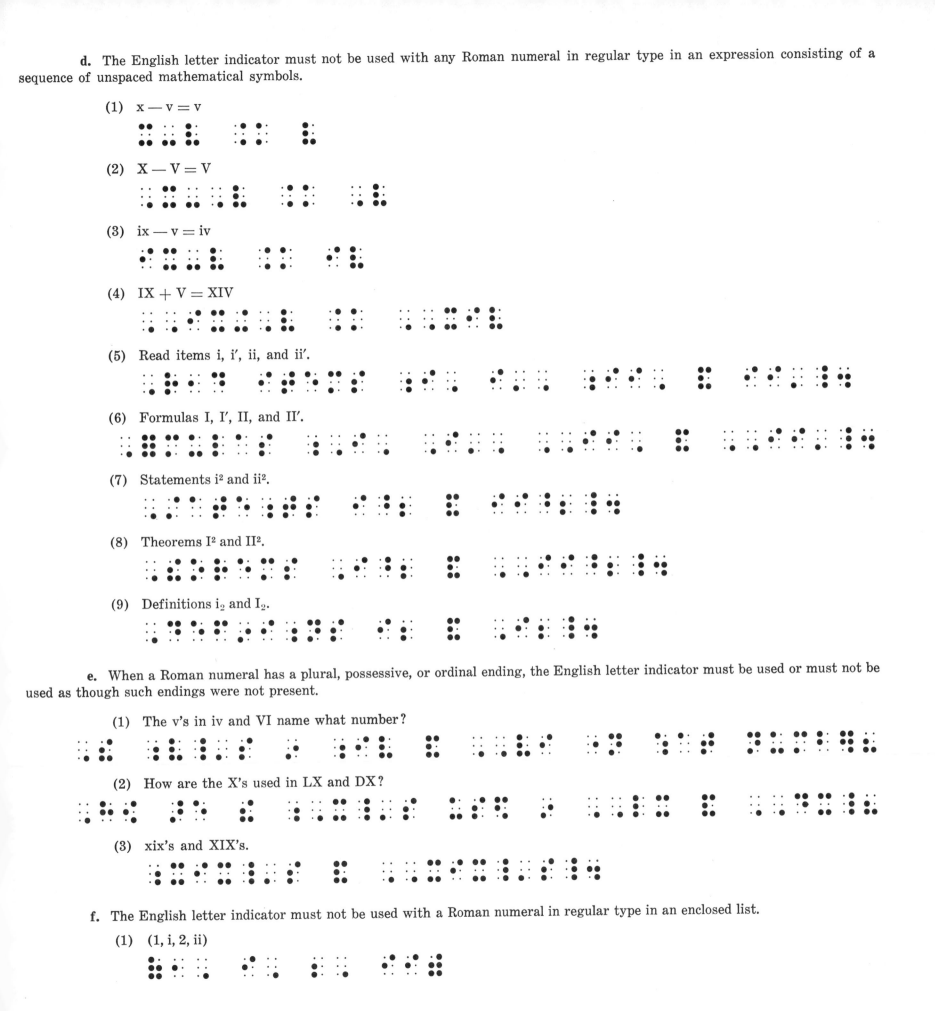

(2) X — V = V

(3) ix — v = iv

(4) IX + V = XIV

(5) Read items i, i′, ii, and ii′.

(6) Formulas I, I′, II, and II′.

(7) Statements i² and ii².

(8) Theorems I² and II².

(9) Definitions i₂ and I₂.

e. When a Roman numeral has a plural, possessive, or ordinal ending, the English letter indicator must be used or must not be used as though such endings were not present.

(1) The v's in iv and VI name what number?

(2) How are the X's used in LX and DX?

(3) xix's and XIX's.

f. The English letter indicator must not be used with a Roman numeral in regular type in an enclosed list.

(1) (1, i, 2, ii)

(2)   (1, I, 2, II)

g. The English letter indicator must not be used with a Roman numeral in regular type enclosed in signs of grouping.

(1) 1. Add:

(i)   10,742 + 4,976

(ii) 943 + 4632 + 1000

(2) Locate quadrants (I) and (II).

h. When a Roman numeral is in direct contact with only its opening or closing sign of grouping, the English letter indicator must be used or must not be used as though the grouping signs were absent. However, the English letter indicator must not be used when a grouping sign carries a prime, a superscript, or a subscript.

(1) The problems (i and ii) are difficult.

(2) (M is a Roman numeral)

(3) (name the Arabic numeral for MCM)

(4) (v = 5)

(5) (D = 500)

(6) (xiv = 14)

(7) (MCMLXXII = 1972)

(8) (v + i) × (xx + xv)

(9) $(V + I) \times (XX + XV)$

⠀⠀[braille]

(10) Read sections X), X)′, x)², and x)₂.

⠀⠀[braille]

⠀⠀[braille]

§92. Letter Combinations Similar to Roman Numerals: When it is unclear whether a letter combination is a Roman numeral, the combination must be treated as if it were not a Roman numeral. In such cases, the letters must be treated individually, and the English letter indicator must be used or not used in accordance with the rules for English letters.

(1) What does DC denote?

⠀⠀[braille]

(2) dix has a special meaning.

⠀⠀[braille]

SIGNS OF OPERATION (CONTINUED)

§93. Review of Signs of Operation: No space should be left before or after a sign of operation unless it is preceded or followed by a sign of comparison, an ellipsis, a dash, an unrelated word, or an abbreviation. However, no space must be left between an abbreviation and a fraction line. Signs of operation are mathematical symbols and must be punctuated accordingly.

The following signs of operation have already been introduced:

Plus	$+$	[braille]
Minus	$-$	[braille]
Multiplication		
Cross (Cartesian product)	$\times$	[braille]
Dot	$\cdot$	[braille]
Division (divided by)	$\div$	[braille]
Plus or Minus	$\pm$	[braille]
Minus or Plus	$\mp$	[braille]
Plus Followed by Minus	$+\,-$	[braille]
Minus Followed by Plus	$-\,+$	[braille]

Minus Followed by Minus	— —	⠤⠤
Fraction Lines (over, divided by)		
Horizontal Simple Fraction Line	——	
Diagonal Simple Fraction Line	/	
Horizontal Complex Fraction Line	——	
Diagonal Complex Fraction Line	/	

§94. Additional Signs of Operation:

   a. Ampersand (and, logical conjunction): &

When the ampersand is used in mathematical context, it must be treated as a sign of operation, and the symbol shown above must be used. However, when the ampersand is used in abbreviations or other literary context, the symbol and rules of English braille apply.

   (1) A & B

   (2) The & denotes *logical conjunction*.

   (3) AT&T

   (4) The B & O Railroad.

   b. Asterisk   *

   Crosshatch—number sign, tic-tac-toe, pounds (weight)   #

   Paragraph Mark   ¶

   Section Mark   §

The asterisk, crosshatch, paragraph, and section marks must be represented by the symbols of Nemeth code; English braille symbols must not be used. If these signs of operation occur as superscripts or subscripts, their position must be shown.

The numeric indicator must be used before a numeral or a decimal point and a numeral following an asterisk, crosshatch, paragraph, or section mark.

(1) f ∗ g

(2) (1 + 2) ∗ (3 + 4)

(3) 1 ∗ 2

(4) .1 ∗ .2

(5) x∗ > x

(6) $2\pi x_k^* \cdot \Delta x_k \cdot 2y_k^*$

(7) A′∗

(8) x # y = y # x

(9) 1 # 2 = 2 # 1

(10) In R#, # denotes a 1-place operation symbol.

(11) A ¶ B

(12) 3 ¶ 4 = 4 ¶ 3

(13) A § B

(14) 3 § 4 = 4 § 3

c. **Back Slash (divides, is a factor of):** \

(1) b\a can be read as "b divides a."

(2) 3\6 denotes "3 is a factor of 6."

d. **Dagger:**

  Single †

  Double ‡

(1) $A \dagger B = B \dagger A$

(2) $A \ddagger B = B \ddagger A$

e. **Dot (and, times):** ·

The dot may be used as a multiplication sign or to denote "and."

(1) In logic, $p \cdot q$ is read "p and q."

f. **Hollow Dot:** ∘

The hollow dot may be used as a sign of operation or as a superscript to represent degrees of temperature or angle.

(1) $f \circ g$

(2) $a \circ (b \circ c) = (a \circ b) \circ c$

(3) $f_1 \circ f_2 \circ \ldots \circ f_n$

(4) $40° + 50° = 90°$

(5) $\frac{1}{2}° + 1\frac{1}{2}° = ?°$

(6) $28°6'37''$

(7) A 30°-60°-90° triangle.

(8) $\theta_2^°$

(9) $100°$ C. $= 212°$ F.

(10) $45°$ C $+ 5°$ C $= 50°$ C

(11) N. $35°$ W.

(12) $(60°, 70°, 80°)$

(13) $45°, 90°$.

g. Intersection (cap): $\cap$

(1) $A \cap B = B \cap A$

(2) $(A \cap B) \cap C = A \cap (B \cap C)$

(3) Prove $\cap_i A_i = U$.

h. Logical Product (and, meet): $\wedge$

(1) $p \wedge q \wedge r$

(2) $(p_1 \wedge p_2 \wedge p_3 \wedge \ldots \wedge p_n)$

⠀[braille]

i. Logical Sum (or, join): $\vee$ ⠀[braille]

    (1) $p \vee q \vee r$

⠀[braille]

    (2) $[p \vee (q \vee r)]$

⠀[braille]

j. Minus With Dot Over (proper difference): $\dot{-}$ ⠀[braille]

    (1) $x \dot{-} y = 0$

⠀[braille]

    (2) $x \dot{-} y' = pd(x \dot{-} y)$

⠀[braille]

k. Tilde (not):

    Simple $\sim$ [braille]

    Extended $\sim\!\sim$ [braille]

In logic, the tilde is used as a sign of operation meaning "not."

When two symbols for the tilde follow one another, the multipurpose indicator [braille] must be inserted between them to indicate that they are written horizontally.

    (1) $\sim p$

⠀[braille]

    (2) $\sim p \vee q$

⠀[braille]

    (3) $\sim p \wedge \sim q \wedge \sim r$

⠀[braille]

    (4) $\sim (\sim p)$

⠀[braille]

    (5) $\sim \sim p \vee q$

⠀[braille]

(6) $\smile\smile$ s ∨ t

⠿⠿⠿⠿⠿⠿⠿⠿⠿⠿⠿⠿

l. **Union (cup):**   ∪   ⠸⠢

(1) $A \cup B = B \cup A$

(2) $(A \cup B) \cup C = A \cup (B \cup C)$

(3) $\{a, b, c, d\} \cup \{c, d\}$

(4) $A(S_1 \cup S_2) = A(S_1) + A(S_2)$

(5) Prove that x is an element of $\cup_i A_i$.

m. **Vertical Bar (is a factor, divides):** | ⠳

The vertical bar is used both as a sign of grouping and as a sign of operation.

(1) In b | a, b is a factor of a.

(2) 6 | 12 can be read as "6 divides 12."

(3) $x + 2 \mid x^2 + 7x + 10$

n. **Vertical Bar Negated (does not divide):**   ∤   ⠴⠳

(1) $5 \nmid n$

§95. **Signs of Operation and Boldface Type:** The signs of operation listed below are to be used to show boldface type only when the distinction between the regular and the boldface forms of the same sign has mathematical significance. Each symbol consists of dots

141

4-5-6 followed by the appropriate sign of operation. In this case, dots 4-5-6 must be considered not as the boldface type-form indicator but as part of its related symbol. Dots 4-5-6 must not be used with any other sign of operation.

Boldface Plus $+$

Boldface Minus $-$

Boldface Plus Followed by Boldface Minus $+\ -$

Boldface Plus Followed by Regular Minus $+\ -$

Regular Plus Followed by Boldface Minus $+\ -$

Boldface Minus Followed by Boldface Plus $-\ +$

Boldface Minus Followed by Regular Plus $-\ +$

Regular Minus Followed by Boldface Plus $-\ +$

(1) $a + b = b + a$

(2) $a + - c = b - + d$

REFERENCE SYMBOLS

§96. **Reference Symbols and Punctuation:** The asterisk, dagger, paragraph mark, section mark, and star must be represented by the symbols listed below; English braille symbols must not be used. Some of these signs are also used as signs of operation. However, when used as reference symbols, they must be transcribed in accordance with the following rules.

A reference symbol or numeral printed in a superscript position must not be shown as a superscript in braille. Reference symbols must be punctuated mathematically.

Asterisk *

Dagger

  Single †

  Double ‡

Paragraph Mark ¶

Section Mark

  Single §

  Double §§

Star ☆

§97. References to Footnotes:

a. Reference Symbols Denoting Footnotes: When a printed symbol referring to a footnote is attached to the beginning or end of a word, mathematical expression, etc., the reference symbol must follow that item with a space between in braille and must appear on the same braille line. When such a reference symbol is unattached, it must be positioned as it appears in print. No space should be left between a footnote reference symbol and its related punctuation mark.

(1) Find the *quarterly interest.

(2) Find the quarterly* interest.

(3) Let R† be a set.

(4) Let R be a set. †

(5) Find the quotient*.

(6) The asterisk (*) denotes a footnote.

b. Numbered or Lettered Footnotes and the General Reference Indicator:  When a footnote reference is denoted by a numeral alone, the general reference indicator and the numeric indicator must be placed before the note numeral. When a footnote reference is denoted by a letter alone, the general reference indicator must be placed before the note letter. The English letter indicator must not be used.

An attached footnote reference numeral or letter must follow the corresponding item. An unattached footnote reference numeral or letter must be positioned as it appears in print. Except for its punctuation, the general reference indicator and its numeral or letter must be preceded and followed by a space.

(1) Find the interest[1] and annuity[2].

(2) In $\sqrt[3]{a}$, the [1]index of the radical is 3.

(3) If B is a formula and y is a variable, [1] then (y)B is a formula.

(4) We sketch two proofs[a] of Theorem 15.

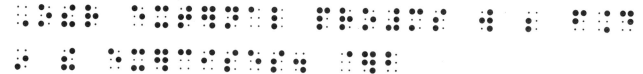

(5) Other external problems will be found in the exercises.[b]

c. Placement of Footnotes: In transcribing footnotes, the reference symbol and its related footnote must be positioned and indented in accordance with the rules of the *Code of Braille Textbook Formats and Techniques*.

(1)   The figure shows a spherical light wave from object O falling on a concave* spherical mirror.

_____

* The inner surface of a spherical shell is concave; the outer surface is convex.

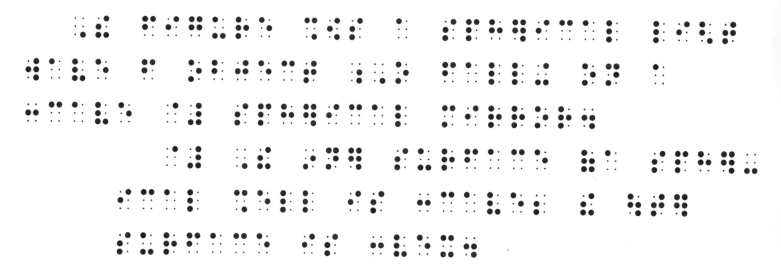

(2) 1. Find the interest[1] and the annuity[2].

_____

[1]Appendix, Table 4.
[2]Appendix, Table 5.

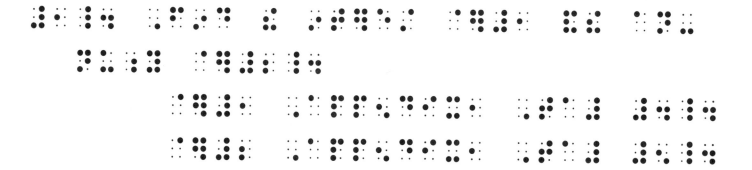

§98. References to Items Other Than Footnotes:

a. A reference symbol may be used with lettered or numbered items to indicate work for extra practice or credit, or to denote references to specific sections, paragraphs, etc. Such a reference symbol must be positioned as it appears in print and must be unspaced from its related letter or numeral. The numeric indicator must be used before a numeral following a reference symbol.

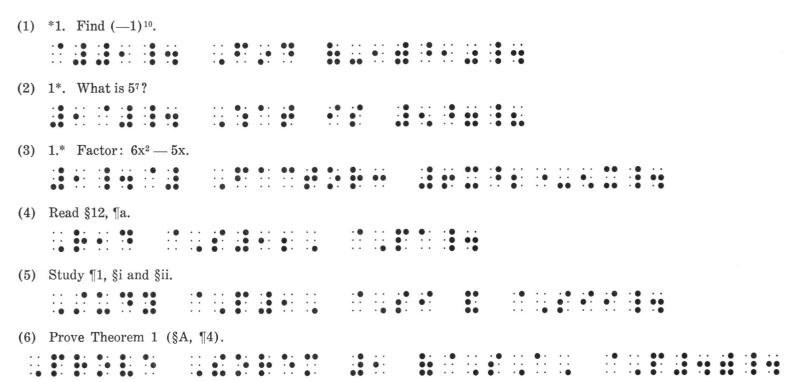

(1) *1. Find $(-1)^{10}$.

(2) 1*. What is 5^7?

(3) 1.* Factor: $6x^2 - 5x$.

(4) Read §12, ¶a.

(5) Study ¶1, §i and §ii.

(6) Prove Theorem 1 (§A, ¶4).

b. When a reference symbol is used to single out one or more words for special emphasis, a space must be left between the reference symbol and the word.

(1) ☆ complex fraction

§99. **Unlisted Reference Symbols:** When print symbols other than those listed are used for reference, the equivalent braille symbols in the Nemeth code must be used. If no equivalent braille symbol exists, a symbol must be devised and explained in a transcriber's note. All such reference symbols must be transcribed in accordance with the rules stated above.

HOMEWORK

Prepare the following homework for submission to your teacher. Proofread carefully.

EXERCISE 8

1. The capitalized letters I, V, X, L, C, D, and M are the number symbols we use to write Roman numerals. What Arabic number does each Roman numeral name?

2. Use Fig. 3 to name the ordered pairs in quadrants I, II, III, and IV.

3. A cornerstone is marked MCMLXXII. What date does it represent?

4. Write in Arabic numerals:
   a. VI   b. XIII   c. MCXL

5. The uncapitalized letters i, v, x, l, c, d, and m are also used to write Roman numerals. What number does each represent?

6. What number does each of the following name: i, ii, iv, vii, x.

7. Solve $V = lwh$ for each of the following (use Figure 3.4):
   i. for l   ii. for w   iii. for h

8. List the definitions given in Chapters I-V and XI-XV.

9. Do Exercises I-a and IV-c.

10. Refer to Theorem 5.9 and show that T has the properties i-ii and iv-v.

11. True or false:
    a. $I = 1$ b. $VII = V + II$
    c. $XLI - IV = XXXVII$ d. $i = 1$
    e. $x + ii = 10 + 2$ f. $xv - ix = xiv$

12. Does "V" $= 5$? Are V and 5 names for the same number?

13. If "x" denotes 10, does "x" $=$ "10"?

14. Refer to Formulas I and I′. Apply the principles to Theorems I and II².

15. Read items i, i′, and i_2.

16. Are the I's added or subtracted in II, IV, VI? What value do the XX's have in LXX?

17. In sets A, B, and C where
    $$A = \{1, II, 3, IV, 5\}$$
    $$B = \{i, ii, iii, iv, v\}$$
    $$C = \{I, 2, III, 4, V\}$$
    is there a 1-to-1 correspondence between the members of sets A and B? between A and C? between B and C?

18. Write the proofs for (i), (ii), and (iii) of Theorem 3.2. Use the results to explain figures (I) and (II).

19. Use the figures (I and II) to solve the problems (i and ii).

20. Read sections I), I)², and II).

21. The symbol & is used to show conjunction. Translate P&C into a word sentence.

22. If 1, 2, and 3 are elements of a system in which two operations are denoted by the symbol # and the symbol &, which of the following expressions represents the statement # is distributive over &?
    (a) 1 # (2 & 3) = (1 & 2) # (1 & 3)
    (b) 1 # (2 & 3) = (1 # 2) & (1 # 3)
    (c) 1 & (2 # 3) = (1 # 2) & (1 # 3)

23. Explain how the cardinal number of a set M is the same as the cardinal number of a set N, or $\#(M) = \#(N)$.

24. An operation ($*$) has been defined over the set of natural numbers. In each of the following, find $2 * 3$.

   (a) $x * y = (1 + x) + y$
   (b) $x * y = x(2y)$
   (c) $x * y = xy^2$

25. Prove: If f has the property that, for all a, b, and c in X, then

   $$a * (b * c) = (a * b) * c.$$

26. Prove that for any order types α and β, $(\alpha + \beta)^* = \alpha^* + \beta^*$.

27. Find the volume of the kth shell where (x_k^*, y_k^*) is the point of the abscissa $x_k^* = \dfrac{1}{2}(x_k + x_{k+1})$.

28. Find the conditional density of Y_1^*, given Y_2^*.

29. A binary operation $\P$ has the cancellation property if and only if each of $x \P z = y \P z$ and $z \P x = z \P y$ implies $x = y$. Show how this applies to the equality relation. Does $1 \P 3 = 4 \P 3$?

30. Y is a set, $\S$ is an associative operation in Y, and m is a member of Y such that $m \S y = y \S m = y$ for all y in Y. Use this notation for all operations in Y.

31. If $p \dagger q$ is defined as "neither p nor q," show that $[(p \dagger p) \dagger (q \dagger q)]$, if and only if $(p \cdot q)$ is a tautology.

32. Prove: For all integers a, b, and c, if a and b are relatively prime and $b\backslash ac$ then $b\backslash c$. Is this true for $2\backslash 8 \times 4$?

33. Given: a, b, c, and x denote elements of the set of natural numbers. Prove:

   (i) If $b \mid a$ and $a \mid c$, then $b \mid c$.
   (ii) If $b \mid a$ and $b \mid c$, then $b \mid (a + c)$.
   (iii) If p is a prime and $p \mid a^2$, then $p \mid a$.

34. From the given information, show that if $a = h$ and $b = k$, then $a \circ b = h \circ b$, $a \circ b = a \circ k$, and $a \circ b = h \circ k$.

35. State whether each equation is valid for linear functions f, g, and h.

   (a) $(f + g) \circ h = f \circ h + g \circ h$
   (b) $f \circ (g \circ h) = (f \circ g) \circ (f \circ h)$

36. Prove: If $90° = 90°$ and $x° > y°$, then $(90 - x)° < (90 - y)°$.

37. Find the answer:

   (a) $68° - 32° = ?°$
   (b) $\dfrac{3}{4}° + 1\dfrac{1}{4}° = ?°$

38. Find the sum of $30°28'$ and $56°42'$.

39. A $30°$-$60°$-$90°$-triangle is what kind of triangle? Draw a $45°$-$45°$-$90°$-triangle.

40. Water freezes at $32°$ F (32 degrees Fahrenheit). Is this the same as $0°$ C (0 degrees Centigrade)?

41. Let sets $S = \{0, 1, 2, 3\}$ and $T = \{5, 6, 7, 8, 9\}$. Find

   (a) $S \cup T$ (b) $T \cup S$ (c) $S \cap T$ (d) $T \cap S$

42. What laws are illustrated by

   $$A \cup (B \cup C) = (A \cup B) \cup C \text{ and }$$
   $$A \cap (B \cap C) = (A \cap B) \cap C?$$

43. Using Venn diagrams show that $(A \cup B)^c = A^c \cap B^c$.

44. We express the union of three sets as $A_1 \cup A_2 \cup A_3$ and, more generally, of n sets as $A_1 \cup A_2 \cup \ldots \cup A_n$.

45. Given: Statements p and q are true and r is false. Identify each of the following as true or false.

   (a) $p \wedge q$ (b) $p \wedge (q \vee r)$ (c) $(p \wedge q) \vee r$

   (d) $(\sim p \wedge q)$ (e) $\sim p \wedge \sim q \wedge \sim r$

46. True or false: Any proposition is the negation of its own negation, or $p = \sim (\sim p)$.

47. Given: Alice is at home and Tom is at home. Which statements are true:

   (a) $p \cdot q$ (b) $\sim \sim (p \cdot q)$

48. We define the proper difference, $\dot{-}$, by the notation $m \dot{-} 0 = m$ and $m \dot{-} n' = pd(m \dot{-} n)$. That is, $m \dot{-} n = m - n$ if m and n are not greater than or equal to each other, and $m \dot{-} n = 0$ if $m < n$. Obtain $m \dot{-} n$ as the value of $\dot{-}$ at $\langle m, n \rangle$.

49. Special operations are denoted by a boldface plus ($\mathbf{+}$) and a boldface minus ($\mathbf{-}$). Use induction to determine if $a \mathbf{+} b = b \mathbf{+} a$ and $c \mathbf{-} d = d \mathbf{-} c$.

50. Show $a/b = c/d$ iff* $ad = bc$.

51. The diagram shows two fixed points A and B and a ray APB† connecting them.

52. In $\sqrt[n]{a}$, n is the index[1] of the radical. What is a?

---

*The phrase "if and only if" occurs so often in mathematics that the abbreviated form "iff" is used throughout this text.
†Assume that ray APB lies in the plane of the figure.
[1]If no index is indicated, it is understood to be 2.

SYMBOLIC LOGIC

Mathematical or symbolic logic is the systematic study of the basic principles of valid relationships by a method which makes a distinction between the validity of some reasoning and the truth of the premises from which it was derived.

In our work we will be using the words and phrases listed below. Study the designated pages and give examples for each starred item. The exercise following the list is for extra study. Such study is denoted by the use of an asterisk placed before the problem number.

☆ composite proposition (31)

☆ conjunction (32)

☆ disjunction (33)

☆ complete disjunction (34)

*53. Show that definition 3.4, §a, ¶1, is a tautology.

REPRESENTATION OF ARROWS

§100. **General Principles:** A figure in the form of an arrow is represented by braille symbols suggesting the ink-print shape. In representing arrows, the appropriate arrowhead and arrow shaft must be selected from the following list.

Arrowheads

Name	Print
Left Full Barbed	⟨
Left Lower Barbed	＼
Left Upper Barbed	∠
Right Full Barbed	⟩
Right Lower Barbed	⟋
Right Upper Barbed	＼
Left Full Blunted	E
Left Lower Blunted	L
Left Upper Blunted	Γ
Right Full Blunted	ⴺ
Right Lower Blunted	⌐
Right Upper Blunted	⌐
Left Full Curved	(
Left Lower Curved	⟨
Left Upper Curved	∟
Right Full Curved	)
Right Lower Curved	⟩
Right Upper Curved	⟩
Left Full Straight	⊢

Left Lower Straight	⌐	⠄⠛
Left Upper Straight	∟	⠈⠛
Right Full Straight	⊣	⠿
Right Lower Straight	⌐	⠄⠹
Right Upper Straight	⌐	⠈⠻

Arrow Shafts

Ordinary Length Single	—	⠒⠒
Ordinary Length Double	═	⠶⠶
Short Single	–	⠒
Short Double	═	⠶
Long Single	——	⠒⠒⠒
Long Double	══	⠶⠶⠶
Curved	(or)	⠣ ⠜
Dashed	– –	⠒ ⠒
Dotted	· · ·	⠂ ⠂ ⠂
Wavy	∿	⠢⠒⠄

§101. Construction of Arrows: In general, arrows should be transcribed in the order in which their symbols appear.

a. Shape Indicator: ⠫

The shape indicator must be used before an arrow symbol.

b. Arrowheads: An arrowhead may be barbed, blunted, straight, or curved, and may occur at the left, at the right, or at both ends of an arrow shaft. An arrowhead may also appear with only its upper or lower portion.

c. Arrow Shafts: The length of an arrow shaft is indicated by the number of times the braille arrow shaft symbol is used. One braille symbol represents a short shaft, two symbols represent the ordinary shaft length, and three or more symbols are used to indicate a longer shaft.

(1)	→	⠫⠒⠕
(2)	←	⠪⠒⠒

150

(3) ↔

(4) →

(5) ←

(6) ⟷

(7) ⟶

(8) ⟵

(9) ←⟶

(10) ⟹

(11) ⟸

(12) ⟺

(13) —→

(14) ⋯›

(15) ↢⟶

(16) ⊣

(17) ⊢

(18) ⊢⊣

(19) →⟩

(20) ⟨←

(21) ⟨—⟩

(22) ⊤

(23) ⊢

(24) ⊢⊣

(25) ⟶

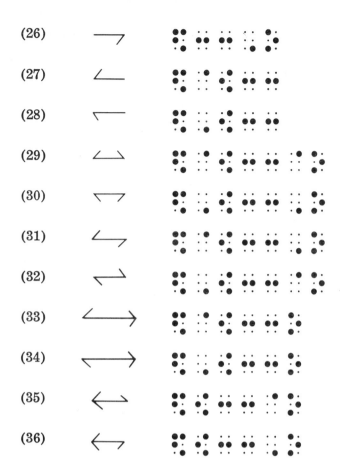

(26) ⌐

(27) ∟

(28) ⌐

(29) ∠⃗

(30) ▽

(31) ⟵

(32) ⇌

(33) ⟶

(34) ⟹

(35) ⟵

(36) ⟵

d. Arrows With Dotted Ends: Arrows may also be represented by a shaft preceded or followed by a solid dot (•) or by a hollow dot (○) .

(1) •⟶

(2) ⟵•

(3) —•

(4) •—

(5) •—•

(6) ○⟶

(7) ⟵○

(8) —○

(9) ○—

(10) ○—○

152

§102. **Arrow Directions:** Arrow directions are represented by the use or nonuse of direction indicators. When required, the appropriate direction indicator must immediately follow the shape indicator.

    a. Horizontal Arrow Directions: Direction indicators are not required with a horizontal arrow which points left, right, or both left and right.

(1)   ⟵

(2)   →

(3)   ⟹

(4)   ⟷

    b. Vertical Arrow Directions: Vertical arrows require the following direction indicators:

Directly-Over Indicator

Directly-Under Indicator

The directly-over indicator must be used before a two-headed vertical arrow pointing up and down, or before a one-headed vertical arrow pointing up only.

The directly-under indicator must be used before a one-headed vertical arrow pointing down.

When a vertical arrow has only one arrowhead, the symbol for the right-arrowhead must be used.

(1)   ↕

(2)   ↑

(3)   ↓

    c. Slanted Arrow Directions: Slanted arrows require the following direction indicators:

Superscript Indicator

Subscript Indicator

The superscript indicator must be used to show that a one-headed left- or right-slanted arrow points upward. The subscript indicator must be used to show that a one-headed left- or right-slanted arrow points downward.

(1)   ↖

(2)   ↗

(3)   ↙

(4)   ↘

When a slanted arrow has two arrowheads, the superscript indicator is used when the left arrowhead points upward; the subscript indicator is used when the left arrowhead points downward.

(5) 

(6) 

d. Curved Arrow Directions: Direction indicators are not required with curved arrows. The direction of curvature is shown by a left- or right-arrowhead. A curved shaft followed by a right-arrowhead represents a counterclockwise arrow; a curved shaft preceded by a left-arrowhead represents a clockwise arrow.

(1) 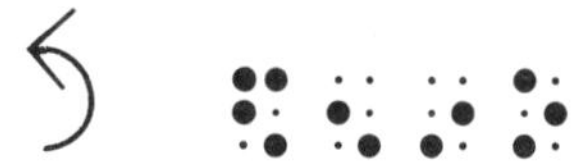

(2) 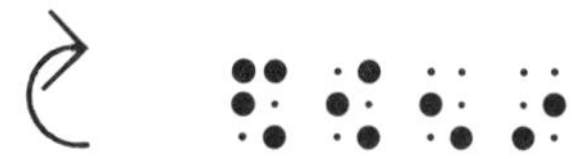

§103. Boldface Arrows: When an arrow is printed in boldface type, the boldface type-form indicator 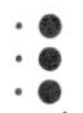 must be placed before the arrowhead or arrow shaft at the beginning of the arrow symbol. When both the boldface type-form indicator and a direction indicator are required, the boldface type-form indicator must follow the direction indicator.

(1)–(6) 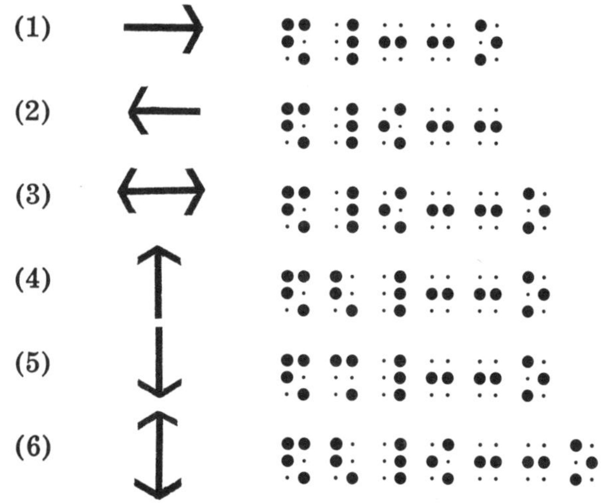

§104. Spacing and Punctuation With Arrows: Arrows are considered signs of comparison and must be spaced and punctuated accordingly.

(1) B ⟵ A

(2) p ⟷ q

(3) $|x - a| < 3 \Longleftrightarrow x - a$

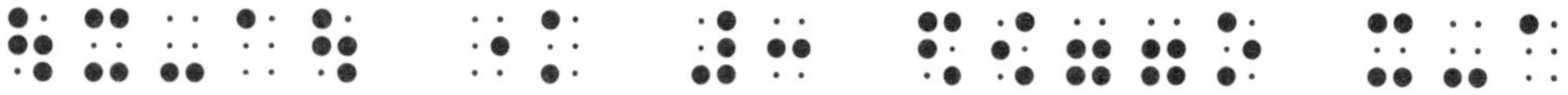

(4) $x \downarrow 2$

⠿ ⠿⠿⠿⠿⠿ ⠿⠿⠿

(5) $(\uparrow, \updownarrow)$

⠿⠿⠿⠿⠿⠿⠿ ⠿⠿⠿⠿⠿⠿⠿⠿

(6) $X = \{x_i\}$ or $x_i \uparrow$.

⠿⠿ ⠿⠿ ⠿⠿⠿⠿⠿⠿⠿⠿ ⠿⠿ ⠿⠿⠿ ⠿⠿⠿⠿⠿⠿⠿

§105. Contracted Form of Right-Pointing Arrow: ⟶ ⠿ ⠿

The contracted form for a right-pointing arrow must be used when a right-pointing arrow with a full barb and a single shaft of ordinary length occurs by itself in regular type. All other right-pointing arrows always require the use of all appropriate symbols.

(1) $A \longrightarrow B$

⠿ ⠿ ⠿ ⠿ ⠿ ⠿

(2) $n{:}v \longrightarrow r$

⠿⠿⠿⠿⠿ ⠿⠿ ⠿

(3) $2H_2O + O_2 \longrightarrow 2H_2O$

⠿⠿ ⠿⠿⠿ ⠿⠿⠿⠿⠿⠿⠿⠿ ⠿⠿ ⠿⠿⠿ ⠿⠿ ⠿⠿⠿⠿⠿⠿

(4) $p \longrightarrow (q \vee r)$

⠿ ⠿⠿ ⠿⠿⠿⠿⠿⠿⠿

(5) $X \Longrightarrow Y$

⠿⠿ ⠿⠿⠿⠿⠿⠿⠿ ⠿⠿

(6) $x \longrightarrow y$

⠿ ⠿⠿⠿⠿⠿⠿ ⠿

(7) $X \Longrightarrow Y$

⠿⠿ ⠿⠿⠿⠿⠿ ⠿⠿

(8) $X \longrightarrow Y$

⠿⠿ ⠿⠿⠿⠿⠿⠿ ⠿⠿

155

§106. **Review of Signs of Comparison:** A space must be left before and after a sign of comparison. However, no space should be left between a sign of comparison and a sign of grouping, a braille indicator, or a punctuation mark which is related to it.

The following simple signs of comparison have already been introduced:

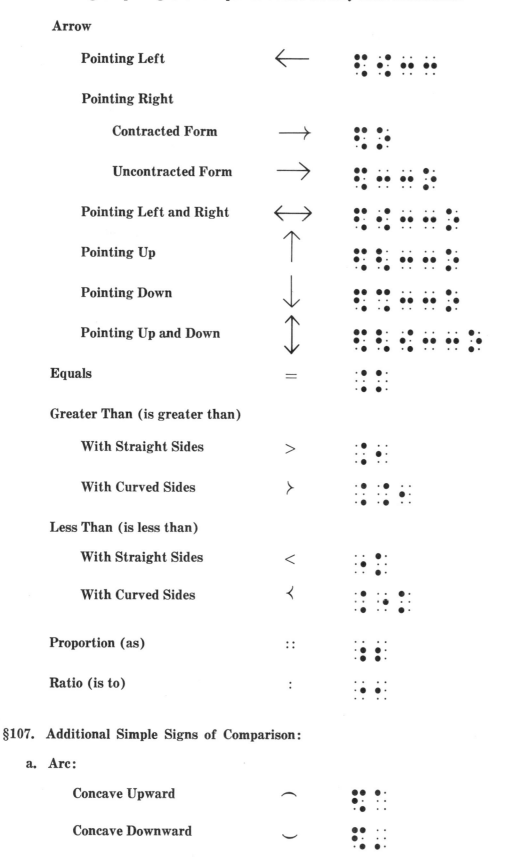

Arrow

    Pointing Left

    Pointing Right

        Contracted Form

        Uncontracted Form

    Pointing Left and Right

    Pointing Up

    Pointing Down

    Pointing Up and Down

Equals

Greater Than (is greater than)

    With Straight Sides

    With Curved Sides

Less Than (is less than)

    With Straight Sides

    With Curved Sides

Proportion (as)

Ratio (is to)

§107. **Additional Simple Signs of Comparison:**

  a. **Arc:**

    Concave Upward

    Concave Downward

(1) x ⌢ y

⠿ ⠿ ⠿ ⠿ (braille)

(2) x ⌣ y

⠿ ⠿ ⠿ ⠿ (braille)

b. **Equivalence (is equivalent to):** ⇌   (braille)

(1) x ⇌ y

(braille)

c. **Identity (is identical with, is congruent to):** ≡   (braille)

This symbol must not be used for *is congruent to* if another sign is used for this purpose in print.

(1) A + B ≡ B + A

(braille)

(2) f(x) ≡ D(x) · q(x)

(braille)

d. **Inclusion (is contained in, is a subset of):** ⊂   (braille)

(1) A ⊂ D

(braille)

(2) (A ∪ E) ⊂ (F ∪ B)

(braille)

e. **Membership (is an element of, belongs to):** ε or ∈ or ∈   (braille)

This symbol is generally used for sets and their elements. It must not be mistaken for the Greek uncapitalized epsilon even though it may be referred to as such.

(1) 5 ε B

(braille)

(2) $\dfrac{8 \times 4}{4}$ ∈ {8}

(braille)

f. Parallel To (is parallel to): ‖

   (1) AB ‖ CD

g. Perpendicular To (is perpendicular to): ⊥

   (1) PQ ⊥ RS

   (2) $x = s + s^{\perp}$

h. Relation (is related to): R

When an R or any other letter or sign is used between two expressions to show relation, the letter or other symbol must be treated as a sign of comparison.

   (1) a R b

   (2) r θ s

i. Reverse Inclusion (contains; in logic, implies): ⊃

   (1) D ⊃ A

   (2) C ⊃ C$_1$ ⊃ C$_2$ ⊃ ...

j. Reverse Membership (contains the element): ∍ or Ǝ or ⊐

   (1) B ∍ 5

k. Tilde:

   Simple (is related to, is similar to)   ∼

   Extended (is related to)   ∼

The tilde may be used as a sign of operation or as a sign of comparison.

(1) PQR $\sim$ P′Q′R′

(2) x $\sim\!\sim$ y

l. **Variation (varies as):** $\propto$

(1) x $\propto$ y

m. **Vertical Bar (such that):** |

The vertical bar may be used as a sign of grouping, as a sign of operation, or as a sign of comparison. When used as a sign of comparison, it usually occurs in an expression within braces used for set notation. However, it may also appear in other situations.

(1) {x | x has the property T}

(2) {w | w = w + 1}

(3) {m | 3(m — 6) = —9}

(4) {(x, y) | x + y < 6}

§108. **Signs of Comparison Compounded Vertically:** When two or more simple signs of comparison are arranged one under the other, the combination becomes a single comparison sign compounded vertically. The symbol for the uppermost sign must be written first and unspaced from the symbol for the next lower sign.

a. **Arrows:** When a right-pointing arrow in regular type with a full barb and single shaft of ordinary length is part of a sign of comparison compounded vertically, its contracted form must not be used.

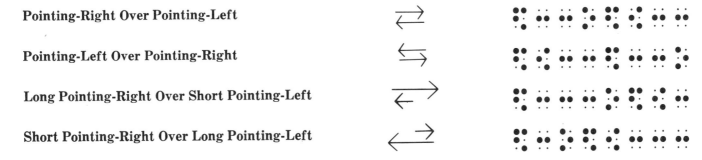

Pointing-Right Over Pointing-Left $\rightleftharpoons$

Pointing-Left Over Pointing-Right $\leftrightharpoons$

Long Pointing-Right Over Short Pointing-Left

Short Pointing-Right Over Long Pointing-Left

Pointing-Right With Upper Barb Only Over
Pointing-Left With Lower Barb Only

Pointing-Right Over Boldface Pointing-Left

Pointing-Left Over Boldface Pointing-Right

Boldface Pointing-Right Over Pointing-Left

Boldface Pointing-Left Over Pointing-Right

Boldface Pointing-Right Over Boldface Pointing-Left

Boldface Pointing-Left Over Boldface Pointing-Right

(1) A + B $\rightleftharpoons$ C + D

(2) HCl $\rightleftharpoons$ H+ + Cl−

b. Equals:

Horizontal Bar   —

Oblique Stroke   / or \

Equals Sign   =

As shown in **c** through **k** below, a single horizontal bar, an oblique stroke, or an equals sign may appear as part of a sign of comparison compounded vertically.   The horizontal bar or oblique stroke is often substituted for the equals sign.

c. Greater Than:

Bar Over Greater Than (is equal to or greater than) $\overline{>}$ or $\geqslant$

Equals Sign Over Greater Than (is equal to or greater than) $\overline{\overline{>}}$ or $\geqq$

Bar Under Greater Than (is greater than or equal to) $\geq$ or $\geqslant$

Equals Sign Under Greater Than (is greater than or equal to) $\geqq$ or $\geqq$

(1) a $\overline{>}$ b

(2) $a \overset{=}{>} b$

⠿ braille

(3) $|x| \geqslant 0$

(4) $|x| \gneqq 0$

d. Inclusion (is a subset of):

Bar Over Inclusion	$\overline{\subset}$	
Equals Sign Over Inclusion	$\overset{=}{\subset}$	
Bar Under Inclusion	$\underline{\subset}$	
Equals Sign Under Inclusion	$\subseteqq$	

(1) $C \overline{\subset} B'$

(2) $C \overset{=}{\subset} B'$

(3) $(D \cap E) \underline{\subset} (E \times E)$

(4) $(D \cap E) \subseteqq (E \times E)$

e. Intersection (cap): The intersection sign is a sign of comparison when modified by a bar or equals sign above or below it. An unmodified intersection sign is a sign of operation (see §94g).

Bar Under Intersection	$\underline{\cap}$	
Equals Sign Under Intersection	$\underset{=}{\cap}$	

(1) $X \underline{\cap} Y$

(2) $X \underset{=}{\cap} Y$

f. Less Than:

Bar Over Less Than (is equal to or less than) $\overline{<}$ or $\overline{\ll}$

Equals Sign Over Less Than (is equal to or less than) $\overline{\overline{<}}$ or $\overline{\overline{\ll}}$

Bar Under Less Than (is less than or equal to) $\underline{<}$ or $\underline{\ll}$

Equals Sign Under Less Than (is less than or equal to) $\underline{\underline{<}}$ or $\underline{\underline{\ll}}$

(1) $v - 1 \overline{<} 5$

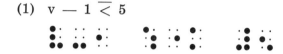

(2) $v - 1 \overline{\overline{<}} 5$

(3) $6 \ll x \ll 9$

(4) $6 \underline{\ll} x \underline{\ll} 9$

g. Logical Product (meet): The logical product sign is a sign of comparison when modified by a bar or equals sign above or below it. An unmodified logical product sign is a sign of operation (see §94h).

Bar Over Logical Product $\overline{\wedge}$

Bar Over and Bar Under Logical Product $\overline{\underline{\wedge}}$

Bar Over and Equals Sign Under Logical Product $\overline{\underline{\underline{\wedge}}}$

Bar Under Logical Product $\underline{\wedge}$

Equals Sign Over Logical Product $\overline{\overline{\wedge}}$

Equals Sign Over and Bar Under Logical Product $\overline{\overline{\underline{\wedge}}}$

Equals Sign Over and Equals Sign Under Logical Product $\overline{\overline{\underline{\underline{\wedge}}}}$

Equals Sign Under Logical Product $\underline{\underline{\wedge}}$

(1) ABCD $\overline{\wedge}$ A'B'C'D'

162

(2) {A} $\underline{\wedge}$ K

⠐⠨⠁⠨⠆⠀⠈⠈⠼⠀⠨⠅

(3) p $\wedge$ q

⠏⠀⠈⠈⠼⠀⠟⠄

h. Logical Sum (join): The logical sum sign is a sign of comparison when modified by a bar or equals sign above or below it. An unmodified logical sum sign is a sign of operation (see §94i).

Bar Over Logical Sum	$\overline{\vee}$	⠐⠈⠬
Bar Over and Bar Under Logical Sum	$\underline{\overline{\vee}}$	⠐⠈⠬⠠
Bar Over and Equals Sign Under Logical Sum	$\underset{=}{\overline{\vee}}$	⠐⠈⠬⠨⠶
Bar Under Logical Sum	$\underline{\vee}$	⠈⠬⠠
Equals Sign Over Logical Sum	$\overline{\overline{\vee}}$	⠨⠶⠬
Equals Sign Over and Bar Under Logical Sum	$\underline{\overline{\overline{\vee}}}$	⠨⠶⠬⠠
Equals Sign Over and Equals Sign Under Logical Sum	$\underset{=}{\overline{\overline{\vee}}}$	⠨⠶⠬⠨⠶
Equals Sign Under Logical Sum	$\underset{=}{\vee}$	⠬⠨⠶

(1) ABC $\overline{\vee}$ A'B'C'

⠠⠁⠠⠃⠠⠉⠐⠈⠬⠠⠁⠄⠠⠃⠄⠠⠉⠄

(2) $F_1 \overline{\overline{\vee}} F_2$

⠠⠋⠆⠀⠨⠶⠬⠀⠠⠋⠼

(3) P(E $\underline{\vee}$ F)

⠠⠏⠷⠠⠑⠀⠈⠬⠠⠀⠠⠋⠾

i. Reverse Inclusion:

Bar Over Reverse Inclusion	$\overline{\supset}$	⠐⠈⠴
Equals Sign Over Reverse Inclusion	$\overline{\overline{\supset}}$	⠨⠶⠴
Bar Under Reverse Inclusion	$\underline{\supset}$	⠈⠴⠠
Equals Sign Under Reverse Inclusion	$\underset{=}{\supset}$	⠴⠨⠶

163

(1) B $\overline{\supset}$ A

⠀⠆ ⠐⠶ ⠀ ⠐⠂⠶⠶ ⠀ ⠐⠁

(2) D $\underline{\underline{\supset}}$ C

⠀⠲ ⠐⠶ ⠀ ⠐⠂⠶⠶⠶⠶ ⠀ ⠐⠉

j. Tilde:

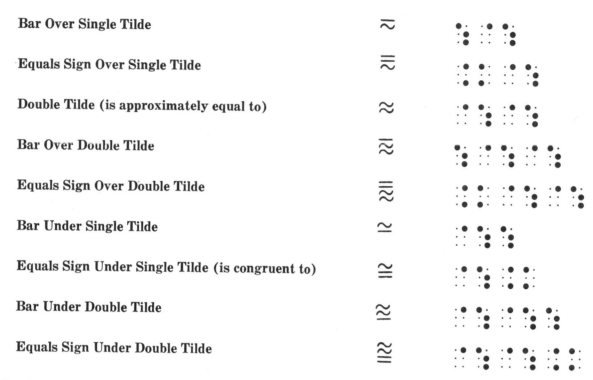

Bar Over Single Tilde	$\bar{\sim}$	
Equals Sign Over Single Tilde	$\approxeq$	
Double Tilde (is approximately equal to)	$\approx$	
Bar Over Double Tilde	$\bar{\approx}$	
Equals Sign Over Double Tilde		
Bar Under Single Tilde	$\simeq$	
Equals Sign Under Single Tilde (is congruent to)	$\cong$	
Bar Under Double Tilde	$\approx$	
Equals Sign Under Double Tilde	$\approxeq$	

(1) 3.14159 $\approx$ 3.1416

(2) ABC $\cong$ DEF

k. Union (cup): The union sign is a sign of comparison when modified by a bar or equals sign above or below it. An unmodified union sign is a sign of operation (see §94l).

Bar Under Union	$\underline{\cup}$	
Equals Sign Under Union	$\underline{\underline{\cup}}$	

(1) A $\underline{\cup}$ B

(2) X $\underline{\underline{\cup}}$ Y

§109. Signs of Comparison Compounded Horizontally: When two or more signs of comparison are arranged side by side, the combination becomes a single comparison sign compounded horizontally. The multipurpose indicator ⠐⠂ must be placed between the unspaced symbols to indicate that they are printed horizontally, not vertically. Unlisted signs of comparison compounded horizontally must be transcribed according to the same principle.

a. **Arrows:**

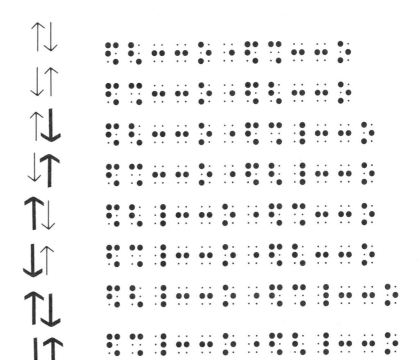

Pointing-Up Followed by Pointing-Down

Pointing-Down Followed by Pointing-Up

Pointing-Up Followed by Boldface Pointing-Down

Pointing-Down Followed by Boldface Pointing-Up

Boldface Pointing-Up Followed by Pointing-Down

Boldface Pointing-Down Followed by Pointing-Up

Boldface Pointing-Up Followed by Boldface Pointing-Down

Boldface Pointing-Down Followed by Boldface Pointing-Up

(1) $+ \mathrm{H_2O} \;\uparrow\downarrow\; - \mathrm{H_2O}$

b. **Greater Than:**

Followed by Less Than $> <$

Followed by Equals Sign Followed by Less Than $> = <$

(1) $n > < 1$

(2) $n > = < 1$

c. **Less Than:**

Followed by Greater Than $< >$

Followed by Equals Sign Followed by Greater Than $< = >$

(1) $n < > 1$

⠀⠀[braille]

(2) $n < = > 1$

⠀⠀[braille]

§110. Negated Signs of Comparison: In print, a sign of comparison may be negated by a vertical line or by a slant line drawn through it. In braille, the symbol ⠢ must be used to represent either of the print negation signs and must be placed immediately before the sign of comparison being negated. Negated signs of comparison not illustrated below must be transcribed according to the same principle.

(1) $4 \times 13 \neq 14$

⠀⠀[braille]

(2) $a_1^2 + b_1^2 \neq 0$

⠀⠀[braille]

(3) $9 \not\in D$

⠀⠀[braille]

(4) $^+4 \ngeq {}^+7$

⠀⠀[braille]

§111. Signs of Comparison and Boldface Type: When it is necessary to show that a sign of comparison is printed in boldface type, dots 4-5-6 are placed before the corresponding symbol in braille. However, the use of dots 4-5-6 to denote boldface type is restricted to the specific signs listed below. They must not be used with any other sign of comparison. Boldface signs of comparison should be used only when the distinction between the regular and boldface forms of the same sign has mathematical significance.

Boldface Arrows (See §103)

Boldface Equals $=$ [braille]

(1)  shows that the reaction begins at the left and is completed to the right.

⠀⠀[braille]

⠀⠀[braille]

(2) $a \times c = b \times d$ if and only if $a = c$ and $b = d$.

⠀⠀[braille]

⠀⠀[braille]

HOMEWORK

Prepare the following homework for submission to your teacher. Proofread carefully.

EXERCISE 9

1. Find functions f and g and a number n such that $f(x) \longrightarrow 0$ and $g(x) \longrightarrow 0$ as $x \longrightarrow n$ and such that
   a. $f(x)/g(x) \longrightarrow 1$ as $x \longrightarrow n$
   b. $f(x)/g(x) \longrightarrow 0$ as $x \longrightarrow n$

2. Construct truth tables for each statement:
   a. $(p \longrightarrow q) \longleftrightarrow (q' \longrightarrow p')$ b. $(p \longrightarrow q) \longleftrightarrow (p \vee q)$

3. From Exercise 7-9 we have $\sqrt{a} > 0$ and $(\sqrt{a})^2 = a$. Prove
   $$x > 0 \text{ and } x^2 = a \Longrightarrow x = \sqrt{a}.$$

4. Complete the formula using $|y - b| < 6 \Longleftrightarrow y - b$.

5. True or false:
   a. $S + O_2 \longrightarrow SO_2 \uparrow$ b. $NaCl \rightleftarrows Na^+ + Cl^-$
   c. $HCl \rightleftarrows H^+ + Cl^-$ d. $KI + I_2 \uparrow\downarrow KI_3$

6. Show that $XY \frown RS$.

7. If two functions are equal for all values of n variables we can write
   $$f(x_1, \ldots, x_n) \equiv g(x_1, \ldots, x_n)$$

   This is an *identity*. Explain.

8. Argue that if $A \subset B$ and $B \subset C$, then $A \subset C$.

9. Argue that if $X \supset Y$ and $Y \supset Z$, then $X \supset Z$.

10. Let $M = \{1, 2, 3, \ldots, 9\}$ and $N = \{2, 4, 6, 8\}$. Identify as true or false:
    (a) $3 \in M$ (b) $3 + 4 \in N$
    (c) $N \ni 8$ (d) $M \ni 9$

11. The vertices of a quadrilateral are $A(-1, 3)$, $B(-2, -1)$, $C(2, -2)$, and $D(3, 2)$. Prove:
    (a) $AD \parallel BC$ (b) $AB \parallel DC$ (c) $AD \perp DC$ (d) $AC \perp BD$

12. Show that if a and b are elements of a set S, one and only one of the relations $a = b$, $a \, R \, b$, $b \, R \, a$ is true.

13. Is a relation $y \, \theta \, x$ a function if its graph has more than one y on any vertical line?

14. Show that $I \sim E_R^2$.

15. Coulomb's first experimental results are represented by
    $$F \propto \frac{1}{r^2}.$$

    Describe the method and apparatus he used.
    What technique did he use to derive
    $$F \propto \frac{q_1 q_2}{r^2} ?$$

16. Determine the solution sets if the universal set is the set of **real** numbers.

 a. $\{m \mid 5(m + 2) = 10\}$ b. $\{v \mid -6(7v + 5) = 12\}$

17. Figure 32 shows all nuclei with $Z \gg 83$ are unstable. Explain.

18. Sketch the graphs of the following relations.

 a. $x \geq -1$ b. $d \geq 2\frac{1}{2}$

 c. $4x^2 + y^2 \leq 16$ d. $-3 \leq y - 2x \leq 3$

19. Prove $\mid w_1 + w_2 \mid \leqq \mid w_1 \mid + \mid w_2 \mid$.

20. Given the following sets

$$E = \{1, 3, 4, 6\}$$
$$F = \{1, 6\}$$
$$G = \{1, 3, 4, 6, 8, 9\}.$$

 Label each statement as either true or false.

 a. $E \subseteq F$ b. $G \subseteq F$ c. $G \supset F$ d. $E \supseteq G$

21. If X and Y are sets and we know that $7 \in X$ and $7 \in Y$, can we conclude $X \subseteqq Y$? $Y \subseteqq X$?

22. Show that two figures F and F' are projective if $F \overline{\overline{\wedge}} F'$.

23. Make a statement about the truth value of p and q when $(p \underline{\vee} q)$ is true and $(p \longrightarrow q)$ is true.

24. Use Eq. (5) to find $(2.98)^3 \approx 26.46$.

25. Use the triangles in Figure 4.3 to prove ACE $\cong$ DBE.

26. What is the effect of the assumption $x < = > b$ in the previous experiment?

LESSON 10

SIGNS OF SHAPE

§112. **Definition**: A sign of shape is a miniature picture of a geometric figure or another object.

$\triangle$ (triangle) $\angle$ (angle) $\bigcirc$ (circle)

§113. **Shape Indicator** ⠫ **and Basic Signs of Shape:**

A basic sign of shape is represented by the shape indicator followed by one or more letters, by a numeral, or by a dot combination suggestive of the ink-print shape.

When the shape is a *regular polygon* (a closed figure with equal sides and equal angles), it is represented by the shape indicator followed by a numeral specifying the number of sides in the figure.

When the shape is an *irregular polygon* (a closed figure with at least two unequal sides and two unequal angles), it is represented by the shape indicator followed by a letter or a combination of letters suggestive of the ink-print shape.

Shape	Figure	Braille
Angle	$\angle$	⠫ ⠪
Arc		
Concave Upward	⌢	⠫ ⠉
Concave Downward	⌣	⠫ ⠒
Arrow		
Right-Pointing		
Contracted Form	→	⠳ ⠕
Uncontracted Form	→	⠫ ⠒ ⠒ ⠕
Left-Pointing	←	⠫ ⠪ ⠒ ⠒
Down-Pointing	↓	⠫ ⠣ ⠒ ⠒ ⠔
Up-Pointing	↑	⠫ ⠜ ⠒ ⠒ ⠩
Circle	$\bigcirc$	⠫ ⠉
Diamond	◇	⠫ ⠫
Ellipse	⬭	⠫ ⠑

Hexagon

    Regular

    Irregular

Intersecting Lines

Is Parallel To

Is Not Parallel To

Is Perpendicular To

Is Not Perpendicular To

Parallelogram

Pentagon

    Regular

    Irregular

Quadrilateral

Rectangle

Rhombus

Square

Star

Trapezoid

Triangle

    Regular (equilateral)

    Inverted

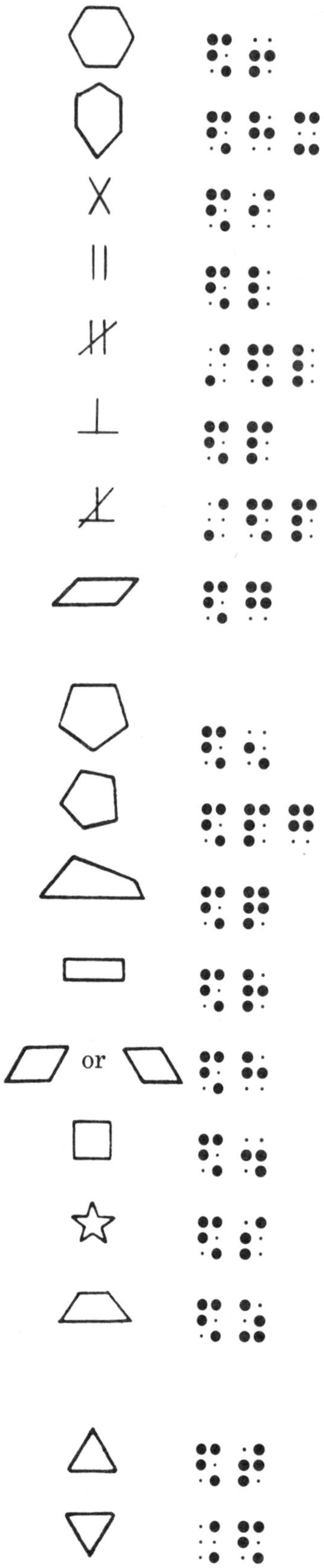

§114. Signs of Shape With Structural Modification: A shape with structural modification is one in which two or more signs of shape are combined to form a composite sign, such as *adjacent angles;* or one in which the general print form of a basic shape is changed to show a more specific form, such as a *right angle*, a *right triangle*, etc.

A shape with structural modification is represented by the basic shape symbol followed by the structural shape-modification indicator ⠂⠄ , by a letter or an uncontracted combination of letters suggestive of the change in the shape, and by the termination indicator ⠰⠆ showing the end of the modification.

Angle

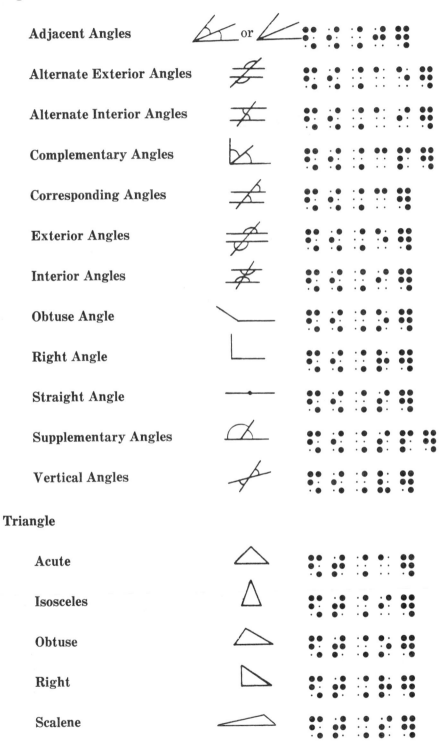

Adjacent Angles

Alternate Exterior Angles

Alternate Interior Angles

Complementary Angles

Corresponding Angles

Exterior Angles

Interior Angles

Obtuse Angle

Right Angle

Straight Angle

Supplementary Angles

Vertical Angles

Triangle

Acute

Isosceles

Obtuse

Right

Scalene

§115. **Signs of Shape With Interior Modification:** A shape with interior modification is a basic shape within which a letter, a numeral, a sign of operation, or other sign appears.

a. A shape with interior modification is represented by the basic shape symbol followed by the interior shape-modification indicator ⠒⠒ ⠿, by the symbol corresponding to the interior sign, and by the termination indicator ⠿ to show the end of the modification.

The numeric indicator must be used before a numeral or before a decimal point and a numeral following the interior shape-modification indicator.

If a right-pointing arrow in regular type with a full barb and single shaft of ordinary length is part of a shape symbol, its contracted form must not be used.

Angle

Angle With Interior Arc

Angle With Interior Clockwise Arrow

Angle With Interior Counterclockwise Arrow

Circle

Circle With Interior Arrow Pointing Right

Circle With Interior Arrow Pointing Left

Circle With Interior Arrow Pointing Up

Circle With Interior Arrow Pointing Down

Circle With Interior Capitalized Letter

Circle With Interior Numeral

Circle With Interior Cross

Circle With Interior Dot

Circle With Interior Minus Sign

Circle With Interior Plus Sign

Circle With Interior Vertical Bar

Rectangle With Interior Horizontal Bar

Square

Square With Interior Diagonal from Upper-Left to Lower-Right

Square With Interior Diagonal from Lower-Left to Upper-Right

Square With Interior Diagonals	⊠	⠨⠫⠰⠙⠒⠱⠻⠼⠒⠿
Square With Interior Dot	☐·	⠨⠫⠰⠄⠻⠿
Square With Interior Horizontal Bar	⊟	⠨⠫⠒⠒⠻⠿
Square With Interior Vertical Bar	⊞|	⠨⠫⠸⠳⠻⠿
Square With Interior Numeral	5	⠨⠫⠰⠼⠢⠻⠿

b. When two or more vertically arranged modifiers occur within a basic sign of shape, the basic shape symbol and the interior shape-modification indicator must be followed by the symbols for the upper and then the next lower interior signs. The termination indicator must be used only after the last modifier symbol.

Circle With Interior Arrow Pointing Right **Over Interior Arrow Pointing Left**	⊖→	⠨⠫⠻ ...
Circle With Interior Arrow Pointing Left **Over Interior Arrow Pointing Right**	⊖←	⠨⠫⠻ ...

c. When two or more horizontally arranged modifiers occur within a basic sign of shape, the basic shape symbol and the interior shape-modification indicator must be followed by the symbols for the interior signs. The multipurpose indicator ⠐⠆ must be

placed between the interior modifiers to show that they are printed horizontally, not vertically. The termination indicator must be used only after the last modifier symbol.

Circle With Interior Arrow Pointing Up **Followed by Interior Arrow Pointing Down**	⊖↑↓	⠨⠫⠻ ...
Circle With Interior Arrow Pointing Down **Followed by Interior Arrow Pointing Up**	⊖↓↑	⠨⠫⠻ ...

§116. Unlisted Signs of Shape:

a. Basic signs of shape and shapes with structural modification not provided for in this code must be formed in accordance with the principles for the construction of such shapes. Contractions must not be used in any letter combination selected to represent a basic shape or its structural modification. A symbol which has been assigned a meaning must not be used. Any unlisted shape, except a regular polygon, must be explained by a transcriber's note giving the name or description of the symbol used. If possible, a drawing of the shape must be included.

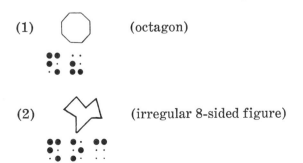

(1) ⬡ (octagon)

(2) ⬙ (irregular 8-sided figure)

(3) 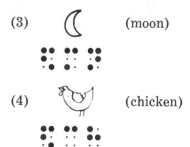 (moon)

⠀⠿⠀⠿⠀⠿

(4) 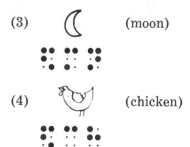 (chicken)

⠀⠿⠀⠿⠀⠿

b. Unlisted shapes with interior modification must be formed in accordance with the principles for the representation of such shapes. Transcriber's notes are required only for symbols that must be devised and are not listed in the code.

(1) 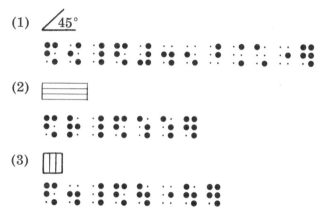 ∠45°

⠀⠿⠀⠿⠀⠿⠀⠿⠀⠿⠀⠿⠀⠿⠀⠿

(2)

⠀⠿⠀⠿⠀⠿⠀⠿⠀⠿⠀⠿

(3)

⠀⠿⠀⠿⠀⠿⠀⠿⠀⠿⠀⠿⠀⠿

§117. Shapes Represented by Drawing: Drawn-in shapes are often more readable than elaborate braille constructions. Since it is not possible to formulate specific rules for the selection of an appropriate form, the decision is left to the experience and judgment of the transcriber.

Shapes may also be represented by a combination of drawing and braille symbols. For example, if a modified shape cannot be represented clearly by braille symbols alone, the shape can be drawn, and the modification shown in braille.

(1)

§118. Filled-In and Shaded Shapes: A filled-in or shaded closed shape (circle, diamond, square, etc.) must be represented as such by the *filled-in shape indicator* ⠨⠿ or the *shaded shape indicator* ⠰⠿ . The appropriate indicator must be placed between the shape indicator and the shape symbol.

(1)

⠀⠿⠀⠿⠀⠿

(2)

⠀⠿⠀⠿⠀⠿

§119. Punctuation and Plurals With Signs of Shape:

    a. Signs of shape must be punctuated mathematically.

        (1) $\angle$, $\triangle$, $\bigcirc$.

        (2) ($\Diamond$, $\triangledown$, $\square$)

        (3) ⦟ , ⊕.

    b. The uncapitalized letter "s" or the apostrophe-s combination occurring inside or after a sign of shape to show its plural or possessive must be placed after the shape symbol.

        (1) ⦤ and ⟁ .

            (Each s is inside the shape.)

        (2) $\angle$s and $\triangle$s.

            (Each s follows the shape.)

        (3) $\angle$'s and $\triangle$'s.

        (4) ($\angle$'s, $\triangle$'s, and $\bigcirc$'s.)

§120. Spacing With Signs of Shape: A sign of shape must be spaced in accordance with its assigned meaning:

    a. A sign of shape representing a sign of operation must be spaced accordingly.

    The multipurpose indicator ⠐ must be used between a sign of operation represented by a regular polygon and a numeral following it.

        (1) x ⊕ y

        (2) 2 ⊕ 3 = 3 ⊕ 2

175

(3) a ⊕ (b ⊕ c)

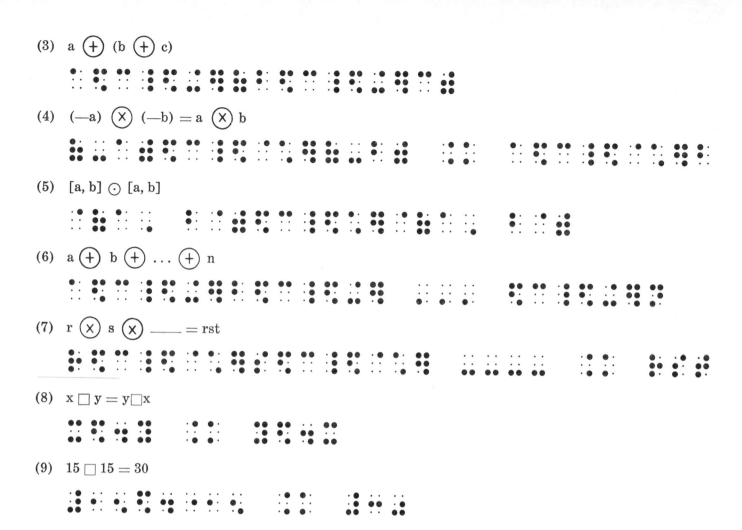

(4) (—a) ⊗ (—b) = a ⊗ b

(5) [a, b] ⊙ [a, b]

(6) a ⊕ b ⊕ ... ⊕ n

(7) r ⊗ s ⊗ ____ = rst

(8) x □ y = y □ x

(9) 15 □ 15 = 30

b. A sign of shape representing a sign of comparison must be spaced accordingly.

(1) x ⌢ y

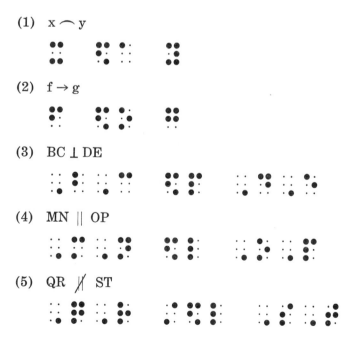

(2) f → g

(3) BC ⊥ DE

(4) MN ∥ OP

(5) QR ∦ ST

c. When a sign of shape is used as a sign of omission or placeholder to represent a numeral, letter, sign of operation, sign of comparison, abbreviation, or any other item, the sign of shape must be spaced as the material which it represents. In any case, a sign of shape must be unspaced from any braille indicator applying to it.

(1) $7 \times \triangle = 4 \times \triangle$ (numeral omitted)

(2) $436 - \Diamond = 102$ (numeral omitted)

(3) $\triangle \times (\square - 46) = 46$ (numerals omitted)

(4) $N = (2 \times \Diamond) + 1$ (numeral omitted)

(5) $\triangle + \square = \square + \triangle$ (numerals omitted)

(6) $(\square + \triangle) + \Diamond = \square + (\triangle + \Diamond)$ (numerals omitted)

(7) $\{\triangle, \square, \bigcirc\} \cup \{\square\}$ (numerals omitted)

(8) $40 \text{ dimes} = \$\triangle$ (numeral omitted)

(9) $\$5.00 = \square\cent$ (numeral omitted)

(10) $\triangledown \% = \triangledown \times .01$ (numeral omitted)

(11) $\dfrac{15}{20} = \dfrac{\square}{\bigcirc}$ (numerals omitted)

(12) $8\dfrac{2}{6} = 8\dfrac{\triangle}{3}$ (numeral omitted)

(13) $\square_8 + \square_8 = 22_8$ (numeral omitted)

(14) $x^2 \times x^4 = x^{\square}$ (numeral omitted)

(15) $24_{\lozenge} + 11_{\lozenge} = 40_5$ (numeral omitted)

(16) $\square$ l. $= 1000$ cc. (numeral omitted)

(17) 11 yds. 16 ft. $= \square$ yds. $\lozenge$ ft. (numerals omitted)

(18) $3 \; \lozenge \; 7 = 10$ (sign of operation omitted)

(19) $50 \; \blacksquare \; 50 = 100$ (sign of operation omitted)

(20) $\dfrac{1}{4} \; \bigcirc \; \dfrac{1}{4} = \dfrac{1}{2}$ (sign of operation omitted)

(21) $50 + 50 \; \bigcirc \; 100$ (sign of comparison omitted)

(22) 99 ▨ 100 represents $99 < 100$ (sign of comparison omitted)

(23) 24 hrs. $= 1 \; \triangle$ (abbreviation omitted)

§121. Identified Signs of Shape:

a. A space must be left between a sign of shape and its identifying numeral, letter, or sequence of letters following it.

(1) $\angle \alpha$

(2) $\angle 1$

(3) △ABC is a right triangle.

(4) ▱ EFGH is a parallelogram.

(5) Angle (∠) BAC is a right angle.

(6) △'s PQR and STU are similar.

b. The spacing before and after a sign of shape and its identification is subject to the spacing rules for the symbols preceding or following it.

(1) $\angle 1 < \angle 2$

(2) $\triangle$ PQR $\sim$ $\triangle$ P'Q'R'

(3) $\triangle$ ADM $\cong$ $\triangle$ BEM

(4) $\triangle$ II $\sim$ $\triangle$ II'

(5) $\angle 2 + \angle 3 = \angle 4$

(6) $\angle$ x $+ \angle$ y

(7) $\angle$ ABD $+ \angle$ DBE $= ?$

(8) $\angle 45° + \angle 45° = ?$

(9) $(\angle 1 + \angle 2) + (\angle 3)$

179

(10) $\dfrac{\triangle \text{ABC}}{\triangle \text{DEF}}$

⠠⠫⠞⠠⠁⠠⠃⠠⠉

(11) $\triangle \text{EFG}/\triangle \text{RST}$

(12) $\angle \text{ECB} = \dfrac{1}{2} \angle \text{ABC}$

(13) $m \angle 2 + m \angle 3 = m \angle 4$

(14) $m \angle \text{ABC} + m \angle \text{CDE}$

(15) $m° \angle \alpha = -42°$

c. The effect of the level indicator before an identified sign of shape in a superscript or subscript extends through the space following the sign of shape. In such cases, the space preserves the superscript or subscript level where the sign of shape appears. Thus, the identifying symbol following the space assumes the same level as its related sign of shape.

(1) $\text{A}_{\triangle \text{ABC}}$

(2) $\text{A}_{\triangle \text{DEF}} = \dfrac{1}{2} bh$

(3) $\text{A}_{\square \text{ACIJ}} + \text{A}_{\square \text{BGNC}}$

(4) $(\text{I}_{\angle \text{PMQ}}) \cup (\angle \text{PMQ})$

d. When an identified sign of shape carries a superscript or subscript, the space required after the sign of shape must follow the superscript or subscript. If the sign of shape is on the baseline of writing, the space following the superscript or subscript terminates the effect of the level indicator and reinstates the baseline level where the sign of shape appears.

(1) $\triangle^2 \text{DEF}$

§122. **Signs of Shape and the English Letter Indicator:**

a. The English letter indicator must not be used with an English letter, a short-form combination, or a Roman numeral in regular type after a space following a sign of shape. However, if the sign of shape has a plural or possessive ending, the general rules for the English letter indicator apply.

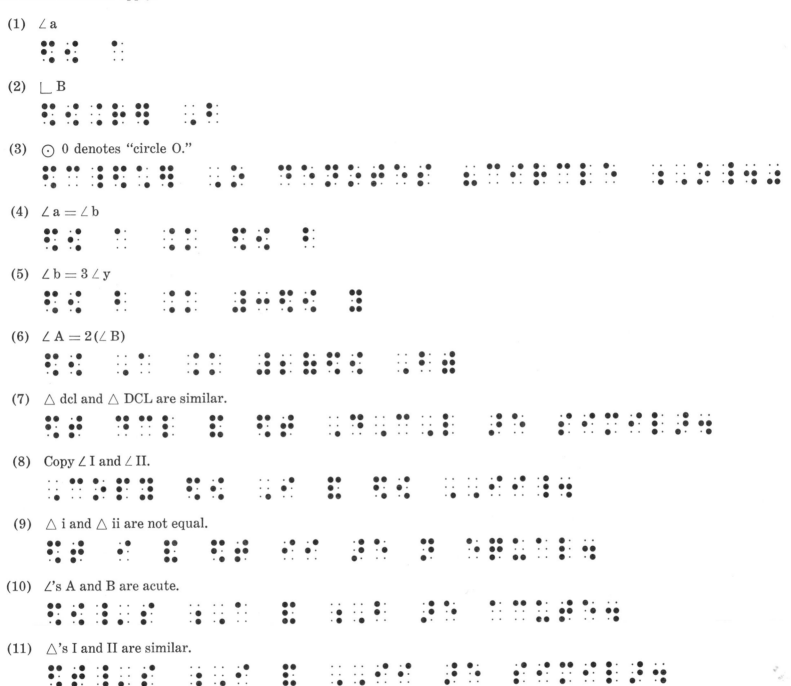

(1) ∠ a

(2) ⌊ B

(3) ⊙ 0 denotes "circle O."

(4) ∠ a = ∠ b

(5) ∠ b = 3 ∠ y

(6) ∠ A = 2(∠ B)

(7) △ dcl and △ DCL are similar.

(8) Copy ∠ I and ∠ II.

(9) △ i and △ ii are not equal.

(10) ∠'s A and B are acute.

(11) △'s I and II are similar.

b. The English letter indicator must not be used with an English letter, a short-form combination, or a Roman numeral in regular type followed by a space which in turn precedes a sign of shape used as a sign of omission. If the sign of shape is not a sign of omission, the general rules for the English letter indicator apply.

(1) x □ y

(the symbol for the "square" is used as a sign of omission)

(2) Find the sum of the n ∠'s.

⠀⠀⠀⠀⠀⠀[braille]

(the symbol for the "angle" is not an omission sign)

§123. **Signs of Shape With Enclosed Lists:** In an enclosed list, an identified sign of shape and the following numeral, letter, or sequence of letters must be considered as a single item, even though a space occurs between them.

The numeric indicator must not be used before a numeral or before a decimal point and a numeral in regular type at the beginning of an item in an enclosed list; however, it must be used when these symbols follow an identified sign of shape.

(1) (∠ 1, 2 ∠ 1, 3 ∠ 1)

⠀⠀⠀⠀⠀⠀[braille]

(2) (∠ 1, ∠ 2, ∠ 3)

⠀⠀⠀⠀⠀⠀[braille]

(3) (1 ∠ a, 2 ∠ b)

⠀⠀⠀⠀⠀⠀[braille]

HOMEWORK

Prepare the following homework for submission to your teacher. Proofread carefully.

EXERCISE 10

1. ∠, ○, ◇, and ▭ are all figures we will study.

2. How do we find the area of a ○?

3. Copy each shape and explain its meaning.

   a.

   b.

   c.

   d.

   e.

   f.

   g.

4. Add ∠30° and ∠20° .

5. Substitute ■ s for the ◯ s:

$$(\bigcirc, \rectangle, \square, \triangle, \bigcirc).$$

6. (◇'s, ▽'s, and △'s.)

7. (s) and /s/ are geometric shapes.

8. If ABCD is a parallelogram and CDFE is a parallelogram, prove:
   (a) ABEF is a ▱.
   (b) FA = EB and FA ∥ EB.

9. If $\square + \triangle = N$, does this mean that $\square = N - \triangle$? Does it also mean that $\triangle = N - \square$?

10. Write $+$ or $-$ in each shape.
    a. $5 \triangle 2 = 7$
    b. $9 \triangle 1 = 8$
    c. $10 \triangle 3 = 7$
    d. $3 \square 2 = 5$
    e. $(a - b) \square a = -b$

11. Write $>$, $<$, or $=$ in each shape.
    a. $3 + 5 \bigcirc 7$
    b. $8 - 1 \bigcirc 10$
    c. $4 + 5 \bigcirc 6 + 2$
    d. $8 - 6 \square 5 + 1$
    e. $4 - 1 \square 2 + 2$

12. $(3 \otimes 2) + 1 = 7$

13. If $250\cent = \$2.50$, then $736\cent = \$\bigcirc$. Similarly, we see that if $\$6.00 = 600\cent$, then $\$9.32 = \square\cent$.

14. 148 people went to a snack bar. 111 were grown-ups. $\triangle\%$ were children.

15. a. $\dfrac{192}{80} = \dfrac{\triangle}{40} = \dfrac{\bigcirc}{\square}$

    b. $23\dfrac{15}{25} = 23\dfrac{\rectangle}{5}$

16. Using the "common factor" method, we see that $x^{n+3} - 5x^n = x^{\bigcirc}(x^{\triangle} - 5)$.

17. 1 qt. = ▭ pt. and 4 qt. = ◯ pt. How are quarts related to pints?

18. Solve the problems.
    a. 2 ft 3 in = $27 \square$
    b. 2 yd = $6 \bigcirc$
    c. $\dfrac{1}{4}$ ft. = $\square$ in.

19. $\triangle ABD \cong \triangle ACE$

20. In $\triangle ABCD$, BC = AD. If diagonals AC and BD intersect at E, prove that $\triangle DEA \sim \triangle CEB$.

21. If ABCD is an isosceles trapezoid, DC ∥ AB, DE ⊥ AB, and CF ⊥ AB, prove that △ DEA ≅ △ CFB.

22. Is ∠ B acute or obtuse?

23. In △ ABC, ∠ A = 3 ∠ C, and ∠ B = 36°.   Find the number of degrees in ∠ C.

24. ∠ a + ∠ b + ∠ c = 180°

25. If △ ABC = $\frac{1}{2}$ ▱ ABEC and the area of ▱ ABEC = bh, then the area of △ ABC = $\frac{1}{2}$ bh.

26. Find the sums.
   a. ∠ 30° + ∠ 25° = ?
   b. In △ ABC, m ∠ A + m ∠ B + m ∠ C = ?

27. What does □² ABCD mean?

28. Prove A$_{▱ ABCD}$ = A$_{△ ADE}$.

29. Draw a figure illustrating the following statement:
   A$_{△ 1}$ + A$_{△ 2}$ = A$_{△ 3}$.

30. Show that ∠ acr and ∠ afn are equal.

31. ∠ C = ∠ D and ∠'s C and D are both obtuse.

32. ○ i and ○ ii have diameters of the same size.

   ○'s i and ii therefore also have equal radii.

33. If y > 0, then x □ x + y.   (Use >, <, or =.)

34. (∠ 5, ∠ 6, ∠ 7).

35. (5 ∠ 3, 2 ∠ 2, 6 ∠ 1).

MODIFIERS AND MODIFIED EXPRESSIONS

§124. **Definition**: A modifier is a symbol or a combination of symbols occurring directly over or under its related symbol or expression.

$$\overline{34} \qquad \tilde{x} \qquad \underline{x + y}$$

The most commonly used modifiers are listed below. Other symbols of the code may also be used as modifiers.

Modification Indicators

    Multipurpose Indicator

    Directly-Over Indicator

    Directly-Under Indicator

    Termination Indicator

Modifiers

    Arc

        Concave Upward   ⌢

        Concave Downward   ⌣

    Arrow

        Barbed at Right

            Contracted Form   →

            Uncontracted Form   →

        Barbed at Left   ←

        Barbed at Both Ends   ⟷

        Barbed at Right and Dotted at Left   •→

        Barbed at Left and Dotted at Right   ←•

        Dotted at Right (no barb)   —•

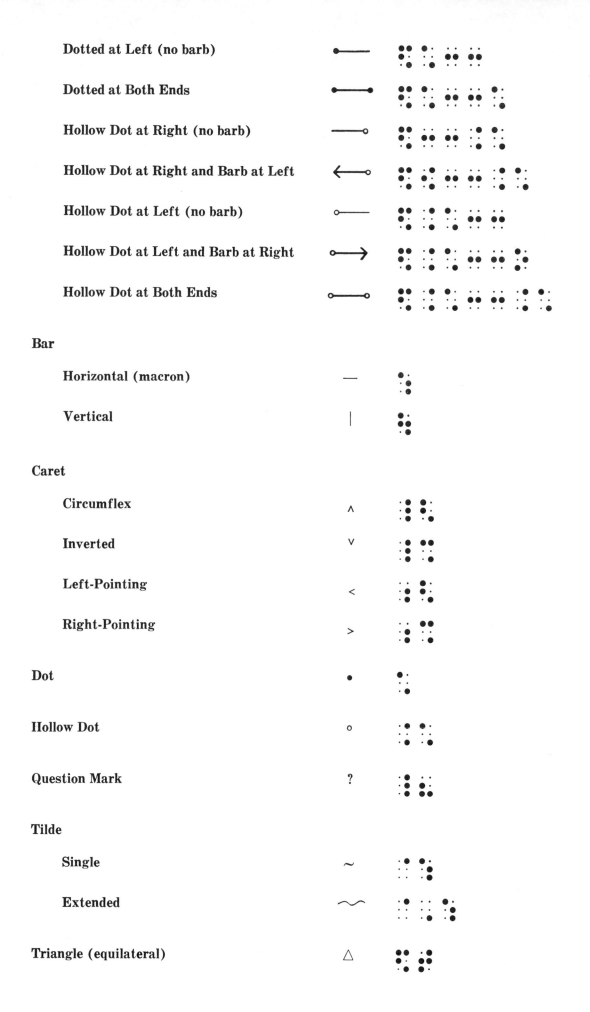

Dotted at Left (no barb)

Dotted at Both Ends

Hollow Dot at Right (no barb)

Hollow Dot at Right and Barb at Left

Hollow Dot at Left (no barb)

Hollow Dot at Left and Barb at Right

Hollow Dot at Both Ends

Bar

Horizontal (macron)

Vertical

Caret

Circumflex

Inverted

Left-Pointing

Right-Pointing

Dot

Hollow Dot

Question Mark

Tilde

Single

Extended

Triangle (equilateral)

§125. Construction of Simple Modified Expressions:

a. The Five-Step Rule: The following five-step rule must be used for the transcription of a modified expression. (See exception in **c** below.)

i. The multipurpose indicator ⠐ must be placed immediately before the expression to be modified.

ii. The expression to be modified must be written second.

iii. The directly-over indicator ⠣ or the directly-under indicator ⠩ must be written third to show the position of the modifier.

iv. The modifying symbol must be written fourth.

v. The termination indicator ⠻ must be written last to show the end of the modification.

b. The spacing before and after a modified expression is subject to the spacing rules for the symbols preceding or following it. Two or more symbols in a modifier must be spaced in accordance with their appropriate spacing rule.

(1) $\overline{34}$

(2) $1.142857\overline{142857}$

(3) $1.3\overline{7}$

(4) $\dfrac{3}{7} = .\overline{428571}$

(5) $\overline{PQ}$

(6) $\overline{OP} + \overline{QR} = \overline{OR}$

(7) $\overline{AB}^2 + \overline{BC}^2$

(8) $\overline{x'}$

(9) $\overline{R''S''}$

(10) $m\overline{BC} = a$

(11) $\dfrac{\overline{PR}}{\overline{OR}}$

(12) $\overline{x+y}$

(13) $\tilde{u} = 0.8$

(14) $f \longrightarrow \tilde{f}$

(15) $\tilde{A} \cup \tilde{B}$

(16) $\overbrace{x + y}$

(17) $\overbrace{(A \cap B \cap C)}$

(18) $\overbrace{r+s+t}$

(19) $\angle ABD = \dfrac{1}{2}\,\widehat{DC}$

(20) $\underline{x}$

(21) $\underline{3}$

(22) $\underline{x+y}$

(23) $A(\underline{sn})$

(24) $\underline{579}$

(25) $\underline{R}^+$

(26) $\underset{v}{x}$

(27) $\underset{\smile}{AB}$

(28) $\underset{i<j}{\Sigma}\ a_{ij}$

(29) $\underset{i>j}{\Pi}\ (x_i - x_j)$

(30) $\underset{\alpha\,\epsilon\,\Lambda}{\times}\ \underset{\alpha}{A}$

(31) $\underset{A\subset F}{\cup}$

(32) $(\widetilde{x},\ \widetilde{y})$

(33) $\widetilde{x}$ and $\widetilde{y}$.

c. Contracted Form of Modified Expressions: When a *single* digit or a *single* letter (in any type form or any alphabet) is modified only by a single horizontal bar directly over it, the symbol for the bar must be placed immediately after the digit or letter modified, and the five-step rule must not be used. In all other cases, the five-step rule in **a** above must be applied.

(1) $\overline{7}$

(2) $5\overline{67}$

(3) $\dfrac{7}{15} = .4\overline{6}$

(4) $2 \cdot 3 = \overline{2} \cdot 3 = \overline{2 \cdot 3}$

(5) $\overline{C} = 100 \times 1000$

(6) $\overline{s}$

(7) $\overline{\alpha}$

(8) $F = 2\pi \overline{r}l$

(9) $P(\overline{x}) = \overline{P(x)}$

(10) $g(\overline{x}\overline{y}) = g(\overline{xy})$

(11) $P(\overline{a+bi}) = \overline{0} = 0$

(12) $\overline{x}'$

(13) $\overline{x}^2$

(14) $a_0\overline{x}^n + a_1\overline{x}^{n-1}$

(15) $\overline{A} = [\overline{a}_i]$

(16) $(\overline{x}, \overline{y})$

(17) The $\overline{7}$'s are repeated.

⠀⠀⠀ (braille)

(18) $\overline{x}$'s and $\overline{y}$'s

⠀⠀⠀ (braille)

d. Binomial Coefficient: The binomial coefficient does not follow the five-step rule for modified expressions. The directly-under indicator ⠒ separates the two expressions composing the binomial coefficient. That is, the opening parenthesis is followed by the upper expression. The directly-under indicator is placed next and is followed by the lower expression and the closing parenthesis.

(1) $\binom{n}{q}$

⠀⠀⠀ (braille)

(2) $\binom{a_x}{b_y}$

⠀⠀⠀ (braille)

§126. **Expressions With More Than One Modifier:**

a. When two or more modifiers occur one above the other and apply to exactly the same expression, the second, third, etc. modifiers are "modifiers of higher order." In such cases, the directly-over indicator ⠡ or the directly-under indicator ⠠⠤ must be doubled, tripled, etc. before each modifier to indicate its position. The termination indicator ⠻ must be used only after the last modifier shown.

(1) $\overset{\overline{a=3}}{x+y}$

⠀⠀⠀ (braille)

(2) $\underset{\underset{b=2}{a=3}}{x+y}$

⠀⠀⠀ (braille)

Exception: When two or more parallel horizontal bars are the same length and apply to exactly the same expression, they must be treated as a single modifier. In such cases, the directly-over or the directly-under indicator must be used only once, and the symbol for the bar should be used as many times as necessary to correspond to the print text.

Note: Two parallel horizontal bars must not be interpreted as the equals sign, and three parallel horizontal bars must not be interpreted as the identity sign unless they occur above or below a sign of comparison. In such cases, the combination must be treated as a sign of comparison compounded vertically (see §108).

(3) $\overset{=}{x}$

⠀⠀⠀ (braille)

(4) $(\overline{\overline{A}})$

⠀⠀⠀ (braille)

191

(5) $\overline{\overline{7}} \cdot \overline{\overline{2}} = \overline{\overline{7 \cdot 2}}$

⠀(braille)

(6) $\underline{\underline{x}}$

⠀(braille)

(7) $\overline{\overline{>}}$ is a sign of comparison compounded vertically.

⠀(braille)

⠀(braille)

b. When two or more modifiers do not apply to exactly the same symbols but cover different portions of the same expression, the longer modification must enclose the entire modified expression, and each inner expression must be modified individually. The five-step rule and the contracted form of transcription may be used together.

(1) $(\overline{\overline{aA} + \overline{bB}})$

⠀(braille)

(2) $\overline{7} + 2 = \overline{7 + \overline{2}}$

⠀(braille)

(3) $\overline{A \cap \overline{B \cap \overline{\overline{C}}}}$

⠀(braille)

(4) $\overline{\overline{\overline{x}} \times \overline{\overline{x}}}$

⠀(braille)

§127. Simultaneous Modifiers: When an expression is simultaneously modified both above and below, the modifier below must be shown first and the modifier above, second. However, the termination indicator must be used only at the end of the entire modification.

(1) $\overline{x} \atop {>}$

⠀(braille)

(2) $\overline{x + y}$

⠀(braille)

(3) $\overline{\overline{N}} \atop {\underline{\underline{}}}$

⠀(braille)

(4) $\displaystyle\sum_{k=1}^{n} (2k) = n(n+1)$

(5) $\displaystyle\prod_{k=2}^{6} a_k$

(6) $\displaystyle\sum_{i,\,j=1}^{n} a_{ij}x_i x_j$

(7) $\displaystyle\sum_{i=1}^{k}\ \sum_{j=1}^{k}$

(8) $\displaystyle\sum_{x_1=0}^{1}\ \sum_{x_2=0}^{1}$

(9) $\displaystyle\bigcup_{r=1}^{n} A_r = A_1 \cup A_2 \ldots$

(10) $\displaystyle\overline{\overline{\prod_{x\epsilon a} c'x}}$

(11) $\displaystyle\prod_{\substack{j=1\\ j\neq k}}^{n}$

(12) $\displaystyle\overline{x+y}\ \substack{b=2 \\ a=3}$

§128. Modified Expressions and Superscripts and Subscripts:

a. A modifier and its related expression must always be placed on the same level of writing. When a modifier affects both an expression on the baseline of writing and its superscript or subscript, the baseline indicator must be used after the superscript or subscript and before the directly-over or the directly-under indicator to indicate the level where the expression as a whole appears. However, it is not necessary to indicate a return to the baseline after a numeric subscript not requiring a subscript indicator.

Note: The contracted form of transcription must not be used when a horizontal bar extends above a superscript or subscript.

(1) $\overline{x^2}$

(2) $\overline{\overline{A^n}}$

⠀ ⠀ ⠀ ⠀ ⠀ ⠀ ⠀ ⠀

(3) $(\overline{3^{-1}}) \; \varepsilon \; P$

⠀ ⠀ ⠀ ⠀ ⠀ ⠀ ⠀ ⠀ ⠀ ⠀ ⠀ ⠀

(4) $\overline{OD^2} + \overline{OP^2}$

⠀ ⠀ ⠀ ⠀ ⠀ ⠀ ⠀ ⠀ ⠀ ⠀ ⠀ ⠀ ⠀ ⠀ ⠀ ⠀ ⠀

(5) $\overline{x_n}$

⠀ ⠀ ⠀ ⠀ ⠀ ⠀ ⠀ ⠀

(6) $\overline{P_n P_{n+1}}$

⠀ ⠀ ⠀ ⠀ ⠀ ⠀ ⠀ ⠀ ⠀ ⠀ ⠀ ⠀ ⠀

(7) $\sum\limits_{i=1}^{6} \overline{P_{i-1} P_i}$

⠀ ⠀

(8) $\overline{x_1}$

⠀ ⠀ ⠀ ⠀ ⠀ ⠀

(9) $\overline{x_1} + \overline{y_1}$

⠀ ⠀ ⠀ ⠀ ⠀ ⠀ ⠀ ⠀ ⠀ ⠀ ⠀ ⠀

(10) $\overline{P_1 P_2}$

⠀ ⠀ ⠀ ⠀ ⠀ ⠀ ⠀ ⠀ ⠀

(11) $\overline{P_1 Q}^2 + \overline{Q P_2}^2$

⠀ ⠀

(12) $R_1 - R_2 = (\overset{\frown}{R_1 - R_2})$

⠀ ⠀ ⠀ ⠀ ⠀ ⠀ ⠀ ⠀ ⠀ ⠀ ⠀ ⠀ ⠀ ⠀ ⠀ ⠀ ⠀ ⠀

(13) $\underline{Z}^{\circ}$

⠀ ⠀ ⠀ ⠀ ⠀ ⠀ ⠀ ⠀ ⠀ ⠀ ⠀

(14) $\underline{N}_k$

⠀ ⠀ ⠀ ⠀ ⠀ ⠀ ⠀ ⠀

b. When a letter modified either by the five-step rule or by the contracted form of transcription is followed by a numeric subscript, the subscript indicator is required.

(1) $\overline{N}_1$

(2) $\overline{\alpha}_2$

c. When an expression carrying a superscript or subscript is immediately followed, without a space, by a modified expression written on the baseline of writing, the baseline indicator must be used to terminate the effect of the level indicator, except when the expression follows a numeric subscript not requiring the subscript indicator. If the modified expression on the baseline requires application of the five-step rule, both the baseline indicator and the multipurpose indicator must be used.

(1) $x^2\overline{y}$

(2) $\overline{x}_n\overline{y}_p$

(3) $x_1\,\overline{y}_1$

(4) $x_1\overline{y_1}$

(5) $3x^2\,\overline{\Delta x} + 3x\,\overline{\Delta x}^{\,2}$

(6) $a_k\overline{b_1\ldots b_p}$

(7) $a_i\;\;\underset{j\neq i}{\Pi}\;\;(A-r_jI)$

d. When a modified expression occurs in a superscript or subscript, the appropriate level indicator must be placed before the multipurpose indicator. If the modified expression occurs in the middle or at the end of the superscript or subscript, the appropriate level indicator must be repeated before the multipurpose indicator to show continuation of the same level of writing. It is not necessary to repeat the level indicator when the contracted form of transcription is used and the multipurpose indicator is absent.

(1) $S^{\widetilde{x}}$

(2) $S^{\widetilde{x}+\widetilde{y}}$

(3) $S_{\widetilde{x}}$

(4) $S_{\widetilde{x}+\widetilde{y}}$

(5) $\underset{\widetilde{x}}{A}_1$

(6) $\overline{P_{(x^2)}}$

(7) $A^{\overline{x}}$

(8) $e^{a\overline{x}}$

(9) $A_{\overline{x}}$

(10) $A_{\overline{x}+\overline{y}}$

(11) $3_{\overline{x}} - 2_{\overline{x}}$

(12) $\underset{\overline{n}}{\,}A_1$

(13) $\overline{a_{\overline{n}}+b_{\overline{b}}}$

(14) $\overline{x_{\overline{a}}+y^{\overline{n}}}$

§129. **Arrows as Modifiers:**

a. An arrow must be treated as a modifier when it occurs directly over or directly under a symbol other than a sign of comparison. An arrow which occurs above or below a sign of comparison must be treated as part of a sign of comparison compounded vertically (see §108).

When a right-pointing arrow in regular type with a full barb and single shaft of ordinary length is used as a modifier above or below a mathematical expression, the arrow must be transcribed in its contracted form. However, if such a right-pointing arrow is itself modified, or is part of a compound modifier, its contracted form must not be used. All other arrows require all their appropriate symbols.

(1) $\overrightarrow{AB}$

(2) $\underset{\rightarrow}{T}$

(3) $\overrightarrow{AB}\text{—}\overrightarrow{CD}$

(4) $|\overrightarrow{O_1P}| + |\overrightarrow{P_1P_2}|$

(5) $\lambda\,\overrightarrow{BA} + \lambda\,\overrightarrow{BC}$

(6) $x \xrightarrow{fog} y$

(7) $x \xrightarrow{g} y \xrightarrow{f} z$

(8) $\overrightarrow{F}$

(9) $\overleftarrow{AB}$

(10) $\overleftrightarrow{XZ} \parallel \overleftrightarrow{RS}$

(11) $\overleftrightarrow{AB} + \overleftrightarrow{CD}$

(12) $\overleftrightarrow{AB}$

(13) $\overrightarrow{OB} \cup \overrightarrow{OC}$

⠀⠀⠀⠀(braille)

(14) $\overleftarrow{AB}$

⠀⠀⠀⠀(braille)

(15) $\overrightarrow{AB}$

⠀⠀⠀⠀(braille)

(16) $\overleftarrow{AB}$

⠀⠀⠀⠀(braille)

(17) $\overset{\circ\!-\!\circ}{AB}$

⠀⠀⠀⠀(braille)

(18) $\underset{\leftarrow}{T}$

⠀⠀⠀⠀(braille)

b. When identical arrows are used above vectors in boldface type throughout the text, they must be omitted from the braille transcription unless the author specifically refers to them as a notational device. If the arrows are to be omitted in braille, a transcriber's note must be included explaining that the arrows are present in print.

(1) $b + a = \overrightarrow{\mathbf{OP}}$

⠀⠀⠀⠀(braille)

(OP is in boldface type, arrow omitted, T.N. required)

(2) $b + a = \overrightarrow{OP}$

⠀⠀⠀⠀(braille)

(OP is in ordinary type; arrow shown; T.N. not required)

(3) $v[\overrightarrow{\mathbf{EF}}]$ and $r[\overrightarrow{st}]$

⠀⠀⠀⠀(braille)

⠀⠀⠀⠀(braille)

(Both arrows must be shown since they are not of uniform construction. T.N. not required)

§130. Dots as Modifiers:

a. In print the recurrence of one or more digits in a decimal numeral may be indicated by one dot over each recurring digit. However, in braille only one dot is used as a modifier. The dot is placed after the last modified digit in the recurring sequence.

(1) $\dot{.4}$

(2) $\dfrac{1}{6} = 0.166\dot{6} \ldots$

(3) $1.\overset{\ldots}{375}$

(4) $\dfrac{1}{11} = 0.909\ddot{0}9$

b. When one or more dots occur over or under a single mathematical expression, the symbol for the dot must be used as many times as necessary to conform with the print text.

(1) $\ddot{x} = \dfrac{d^2x}{dt^2}$

(2) $\dddot{x}$

(3) $x\dddot{y} - \dddot{y}x$

(4) $\sqrt{\ddot{x}^2 + \ddot{y}^2}$

(5) $\underset{..}{x}$

199

§131. Horizontal Grouping Signs as Modifiers: A horizontal grouping sign over or under a mathematical expression must be treated as a modifier. It is recommended that such grouping signs be drawn.

However, horizontal grouping signs may also be represented by braille symbols, in which case the entire modified expression must be transcribed in accordance with the five-step rule. The opening sign of grouping must be used when the modifier is above, and the closing sign of grouping when the modifier is below.

(1) $\overset{\frown}{x+y}$

⠀ (braille)

(2) $\underset{\smile}{x+y}$

⠀ (braille)

(3) $\overline{x+y}$ (with top bracket)

⠀ (braille)

(4) $\underline{x+y}$ (with bottom bracket)

⠀ (braille)

23 zeros

(5) $.000\overbrace{}...016617$

⠀ (braille)

§132. Modified Signs of Comparison: A modified sign of comparison consists of a simple sign of comparison, such as the equals sign or the tilde, modified by a caret, dot, triangle, question mark, vertical bar, or any symbol except another sign of comparison. Such a combination must be transcribed in accordance with the five-step rule for modified expressions. However, when a simple sign of comparison occurs above or below another simple sign of comparison, the combination must be transcribed as a sign of comparison compounded vertically, and the five-step rule must not be used (see **§108**).

A modified sign of comparison may also consist of a horizontal bar modified by a dot under it or by a caret directly over or under it. However, if the horizontal bar is modified by a dot over it, the combination is a sign of operation (see **§94j**).

The following list contains the modified signs of comparison most commonly used. Unlisted modified comparison signs must be transcribed in accordance with the same principles.

Equals Sign

Caret Over	$\overset{\wedge}{=}$	(braille)
Caret Under (is projective to)	$\underset{\wedge}{=}$	(braille)
Inverted Caret Over	$\overset{\vee}{=}$	(braille)
Left-Pointing Caret Over	$\overset{<}{=}$	(braille)
Right-Pointing Caret Over	$\overset{>}{=}$	(braille)
Dot Over (is approximately equal to)	$\overset{\cdot}{=}$	(braille)

200

Dot Over and Dot Under	$\doteqdot$	
Two Dots Over and Two Dots Under	$\Bumpeq$	
Hollow Dot Over (is equal in degrees to)	$\overset{\circ}{=}$	
Equilateral Triangle Over	$\overset{\triangle}{=}$	
Question Mark Over	$\overset{?}{=}$	
Question Mark Under	$\underset{?}{=}$	
Vertical Bar Over	$\overset{|}{=}$	

Simple Tilde

| Dot Under | $\underset{\cdot}{\sim}$ | |
| Dot Over | $\overset{\cdot}{\sim}$ | |

Horizontal Bar

Caret Over	$\overset{\wedge}{-}$	
Caret Under (is perspective to)	$\underset{\wedge}{-}$	
Dot Under	$\underset{\cdot}{-}$	

(1) $\sqrt{3} \doteq 1.732$

(2) $A \doteq 3.14r^2$

(3) $\angle b \overset{\circ}{=} \frac{1}{2}\overset{\frown}{EB}$

(4) $5(3) + 2(-2) \overset{?}{=} 11$

(5) $A \overset{D}{=} B$

Multipurpose Indicator ⠀⠐

§133. **Review of the Multipurpose Indicator:** The multipurpose indicator has already been introduced in the following situations (in these situations it must not be regarded as the baseline indicator):

    a. The multipurpose indicator must be used between two symbols for the tilde to indicate that they are written horizontally (see §94k).

    b. The multipurpose indicator must be used between two unspaced signs of comparison to indicate that they are printed horizontally and not vertically (see §109).

    c. The multipurpose indicator must be used between two horizontally arranged modifiers within a sign of shape (see §115c).

    d. The multipurpose indicator must be used between a regular polygon representing a sign of operation and a numeral immediately following it (see §120a).

    e. The multipurpose indicator must be used before a modified expression (see §125a.)

§134. **Additional Uses of the Multipurpose Indicator:**

    a. When both a letter and a numeral following the letter appear on the baseline of writing, the multipurpose indicator must be used before the numeral to show that it is not a subscript to the letter. However, a letter used to represent a numeral in a nondecimal numeration system must be regarded as a numeral, and the multipurpose indicator must not be used.

    (1)   x3

    (2)   R10

    (3) $4\theta = 120° + n360°$

    (4) $C = \pi 2r$

    (5) $\omega 2 = \omega \neq 2\omega$

    (6)   Serial number GE5678H9

    (7) $2TE14_{12}$ is a base-12 numeral.

(8) $140TE4T5_{12}+E5_{12}$

b. When a letter on the baseline of writing is immediately followed by a decimal point and a numeral, the multipurpose indicator must be placed between the letter and the decimal point to show that the decimal point and numeral are not subscripts to the letter.

(1) x.4

c. The multipurpose indicator must be used after a numeric subscript if the subscript is followed by a numeral on the baseline of writing.

(1) x_710

(2) $\dfrac{A_0}{2} = A_02^{-0.05T}$

(3) $x_2 = n_15^{-1} - 1n_25^{-1}$

d. The multipurpose indicator must be used after a decimal point if the symbol following the decimal point is *not* a numeral. However, the multipurpose indicator must not be used when the decimal point is followed by a comma or the punctuation indicator.

(1) $0.a_1a_2a_3 \ldots a_n$

(2) $0.\alpha_1\alpha_2\alpha_3 \ldots \alpha_n$

(3) .%

(4) $\dfrac{1}{2} = .\underline{\ ?\ }$

(5) $4\% = .\underline{\hspace{1.5cm}}$

(6) 5. + .6 = 5.6

(7) (5.)

(8) Can you explain 1., 10., and 100.?

e. The multipurpose indicator must be used between two unspaced vertical bars when the first bar is a closing sign of grouping, and the second bar is an opening sign of grouping.

The multipurpose indicator must also be used between two vertical bars which are grouping symbols when one bar is shorter and/or thicker than the other.

(1) | x | | y |

⠀

(2) || x || || y ||

⠀

(3) | | x | |

⠀

(Outside bars are longer than inside bars.)

(4) | | | x | | |

⠀

(Inside bars are longer than both sets of outer bars.)

(5) | x | |
         | x = 0

⠀

(Third bar extends to the subscript level.)

HOMEWORK

Prepare the following homework for submission to your teacher. Note: the transcriber's note required on page 206 should be placed at the appropriate point in the transcription. Proofread carefully.

EXERCISE 11

Find the fractional equivalent of each repeating decimal.

1. 2.43$\overline{43}$

2. 0.2367$\overline{78}$

3. 1.142857$\overline{142857}$

4. .249$\dot{9}$

5. 7.13$\overline{13}$ ...

6. 6.2532$\overline{53}$ ...

7. In quadrilateral ABCD, $\overline{DC} \parallel \overline{AB}$, and $\overline{AB}$ equals $\overline{DC}$. The measures of certain angles are represented by a, b, and c. Write the proof that $b = c$.

8. In $\square$DEFG, $m\overline{DE} = 75$ and $m\overline{EF} = 20$. If $m\overline{HJ} = m\overline{EF}$ find $m\overline{HJ} + m\overline{DE}$.

9. In the figure given, if $\overset{\frown}{AB} = \overset{\frown}{CD}$ in circle O, then $\angle\, AOB = \angle\, BOC$.

10. Does $\dfrac{\overline{ST}}{\overline{UV}}$ equal $\dfrac{\overline{UV}}{\overline{ST}}$?

11. In right triangle ABC, if $\overline{AB}$ is the hypotenuse, is it true that $\overline{BC}^2 + \overline{AC}^2 = \overline{AB}^2$?

12. Using workbook pages 159-161, explain the following:
    a. $\widetilde{r} = 72.9$ (page 159)
    b. $\widetilde{T} \cup \widetilde{V}$ (page 160)
    c. $\overset{\frown}{a+b+c}$ (page 161)

13. Let the functions f and g be defined as $f\colon \underset{\sim}{R} \rightarrow \underset{\sim}{R}$ with $f(x) = 2x+1$, $g\colon \underset{\sim}{R}^+ \rightarrow \underset{\sim}{R}^+$ with $g(x) = x^{\frac{1}{2}}$.

14. Explain the meaning of $\underset{\sim}{C}^* / \underset{\sim}{R}^*$.

15. Give the place value of the underlined material.
    a. 3.57<u>9</u>   b. 62.<u>1</u>75   c. 0.00000<u>1</u>

16. Find the fractional equivalent of each repeating decimal.

    a. $0.11\overline{1}$ b. $2.44\overline{4}$

17. $\overline{x} \times \overline{y} = \overline{xy}$

18. $\overline{\alpha}$ and $\overline{\beta}$ identify the circles.

19. The volume V of a right circular cone is given by the formula
    $$V = \frac{1}{3}\overline{A}h,$$
    where $\overline{A}$ is the area of the base.

20. The volume of a sphere varies directly as the cube of its radius, since
    $$V = \frac{1}{3}\pi\overline{r}^3.$$

21. $z = m\dfrac{\overline{x}^2}{\overline{y}^3}$

22. $\dfrac{\overline{p}_x}{\overline{p}_y}$ should be used for checking your work.

23. How many $\overline{6}$'s are needed to fill the blanks in the above example?

24. Is it true that the arbitrary set $\overline{[A \cap X \cup (B \cap \overline{X})]}$ is equal to $(\overline{A} \cap X) \cup (\overline{B} \cap \overline{X})$?

25. All values of y are located on the regression line $\hat{y} = \alpha + \beta x$.

26. The probability of the event A, written P(A), is defined as

$$P(A) = \sum_A f(x)$$

where $\sum_A f(x)$ means sum $f(x)$ over those values x_i that are in A.

27. The variance is the sum of $\Sigma \alpha_i^2 \, \sigma_i^2$ with the product of $\underset{i \neq j}{\sum_i \sum_j}$ and $\alpha_i \alpha_j \sigma_{ij}$.

28. Can you obtain the maximum likelihood estimators $\hat{\bar{r}}$ of the $\bar{r}_{ij}$ by replacing the θ_i by $\hat{\bar{\theta}}_i$?

29. Explain $\bar{\bar{y}} \times \bar{\bar{z}}$ in words.

30.
$$\underset{i<j<k}{\sum_{i,\,j,\,k}}$$

31. A sum of terms such as $n_3+n_4+n_5+n_6+n_7$ is often designated by the symbol $\sum\limits_{i=3}^{7} n_i$.

32. The probability of A_i is $\sum\limits_{j=1}^{s} \dfrac{n_{ij}}{n}$.

33. Mark point $(\hat{\mu}, \hat{\sigma}^2)$ on the graph in Figure 11.2.

34. To get the reduced normal equations, cross the row and column corresponding to $\hat{\beta}_3$ from X'X and from X'Y.

35. If $\bar{a}_1 = 72$, find $\bar{a}_7$.

36. $W = \dfrac{2}{3}\pi r^3 \underline{w}\left(h+\dfrac{3}{8}\,r\right).$

37. If $a^{\tilde{n}} \cdot a^{\tilde{m}}$ equals $a^{\tilde{n}+\tilde{m}}$, what is the product of $x^{\tilde{3}}$ and $x^{\tilde{2}}$? What is the product of x^7 and x^9?

38. Let A, B, C, D be the vertices, in order, of a quadrilateral. Let A′, B′, C′, D′ be the mid-points of the sides $\overline{AB}$, $\overline{BC}$, $\overline{CD}$, and $\overline{DA}$, in order. Prove that A′B′C′D′ is a parallelogram. (*Hint:* First show that $\overrightarrow{A'B'}$ equals $\overrightarrow{D'C'}$ equals $\dfrac{1}{2}\overrightarrow{AC}$.)

39. $\overrightarrow{P_1P_2}$ if P_1 is the point $(1, 3)$ and P_2 is the point $(2, -1)$.

40. $\overrightarrow{OP_3}$ if O is the origin and P_3 is the mid-point of the vector $\overrightarrow{P_1P_2}$ joining $P_1\,(2, -1)$ and $P_2\,(-4, 3)$.

41. R equals $\overrightarrow{OP}$ equals $\overrightarrow{OM}$ plus $\overrightarrow{MC}$ plus $\overrightarrow{CP}$.

42. $\overrightarrow{OP} = ix+jy.$

43. $\overrightarrow{OP}$ equals $\overrightarrow{OT}$ plus $\overrightarrow{TP}$.

44. What is the fractional equivalent of $2.43\overset{..}{1}\overset{}{3}\overset{..}{1}$?

45. Give the sum of $\overset{...}{a}$ and $\overset{...}{b}$.

46. $\overset{.}{a}+\overset{...}{a} = ?$

47. $x^n = \underbrace{x \cdot x \cdot x \cdot \ldots \cdot x}$

48. $\dfrac{48}{48} \overset{?}{=} \dfrac{4}{4},\ 1 = 1.$

49. Find the surface area of a sphere if $S = 4\pi r^2$, $\pi = \dfrac{22}{7}$, and $r = 21$ cm.

50. If 2793t4e6 is a numeral in base-twelve, what is its equivalent in base-ten?

51. If z.6 equals $7\dfrac{3}{5}$, what do you know about z?

52. $D_8 6_3 = Y^2$

53. The orbital speed of the planet Mercury is 29.73 miles per second and the orbital speed of Jupiter is 8.11 miles per second. The difference is 29.73—8.11 = □.△.

54. Does $|{-}2\,|\,|{+}3\,| = {+}6$? Does $|{-}92\,|\,|{-}5\,| = {-}460$?

55. $\dbinom{n}{k} = C_n^k$

LESSON 12

MISCELLANEOUS SYMBOLS

§135. Unspaced Miscellaneous Symbols: No space should be left between the symbols listed below and any other symbol or quantity to which they apply. However, a space must be left between these symbols and a word, an abbreviation, a sign of comparison, or other symbol which specifically requires a space before or after it.

a. Caret (circumflex): ∧

The caret may be used as a modifier above or below a mathematical expression or as a place indicator with the decimal point (to show the position to which the decimal point has been moved). Used as a place indicator, it must be treated as a numeric symbol.

(1) $.37_\wedge 68$

(2) $1.2_\wedge$

(3) $\hat{x}$

(4) The caret (∧) shows the place to which the decimal is moved.

b. Crossed d: đ

Crossed h: ħ

Crossed Lambda: ƛ

Crossed R: ℞

(1) $2đv$

(2) $2\pi ħv = \phi e$

(3) $(v > \phi ħ)$

(4) $ħ = 6.625 \times 10^{-27}$ erg sec.

(5) $3\dot{x}\ldots n\dot{x}$

(6) $\dfrac{\hbar}{R}$

(7) $n = 3R\!\!\!/$

(8) $R\!\!\!/\,(P_1P_2, P_3P_4)$

(9) $R\!\!\!/$: 24 grams

c. **Del (nabla, gradient):** $\triangledown$

When this symbol is used as a sign of omission, it must be spaced accordingly (see **§120c**). In all other cases, it must be spaced in accordance with the rule above.

(1) $\triangledown f(1, 2) = x\underline{i}-3j$

(2) The symbol "$\triangledown$" is called "del."

(3) $\|\triangledown f(a)\|$

(4) $s\triangledown t+t\triangledown s$

(5) $\triangledown(r^n)$

(6) $T \cdot \triangledown (r_1 + r_2) = 0$

d. **Empty Set (null set, void set):**

      Represented by Zero With a Slant or Vertical Bar $\varnothing$ or ϕ
         Through It

      Represented by Facing Braces $\{\ \}$

The print symbols ∅ and ⦰ which are used to denote the empty set must not be mistaken for the Greek uncapitalized phi (ϕ) which they resemble.

When facing braces are used to denote the empty set, one space must be left between the braces.

(1) $A \cap \emptyset = \emptyset$

(2) $\phi \subseteq A$

(3) $S \cup \{\ \}$

(4) $\{\ \} \cap \{\ \}$

(5) $R = \emptyset, R = \{\ \}$

(6) The solution set is $\emptyset$.

e. Factorial Sign: !

(1) $n!$

(2) $\binom{n}{r} = \dfrac{n!}{(n-r)!\,r!}$

(3) $_5C_1 = \dfrac{5!}{1!\,4!}$

f. Infinity: ∞

(1) $a - (+\infty) = -\infty$

(2) $(+\infty) + (+\infty) = +\infty$

(3) 1^∞

⠀⠀⠀⠀⠀⠀⠀⠀⠀⠀⠀⠀⠀⠀⠀

(4) $S_\infty = \dfrac{a}{1-r}$

(5) $\displaystyle\sum_{n=-\infty}^{\infty} f(n)$

(6) $-\infty < x < \infty$

(7) $n \to \infty$

(8) $\langle -\infty, +\infty \rangle = R$

(9) $f'(x) = 0 \text{ or } \infty.$

g. Integral:

Single Integral	$\int$	
Double Integral	$\iint$	
Triple Integral	$\iiint$	
Upper Integral	$\overline{\int}$	
Lower Integral	$\underline{\int}$	

The horizontal bar directly over or under the integral sign must not be treated as a modifier. The symbols for the upper and lower integral signs must be transcribed as shown in the list above. Modifiers other than the horizontal bar must be transcribed according to the five-step rule for the transcription of modified expressions.

(1) $\displaystyle\int (du+dv) = \int du + \int dv$

(2) $d \int f(x) dx$

⠿ ⠿ ⠿ ⠿ ⠿ ⠿ ⠿ ⠿

(3) $V = \iiint dx\ dy\ dy$

⠿ ⠿ ⠿ ⠿ ⠿ ⠿ ⠿ ⠿ ⠿

(4) $\int_a^b f(x) dx = F(x)\Big]_a^b$

⠿ ⠿

(5) $\int_1^3 \dfrac{dx}{x^2 - 2x + 5}$

⠿ ⠿ ⠿ ⠿ ⠿ ⠿ ⠿ ⠿ ⠿ ⠿ ⠿ ⠿ ⠿ ⠿ ⠿ ⠿ ⠿ ⠿

(6) $\int_1^2 \int_0^{x-1} y\ dy\ dx$

⠿ ⠿ ⠿ ⠿ ⠿ ⠿ ⠿ ⠿ ⠿ ⠿ ⠿ ⠿ ⠿ ⠿ ⠿ ⠿ ⠿

(7) $\overline{\int_a^b} f(x) dx = 0$

⠿ ⠿ ⠿ ⠿ ⠿ ⠿ ⠿ ⠿ ⠿ ⠿ ⠿ ⠿ ⠿ ⠿

(8) $\underline{\int_a^b} f(x) dx = 0$

⠿ ⠿ ⠿ ⠿ ⠿ ⠿ ⠿ ⠿ ⠿ ⠿ ⠿ ⠿ ⠿ ⠿

(9) $\int_0^\infty f(x) dx$

⠿ ⠿ ⠿ ⠿ ⠿ ⠿ ⠿ ⠿ ⠿ ⠿ ⠿ ⠿ ⠿

(10) $\int_{x=a}^{x=b} f(t) dt$

⠿ ⠿ ⠿ ⠿ ⠿ ⠿ ⠿ ⠿ ⠿ ⠿ ⠿ ⠿ ⠿ ⠿ ⠿ ⠿ ⠿

(11) $\iint_Q f(x,\ y) dy\ dx$

⠿ ⠿ ⠿ ⠿ ⠿ ⠿ ⠿ ⠿ ⠿ ⠿ ⠿ ⠿ ⠿ ⠿

h. Partial Derivative (round d): ∂ ⠿ ⠿

(1) $\dfrac{\partial f}{\partial x}$

⠿ ⠿ ⠿ ⠿ ⠿ ⠿ ⠿ ⠿ ⠿ ⠿ ⠿

(2) $\dfrac{\partial P}{\partial x} + \dfrac{\partial Q}{\partial y}$

⠐⠦⠰⠠⠏⠰⠀... (braille)

(3) $\dfrac{\partial h}{\partial u} = \dfrac{\partial f}{\partial x}\,\dfrac{\partial x}{\partial u}$

⠐⠦... (braille)

(4) $\dfrac{\partial^2 g(u,v)}{\partial u\,\partial v}$

⠐⠦... (braille)

(5) $\partial/\partial y(\partial b/\partial x)$

⠐⠦... (braille)

i. Quantifiers:

Existential Quantifier

There Exists, for Some	$\exists$	⠈⠮
There Exists Uniquely for Exactly One	$\exists\,\vert$	⠈⠮⠳

Universal Quantifier

For All, For Each, For Every	$\forall$ or $\forall$	⠈⠮

(1) $\exists\, x,\ x < \dfrac{1}{n}$

⠈⠮⠭⠂⠀⠀⠭⠀⠀⠐⠅⠀⠼⠁⠲⠝ (braille)

(2) $(\exists x)\,(\exists y)\,[x + y = 85]$

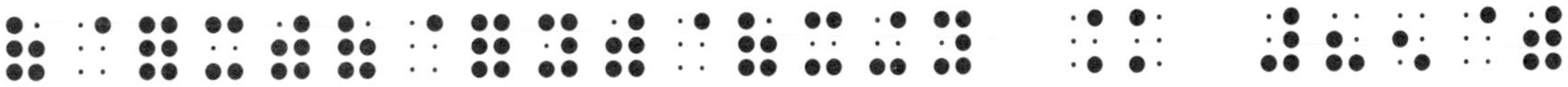

⠐⠣⠈⠮⠭⠐⠜⠐⠣⠈⠮⠽⠐⠜⠨⠣⠭⠖⠽⠀⠀⠨⠶⠓⠑⠨⠜ (braille)

(3) $(\exists_x\ \varepsilon\ A)$

⠐⠣⠈⠮⠭⠀⠈⠑⠀⠠⠁⠐⠜ (braille)

(4) $\exists\vert_x$

⠈⠮⠳⠢⠭ (braille)

(5) $\exists\vert_v\ \vert\ v = {-}v$ means "there exists exactly one v such that v equals —v."

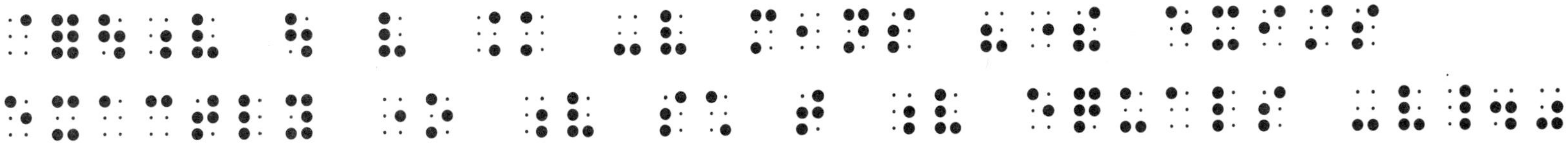

⠈⠮⠳⠢⠧⠀⠳⠀⠧⠀⠐⠶⠀⠤⠧⠀⠰⠦... (braille)

�... (braille)

(6) $\forall_x \, \epsilon \, A$

⠀⠀⠀⠀⠀⠀(braille)

(7) $(\forall_x)$

⠀⠀⠀⠀⠀⠀(braille)

(8) $\forall_x \forall_y - \dfrac{y-x}{x+y}$

⠀⠀⠀⠀⠀⠀(braille)

(9) $\forall_x \, \forall_{y \neq 0} \, (x \div y)$

⠀⠀⠀⠀⠀⠀(braille)

§136. **Spaced Miscellaneous Symbols**: A space must be left before and after the symbols listed below even when these symbols are preceded or followed by a sign of operation. However, no space should be left between these symbols and a sign of grouping, a braille indicator, or a punctuation mark which applies to them.

a. At Sign: @ ⠀(braille)

(1) He sold 5 pens @ 45¢ each.

⠀⠀⠀⠀⠀⠀(braille)

(2) The symbol (@) means "at".

⠀⠀⠀⠀⠀⠀(braille)

b. Check Mark: √ ⠀(braille)

A space must be left before and after a single check mark. A sequence of two or more check marks must be written unspaced, but the combination as a whole must be preceded and followed by a space.

(1) √ $1+2=3$

⠀⠀⠀⠀⠀⠀(braille)

(2) $-6 = {}^-6$ √.

⠀⠀⠀⠀⠀⠀(braille)

(3) √√ pens

⠀⠀⠀⠀⠀⠀(braille)

(4) (√) butter, (√√) milk.

⠀⠀⠀⠀⠀⠀(braille)

c. Ditto Marks: "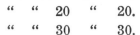

A ditto mark must be centered beneath the material to which it applies. It must be separated from any expression which precedes or follows it by at least one space.

    (1)   1 times 10 equals 10.
            "   "   20   "   20.
            "   "   30   "   30.

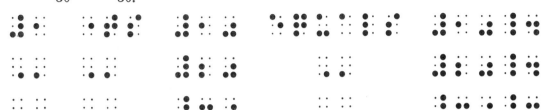

    (2)   10 times 1 equals 10.
            "   "   2   "   20.
            "   "   3   "   30.

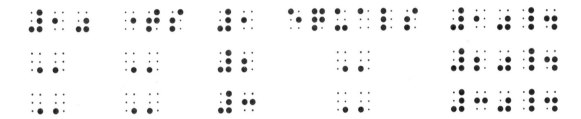

d. Since (because):

    (1) $\because$ x = y, x^2 = y^2.

    (2)   ($\because$) RS = RT

e. Therefore:

    Normal $\therefore$

    Negated (it does not follow that)   /$\therefore$

    (1) $\therefore$ CM $\perp$ AB

    (2) $\therefore$ The solution set is {±3}.

    (3)   /$\therefore$ R = S

f. Boldface Vertical Bar (end of proof):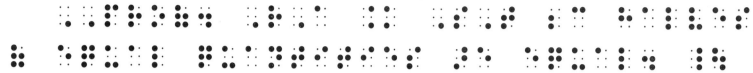

When the single boldface vertical bar means *end of proof,* the bar must be preceded and followed by a space.

(1) PROOF. RA = ST because halves of equal quantities are equal.|

§137. **Special Spacing With Miscellaneous Symbols:**

a. Angstrom Unit: Å

The angstrom unit must be treated as an abbreviation and spaced accordingly. That is, a space must be left before and after the angstrom unit even when it is preceded or followed by a sign of operation. However, a space must not be left between the angstrom unit and a sign of grouping, a horizontal or diagonal fraction line, a braille indicator, or a punctuation mark which applies to it.

(1) $1/10,000\mu = 1\overset{\circ}{A}.$

(2) $1\overset{\circ}{A} + 2\overset{\circ}{A} = 3\overset{\circ}{A}$

(3) $(500\text{-}1000)\overset{\circ}{A}$

(4) An angstrom unit ($\overset{\circ}{A}$) equals 1×10^{-10} meter.

(5) $(\lambda > 7,000\ \overset{\circ}{A})$

(6) $$\dfrac{(2)\,(2\overset{\circ}{A})}{4 \times 10^6\ \overset{\circ}{A}}$$

b. Slash (diagonal line): /

The slash may be used as a sign of operation in fractions, between words, within dates, or in any kind of abbreviation. In all situations, it must be represented by the symbol above; the English braille symbol must not be used.

No space should be left between the slash and any word, part of a word, abbreviation, or numeral to which it applies. In addition, contractions must not be used in any capitalized or uncapitalized word, part of a word, or abbreviation in direct contact with the slash. However, contractions may be used if a punctuation mark or a grouping sign permitting the use of the contraction separates the slash from the word, part of a word, or abbreviation.

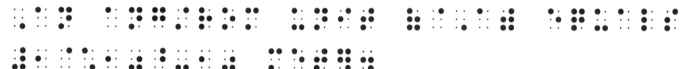

(1) and/or

(2) The rise/run ratio is 5.

(3) The red/white probabilities are the same.

(4) The input/output ratio is equal.

(5) The (input)/(output) ratio is equal.

(6) How many min/hour did he travel?

(7) How many min./hour did he travel?

(8) He worked in the Bio./Chem. lab.

(9) c/o means "care of".

(10) PL/I means "Program Learning I".

(11) The date is 1/30/72.

c. Tally Mark: | ⠅

Tally marks must be grouped in braille just as they are grouped in print. When a group of tally marks is crossed through, the cross-tally must be treated as an additional tally mark which should be added to its group.

One space must be left before and after a group of tally marks even when the group is preceded or followed by a sign of operation. However, when the combination of symbols cannot be accommodated on one braille line, transition to another braille line may take the place of the required space. No space should be left between a group of tallies and a braille indicator, a sign of grouping, or a punctuation mark applying to it.

When a tally mark is followed by punctuation requiring the punctuation indicator, the multipurpose indicator ⠱ must be placed between the tally mark and the punctuation indicator.

(1) ||||| ||||| |||

(In print there are no cross-tallies)

(2) |||| |||| |||

(In print the first two groups of tallies have a cross-tally)

(3) $22_7 = $ ||||||| ||||||| ||

(4) ||| + ||| = ||||||

(5) (|||||) + (|||)

(6) (||| + |||)

(7) ||||²

(8) ||||, ||||.

SUPERPOSED SIGNS

§138. **Order of Superposed Signs:** Superposed signs are signs which are placed one upon another so that one sign extends beyond the boundary of the other.

a. Since it may be difficult to distinguish the basic sign from the superposed sign, the following order of preference should be used as a guide. A symbol lower on the list must be regarded as being superposed upon a symbol higher on the list.

   i. Integral sign
   ii. Signs of operation
   iii. Horizontal and vertical bars
   iv. Signs of shape
   v. Signs of comparison
   vi. Signs not listed above

§139. Transcription of Superposed Signs:

a. The components of a superposed sign must be unspaced and transcribed in the following order:

    i. The symbol for the higher sign on the list must be written first.

    ii. The superposition indicator ⠒⠄ must be written next.

    iii. The symbol for the lower sign on the list must be written third.

    iv. The termination indicator ⠿ must be written last.

b. If two signs belong to the same category, the superposition may be represented in either order, provided the same order is followed consistently throughout the text.

(1) ⊟

(2) ∉

      or

(3) ≮

      or

§140. Integral Modified by Superposition:

The most common integrals with superposed symbols are listed below. Unlisted integrals modified by superposition must be transcribed in accordance with the rules for superposed signs. These signs must be spaced and punctuated as unmodified integral signs.

Integral With Superposed Circle $\oint$

Integral With Superposed Infinity $\oint$

Integral With Superposed Rectangle $\oint$

Integral With Superposed Square $\oint$

(1) $\oint$

(2)    $\oint \dfrac{dq}{T} < 0$

(3)    $\oint P\ dx + Q\ dy$

219

(4) $\oint_3 y^2dx+x\ dy$

⠿ (braille)

(5) $\oint f(x,\ y)dy$

⠿ (braille)

§141. Signs of Comparison Modified by Superposition: The most common signs of comparison with superposed signs are listed below. Unlisted signs of comparison modified by superposition must be transcribed in accordance with the rules for superposed signs. They must be spaced and punctuated as any other sign of comparison.

Dot

Between Bars of Equals Sign	$\dot{=}$	(braille)
Within Inclusion Sign	$\in$	(braille)
Within Reverse Inclusion Sign	$\ni$	(braille)

Equals Sign

Through Inclusion Sign	$\in$	(braille) or (braille)
Through Reverse Inclusion Sign	$\ni$	(braille) or (braille)

Greater Than

Nest of Two With Straight Sides (is large compared with)	$\gg$	(braille)
Nest of Two With Curved Sides	$\gg$	(braille)

Horizontal Bar

Through Inclusion Sign	$\in$	(braille)
Through Reverse Inclusion Sign	$\ni$	(braille)

Less Than

Nest of Two With Straight Sides (is small compared with)	$\ll$	(braille)
Nest of Two With Curved Sides	$\ll$	(braille)

Vertical Bar

Through Shaft of Right-Pointing Arrow

Through Shaft of Left-Pointing Arrow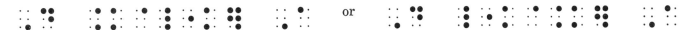

(1) $\pi \doteq 3.14$

(2) $D \in A$ or

(3) $r \gg a$

(4) $T \supset u$

(5) $l \ll n$

(6) $A \longrightarrow B$

§142. Signs of Shape Modified by Superposition: A shape modified by superposition is a basic sign having a superposed sign which extends beyond the boundary of the basic shape. Such signs are transcribed in accordance with the rules for superposed signs in §139. Signs of shape modified by superposition must be spaced and punctuated as other signs of shape.

(1) Describe  A.

(2) Divide the right half of ⊟ into thirds.

HOMEWORK

Prepare the following homework for submission to your teacher. Proofread carefully.

EXERCISE 12

1. In dividing .489 by .3, you must change the divisor to $.3_\wedge$. Select the correct form of the dividend.

   a. $.4_\wedge 89$ b. $.48_\wedge 9$ c. $.489_\wedge$

2. $1/x$ approaches ? as x tends to either $+\infty$ or $-\infty$.

3. Let g and g* be harmonic in Ω, and let $\dfrac{\partial g}{\partial n} = \dfrac{\partial g^*}{\partial n}$ on $\partial \Omega$. Show that $g^* = g + K$, where K is constant.

4. Let $\nabla \cdot F = 0$ in a convex region Ω. Show that F can be expressed there in the form $F = \nabla \times V$, where $\nabla \cdot V = 0$ and $\nabla^2 V = -\nabla \times F$.

5. Show that $(R \cap S) \cap \emptyset = R \cap (S \cap \emptyset)$ if $R = \{1, 3, 5, 7\}$ and $S = \{1, 2, 3, 4\}$.

6. Is the following statement true or false?
$$\{\ \} \subset \{1, 2\}$$

Compute the indicated number.

7. $7!$

8. $\dfrac{10!}{8!}$

9. $\dfrac{6!}{3!2!}$

10. $\dfrac{10!}{5!5!}$

11. Simplify $\dfrac{(x-y)!}{(x-y-1)!}$ given x and y are positive integers with $x > y$ and all denominators are meaningful.

12. Find a 1-form ω, for which $d\omega = (x^2+y^2)\,dxdy$, and use this to evaluate
$$\iint_D (x^2+y^2)\,dxdy$$
where D is the region inside the square $|x|+|y| = 4$ and outside the circle $x^2+y^2 = 1$.

13. Show that the area of a region D to which Green's theorem applies may be given by
$$A(D) = \frac{1}{2}\int_{\partial D} (x\,dy - y\,dx).$$

Read each of the following statements and tell whether the statement is true. Assume that the domain of each variable is $\mathcal{R}$.

14. $(\forall_s)(s \cdot 0 = 0)$

15. $(\exists_a)(a+1 \neq 3)$

16. $(\exists_r)(r-2 = 0)$

17. $(\forall_x)(\exists_y)(x+y \neq y+x)$

Name the coins that might be used in making change from a half-dollar.

18. A basket of grapes @ 20¢.

19. A can of peaches @ 25¢.

20. Find the sum of $2\frac{1}{2}$ inches and 4 inches. Answer: $2+4 = 6, 6+\frac{1}{2} = 6\frac{1}{2}.\checkmark$

21. Answer the following questions.

What part of 24 is 14?
" " " 144 " 48?
" " " 30 " 9?

22. $\because$ $3x+2y = 8$, if we substitute 0 for x we obtain $3(0)+2y = 8$. $\therefore y = 4$.

THEOREM 23. Let f be continuous on the interval [a, b], and let $f'(x)$ exist for $a < x < b$. If, in addition, $f(a) = f(b)$ then there is a point x_0 with $a < x_0 < b$ at which $f'(x_0) = 0$.

If f is a constant function, any choice of the point x_0 will do. If f is not a constant, then it must have either an interior minimum or an interior maximum at some point x_0 on the open interval $a < x < b$; and since f is differentiable there, $f'(x_0) = 0$. ▎

24. In optics we use the micron, the millimicron ($m\mu$), and the Angstrom ($\overset{\circ}{A}$) as units of wavelength. The center of the visible region can be expressed as 0.555 micron, 555 $m\mu$, or 5550 $\overset{\circ}{A}$.

25. Is it conceivable that electromagnetic theory might some day be able to predict the value of $c(3\times10^8$ meters/sec), not in terms of ϵ_0 and μ_0 but directly and numerically without recourse to any measurements?

26. In the mks system S is expressed in (watts)/(meter)^2. Does the direction of S give the direction in which the energy moves?

27. If the marks $||||||||$ equal the numeral 11_{six}, what numeral does $||||||||||$ equal in base six?

28. The boys marked the number of fish they caught in this way:

$$\cancel{||||}\ \cancel{||||}\ \cancel{||||}\ |||\ .$$

How many fish did they catch?

29. Name each ∡ in rectangle QRST.

30. In Gauss's law,

$$\epsilon_0 \oint \mathbf{E} \cdot d\mathbf{S} = q,$$

is E the electric field intensity attributable to the charge?

31. In the figure given, assume that both charges are positive. Show that E at point p in that figure, assuming $r \gg a$, is given by

$$E = \frac{1}{4\pi\epsilon_0}\frac{2q}{r^2}.$$

FUNCTION NAMES AND THEIR ABBREVIATIONS

§143. **Function Names:** The most common function names and their abbreviations are listed below. Abbreviated function names must not be considered ordinary abbreviations. They are mathematical expressions and must be transcribed in accordance with the principles defined below. Unlisted function names or their abbreviations must be transcribed as shown in print and are subject to the same rules.

ABBREVIATED FUNCTION NAME	UNABBREVIATED FUNCTION NAME	BRAILLE EQUIVALENT
amp	**amplitude**	⠁⠍⠏
antilog	**antilogarithm**	⠁⠝⠞⠊⠇⠕⠛
arc (no abbrevation)	**arc**	⠁⠗⠉
arg	**argument**	⠁⠗⠛
colog	**cologarithm**	⠉⠕⠇⠕⠛
cos	**cosine**	⠉⠕⠎
cosh	**hyperbolic cosine**	⠉⠕⠎⠓
cot	**cotangent**	⠉⠕⠞
coth	**hyperbolic cotangent**	⠉⠕⠞⠓
covers	**coversine**	⠉⠕⠧⠑⠗⠎
csc	**cosecant**	⠉⠎⠉
csch	**hyperbolic cosecant**	⠉⠎⠉⠓
ctn	**cotangent**	⠉⠞⠝
ctnh	**hyperbolic cotangent**	⠉⠞⠝⠓
det	**determinant**	⠙⠑⠞
erf	**error function**	⠑⠗⠋
exp	**exponential**	⠑⠭⠏
exsec	**exsecant**	⠑⠭⠎⠑⠉

ABBREVIATED FUNCTION NAME	UNABBREVIATED FUNCTION NAME	BRAILLE EQUIVALENT
grad	gradient	
hav	haversine	
im	imaginary part	
inf	infimum	
lim	limit	
$\overline{\text{lim}}$ or $\overline{\text{limit}}$	upper limit	
$\underline{\text{lim}}$ or $\underline{\text{limit}}$	lower limit	
ln	natural logarithm	
log	logarithm	
max	maximum	
min	minimum	
mod	modulo	
re	real part	
sec	secant	
sech	hyperbolic secant	
sin	sine	
sinh	hyperbolic sine	
sup	supremum	
tan	tangent	
tanh	hyperbolic tangent	
vers	versine	

§144. Contractions With Function Names: Contractions must not be used in any abbreviated function name. Although contractions may be used with unabbreviated function names, an unabbreviated function name must not be contracted when used in conjunction with an abbreviated function name or with related mathematical symbols.

§145. Spacing and Nonuse of the English Letter Indicator With Function Names and Their Abbreviations:

a. A space must be left after a function name or its abbreviation. A space must be left even when the function name or its abbreviation is directly followed by a sign of operation. The expression following the function name or its abbreviation must be spaced in accordance with its appropriate spacing rules.

No space should be left before a function name or its abbreviation unless it is preceded by a symbol requiring a space.

The English letter indicator must not be used with an English letter, a short-form combination, or a Roman numeral in regular type following a function name or its abbreviation.

(1) sin x

(2) arc ab

(3) Sine I

(4) $\cos \theta = \dfrac{1}{\sin \theta}$

(5) ctn —A = —ctn A

(6) 1/cos—cos = tan · sin

(7) $\dfrac{1}{\cos}$ —cos = tan · sin

(8) sin $(\theta + 90°) = \cos \theta$

(9) y = 3tan 2x

(10) $a^2 = 2ac \cos \beta + c^2$

(11) $y = 2\sin x + \sin 2x$

(12) $2\sin x + 3\cos y$

(13) $\sin e\, x - \sin e\, y$

(14) $\sin (\alpha + \beta) + \sin (\alpha - \beta)$

(15) $y' = x\cos \phi - y\sin \phi$

(16) $2\sqrt{x}\,\sin \sqrt{x} + 2\cos \sqrt{x} = C$

(17) $a\sin \dfrac{x}{a} \cdot \dfrac{1}{a} = \sin \dfrac{x}{a}$

(18) $y = \sqrt{\cot x}$

(19) $r[3\cos \theta + 4\sin \theta] = 5$

(20) $7(\cos 20° + i\sin 20°)$

(21) $\sin 2\alpha = 2\sin \alpha$

(22) $6\sin 2A\ \cos 4A$

(23) $\cos 203°\ \csc 203°$

(24) $\{\sin x \mid \sin x + 2 \le +1\}$

(25) $\sin \theta / \cos \theta$

⠿ (braille)

(26) $\dfrac{1+\cos x}{\sin x} + \dfrac{\sin x}{1+\cos x}$

(braille)

(27) $\dfrac{2 \sin \frac{\alpha}{2}}{2 \cos \frac{\alpha}{2}}$

(braille)

(28) $y = \ln |\tan x|$

(braille)

(29) $\ln |\tan (\frac{\pi}{4} + \frac{x}{2})| + C$

(braille)

(30) $\dfrac{1}{2} \ln |\sec 2t + \tan 2t| + C$

(braille)

b. A space must be left between two or more consecutive abbreviated or unabbreviated function names unless they are clearly unspaced in the print text.

(1) $y = \text{arc sin } x$

(braille)

(2) $y = \text{arcsin } x$

(braille)

(3)   What is the arc sine function?

(braille)

(4)   Arc Sine x

(braille)

(5) $n = \log \sin 50° \ 27'$

(braille)

(6) $\cos (\text{arc Tan } x + \frac{\pi}{3})$

(braille)

(7) $\text{Arctan } x + \text{Arccot } x = \dfrac{1}{2}\pi$

⠀⠀⠀⠀⠀⠀⠀⠀⠀⠀⠀⠀⠀⠀⠀⠀⠀⠀⠀⠀(braille)

(8) $\cos \text{arctan } (-1)$

⠀⠀⠀⠀⠀⠀⠀⠀⠀⠀⠀⠀⠀⠀⠀⠀⠀⠀⠀⠀(braille)

(9) $\cos \left[2 \text{ Arc csc } \left(-\dfrac{7}{5}\right)\right]$

⠀⠀⠀⠀⠀⠀⠀⠀⠀⠀⠀⠀⠀⠀⠀⠀⠀⠀⠀⠀(braille)

(10) The logarithm of sin 18° is written log sin 18°.

⠀⠀⠀⠀⠀⠀⠀⠀⠀⠀⠀⠀⠀⠀⠀⠀⠀⠀⠀⠀(braille)

⠀⠀⠀⠀⠀⠀⠀⠀⠀⠀⠀⠀⠀⠀⠀⠀⠀⠀⠀⠀(braille)

§146. Modifiers With Function Names: Modified function names must be transcribed according to the five-step rule for the transcription of modified expressions. When a function name or its abbreviation carries a modifier, the required space after the function name must follow the termination of the modifier.

However, the horizontal bar directly over or under the function name "lim" or "limit" must not be treated as a modifier. The symbols (braille) and (braille) must be used to denote "upper limit," and the symbols (braille) and

(braille) must be used to denote "lower limit."

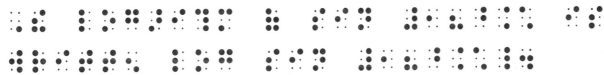

(1) $\overline{\lim}\ f_n(x)$
$\quad n \to \infty$

⠀⠀⠀⠀⠀⠀⠀⠀⠀⠀⠀⠀⠀⠀⠀⠀⠀⠀⠀⠀(braille)

(2) $\overline{\text{limit}}\ f_n(x)$
$\quad n \to \infty$

⠀⠀⠀⠀⠀⠀⠀⠀⠀⠀⠀⠀⠀⠀⠀⠀⠀⠀⠀⠀(braille)

(3) $\underline{\lim}\ f_n(x)$
$\quad n \to \infty$

⠀⠀⠀⠀⠀⠀⠀⠀⠀⠀⠀⠀⠀⠀⠀⠀⠀⠀⠀⠀(braille)

(4) $\underline{\text{limit}}\ f_n(x)$
$\quad n \to \infty$

⠀⠀⠀⠀⠀⠀⠀⠀⠀⠀⠀⠀⠀⠀⠀⠀⠀⠀⠀⠀(braille)

(5) $\lim\ f(x) = 1$
$\quad x \to a$

⠀⠀⠀⠀⠀⠀⠀⠀⠀⠀⠀⠀⠀⠀⠀⠀⠀⠀⠀⠀(braille)

(6) $\lim\ (x-4)^{-1}$
$\quad x \uparrow 4$

⠀⠀⠀⠀⠀⠀⠀⠀⠀⠀⠀⠀⠀⠀⠀⠀⠀⠀⠀⠀(braille)

(7) $\displaystyle\lim_{x \to 0}\ \csc x \ln (1+x)$

(8) $\displaystyle\lim_{\theta \to \theta_0}\ (\tan \theta)$

§147. Superscripts and Subscripts With Function Names:

a. When a function name or its abbreviation carries a superscript or subscript, the required space after the function name must follow the superscript or subscript. A letter, numeral, or other mathematical expression following this space assumes the same level as the function name.

The subscript indicator must not be used when an abbreviated function name carries a numeric subscript only on the first level below the baseline of writing. However, the subscript indicator must be used if an unabbreviated function name carries a numeric subscript.

(1) $\sin^2 x$

(2) $\text{sine}^2 x$

(3) $\sin^2 A + \cos^2 (B+A)$

(4) $\cot^{-1} x + \dfrac{\pi}{2} - \tan^{-1} x$

(5) $\sin^2 90° + \cos^2 90° = 1$

(6) $(1 - \sin^2 x)^2 \cos^2 x$

(7) $\sin^2\theta \times \dfrac{\cos^2\theta}{\sin^2\theta} - 1$

(8) $\dfrac{1 - \dfrac{\sin^2 x}{\cos^2 x}}{\sec^2 x}$

(9) $\log_n .125 = -.6$

(10) $\text{antilog}_a x = N$

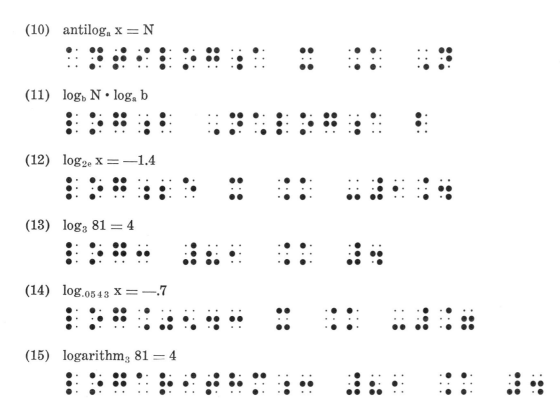

(11) $\log_b N \cdot \log_a b$

(12) $\log_{2e} x = -1.4$

(13) $\log_3 81 = 4$

(14) $\log_{.0543} x = -.7$

(15) $\text{logarithm}_3 81 = 4$

b. When a function name or its abbreviation occurs in a superscript or subscript, the required space following it *does not terminate* the effect of the level indicator. In such cases, the space reinstates the level where the function name or its abbreviation appears. Thus, the letter, numeral, fraction, or other mathematical expression immediately following the space assumes the same level as its related abbreviated or unabbreviated function name.

(1) $y = e^{\sin x}$

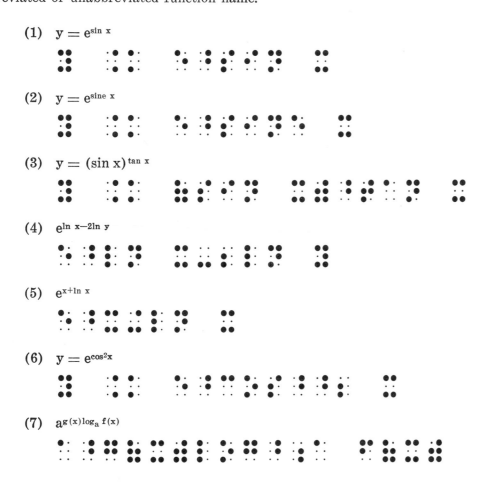

(2) $y = e^{\text{sine } x}$

(3) $y = (\sin x)^{\tan x}$

(4) $e^{\ln x - 2\ln y}$

(5) $e^{x + \ln x}$

(6) $y = e^{\cos^2 x}$

(7) $a^{g(x)\log_a f(x)}$

(8) $3^{\log_3 9}$

⠀⠀⠀⠀[braille]

(9) $e^{\sin x} + e^{\sin y}$

⠀⠀⠀⠀[braille]

(10) $3^{\log_3 7} + 2^{\log_2 5}$

⠀⠀⠀⠀[braille]

(11) $2^{\sec x} = y$

⠀⠀⠀⠀[braille]

(12) $a^{\log_a x} = x$

⠀⠀⠀⠀[braille]

(13) $e^{\sin x} = a > y$

⠀⠀⠀⠀[braille]

§148. Enclosed Lists With Abbreviated or Unabbreviated Function Names: Although the numeric indicator must not be used at the beginning of an item in an enclosed list, it must be used before a numeral or decimal point and a numeral in regular type following a function name or its abbreviation.

(1) $(2\sin 30°, 3\cos 60°)$

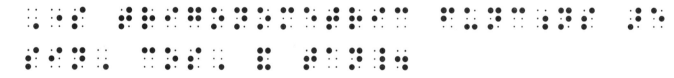

(2) $(\cos .8000, 2\cos .8000)$

§149. Punctuation With Function Names: An abbreviated function name is a mathematical expression and must be punctuated accordingly. An unabbreviated function name must be punctuated in the mathematical or literary mode according to its context.

(1) Some trigonometric functions are sin, cos, and tan.

⠀⠀⠀⠀[braille]

(2) "Arcsin" is the "inverse sine."

⠀⠀⠀⠀[braille]

(3) What is the meaning of logsine?

(4) Some trigonometric functions are sine, cosine and tangent.

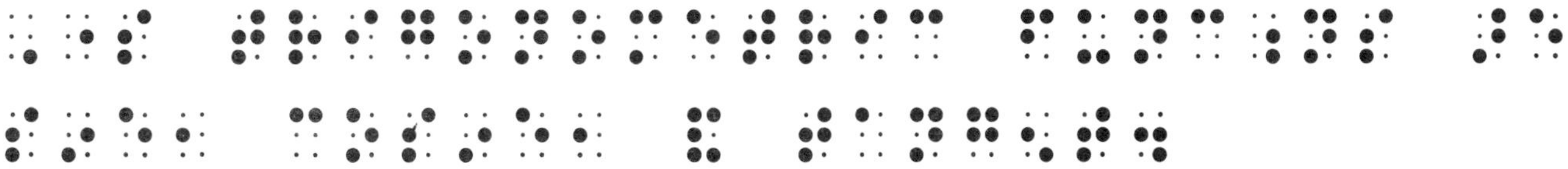

(5) Arc ACB is a major arc.

DIVISION OF MATHEMATICAL EXPRESSIONS BETWEEN BRAILLE LINES

§150. General Principles: Unless absolutely unavoidable, a mathematical expression must not be divided between braille lines or braille pages. In order to avoid a division, if there is insufficient space on the remainder of a line to accommodate the expression, the space must be left blank, and the entire expression must be brought down to the next line.

However, when a mathematical expression is too long to be contained within the margins in effect, a division is unavoidable, and the expression may be divided between braille lines. Such expressions may begin in the remaining space on a line, provided the division is made in accordance with the principles defined below. The placement of all runovers must conform to the margin requirements for itemized, instructional, explanatory, labeled, subdivided, and displayed material (see §§**13a, 28, 29, 47, 69, 89**).

§151. Division of Long Numerals: A long numeral which cannot be contained on one braille line within the margin in effect must be divided after a comma if a comma is present, and a hyphen must be inserted. If the numeral does not contain a comma, the hyphen may be inserted after any digit.

When a numeral is divided between braille lines, the numeric indicator must be used before the first digit of the numeral on the next line.

(1) 100,000,000,000,000,000,000,000

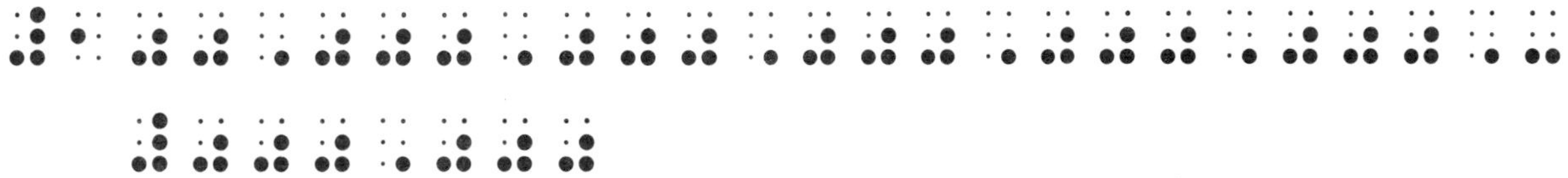

(2) 100000000000000000000000

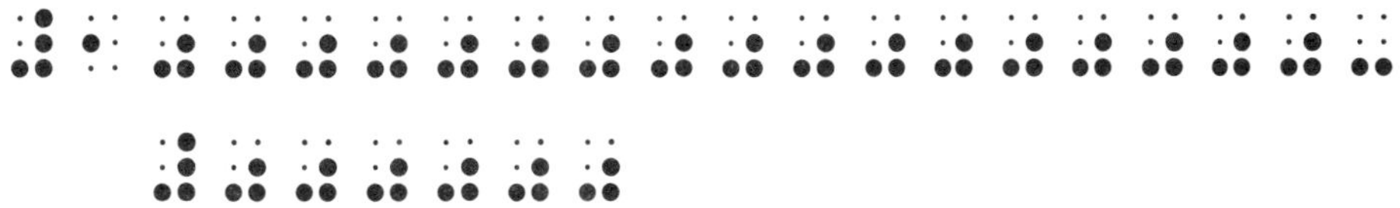

(3) A decillion is 1,000,000,000,000,
000,000,000,000,000,000,000,000.

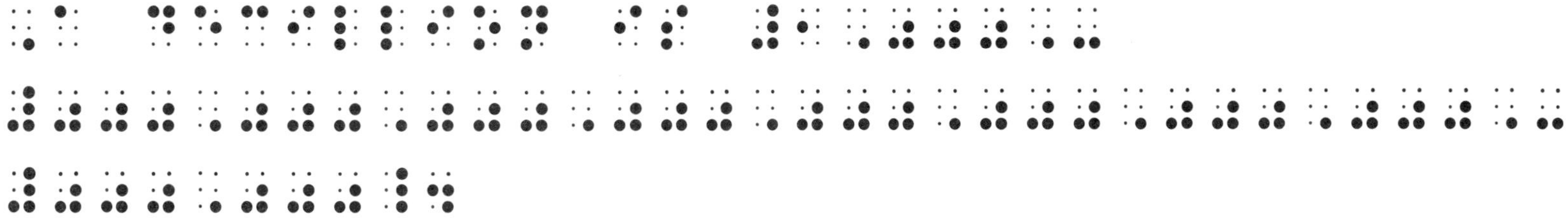

§152. Division of Long Mathematical Expressions:

a. Mathematical expressions, such as enclosed lists, formulas, equations, etc., *which cannot fit on one braille line within the boundaries of the margins used* may be divided between lines in the following order of preference:

i. A division may be made after a comma between items in an enclosed list. When the items in an enclosed list must be divided between braille lines, neither the numeric indicator nor the English letter indicator must be used before a runover on the new line.

(1)   {11, 12, 13, 14, 15, 16, 17, 18, 19, 20}

(2)   Is the set $\{\ldots, 16, 8, 4, 2, 1, \dfrac{1}{2}, \dfrac{1}{4}, \dfrac{1}{8}, \ldots\}$
closed under addition?

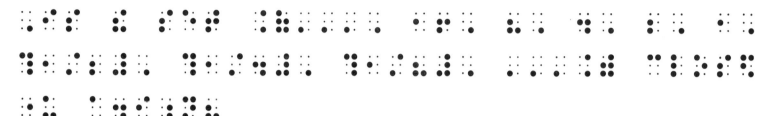

(3)   Does $\{\ldots, -4, -3, -2, -1, 0, 1, 2, 3, 4, \ldots\}$
represent a set of integers?

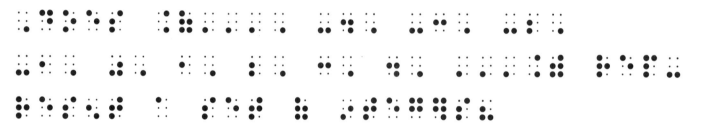

(4) $(\ldots, .10, .09, .08, .07, .06, .05, .04, \ldots)$

ii. A division may be made before a sign of comparison on the baseline of writing, provided it is not part of an item enclosed in grouping symbols, fraction indicators, radical signs, or by the symbols of a modified expression. A transition to a new braille line made before a sign of comparison terminates the effect of any level indicator used on the line above.

(1) $1778 + 1294 + 865 + 905 + 1574 + 485 = 7901$

(2) $2 \times 423 = (2 \times 400) + (2 \times 20) + (2 \times 3)$

234

(3) $\dfrac{3}{5}\left(\dfrac{2}{3}\mathrm{x}-\dfrac{1}{2}\right)>\dfrac{2}{5}\left(\dfrac{1}{4}\mathrm{x}+\dfrac{1}{3}\right)$

(4) $33\dfrac{1}{3}\%+40\%+61\dfrac{2}{3}\% = 134\dfrac{3}{3}\% = 135\%$

(5) 1. In multiplying $5\dfrac{3}{4}\times46$, we find $5\dfrac{3}{4}=5+\dfrac{3}{4}$.

Therefore, $46\times\left(5+\dfrac{3}{4}\right)=(46\times5)+\left(46\times\dfrac{3}{4}\right)=264\dfrac{1}{2}$.

(6) 2. Explain the following. Give examples.

a. $64\mathrm{x}^4+81\mathrm{y}^4=(8\mathrm{x}^2)^2+(9\mathrm{y}^2)^2$

b. $\left(\dfrac{\mathrm{a}^2}{\mathrm{b}}\right)^2\div\left(\dfrac{\mathrm{b}^2}{\mathrm{a}}\right)^3=\dfrac{\mathrm{a}^7}{\mathrm{b}^8}$

iii. A division may be made before a sign of operation on the baseline of writing. If the transition to a new line is made before a minus sign, the numeric indicator must be used after the minus sign when followed by a numeral or a decimal point and a numeral.

(1) $1\frac{5}{6}+9\frac{1}{2}+3\frac{1}{12}+2\frac{1}{4}+3\frac{1}{2}=20\frac{1}{6}$

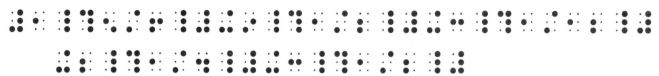

(2) $14x^3-15y^3+5x^2-4y^2+16x-10y+31$

(3) $\angle 1+\angle 2+\angle 3+\angle 4+\angle 5+\angle 6=490°$

(4) $2\frac{3}{4}$ yd$+1\frac{3}{4}$ yd$+\frac{3}{4}$ yd $=5\frac{1}{4}$ yd

(5) $(3\times10^4)+(4\times10^3)+(7\times10^2)+(5\times10)+(4\times1)=N$

(6) {x | x is an even integer} ∪ {x | x
is an odd integer}

(7) $\dfrac{1}{y^2-6y+8}+\dfrac{1}{y^2-16}-\dfrac{5}{y^2+2y-8}=\dfrac{1}{y-4}$

236

(8) $\sqrt{(x+a^2)+(y+a^2)} - \sqrt{(x-a^2)+(y-a^2)} = \pm 2a$

(9) $\dfrac{1}{2} \left| \displaystyle\int_{\alpha}^{\beta} \left\{ x(t)\dfrac{dy}{dt} - y(t)\dfrac{dx}{dt} \right\} dt \right|$

iv. A division may be made before a fraction line belonging to a fraction on the baseline of writing.

(1) $\dfrac{93{,}000 \times 0.0006 \times 2.0 \times 10.56}{32 \times 1.257 \times 10}$

(2) $\dfrac{\left(\dfrac{3}{2}\right) \times \left(\dfrac{1}{2}\right) \times \left(-\dfrac{1}{2}\right)}{1 \times 2 \times 3}$

(3) $\dfrac{e^{1/n} + e^{2/n} + e^{3/n} + \ldots + e^{(n-1)/n} + e^{n/n}}{n}$

(4) $\dfrac{\dfrac{dx}{dt}\dfrac{d^2y}{dt^2} - \dfrac{d^2x}{dt^2}\dfrac{dy}{dt}}{(dx/dt)^3} = \dfrac{d^2y}{dx^2}$

v. A division may be made before the baseline indicator. Thus, if a baseline indicator is required to show a return to the baseline of writing after a superscript or subscript, it must be the first symbol on the new braille line. However, if transition to a new line is made after a numeric subscript not requiring the subscript indicator, the baseline indicator is not required before the runover on the new line.

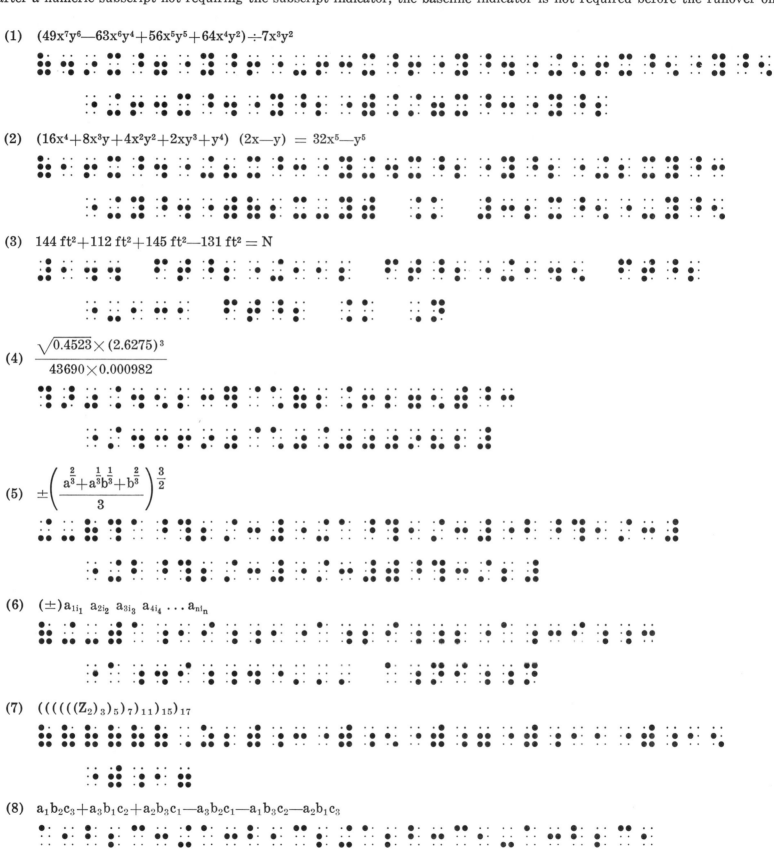

(1) $(49x^7y^6 - 63x^6y^4 + 56x^5y^5 + 64x^4y^2) \div 7x^3y^2$

(2) $(16x^4 + 8x^3y + 4x^2y^2 + 2xy^3 + y^4) \ (2x - y) = 32x^5 - y^5$

(3) $144 \text{ ft}^2 + 112 \text{ ft}^2 + 145 \text{ ft}^2 - 131 \text{ ft}^2 = N$

(4) $\dfrac{\sqrt{0.4523} \times (2.6275)^3}{43690 \times 0.000982}$

(5) $\pm \left(\dfrac{a^{\frac{2}{3}} + a^{\frac{1}{3}}b^{\frac{1}{3}} + b^{\frac{2}{3}}}{3} \right)^{\frac{3}{2}}$

(6) $(\pm)a_{1i_1} \ a_{2i_2} \ a_{3i_3} \ a_{4i_4} \ldots a_{ni_n}$

(7) $((((((Z_2)_3)_5)_7)_{11})_{15})_{17}$

(8) $a_1b_2c_3 + a_3b_1c_2 + a_2b_3c_1 - a_3b_2c_1 - a_1b_3c_2 - a_2b_1c_3$

vi. A division may be made before a superscript or subscript change-of-level indicator, or before a sign of comparison, a sign of operation, or a fraction line within a superscript or subscript.

When an expression is divided before a superscript or subscript change-of-level indicator, the indicator must be placed before the continuation of the expression on the new braille line.

If transition to a new braille line is made within a superscript or subscript, the level in effect is not changed when the division is made before a sign of operation or a fraction line. However, if the transition is made before a sign of comparison, the level in effect is terminated, and the level must be restated before the sign of comparison on the new braille line.

(1) 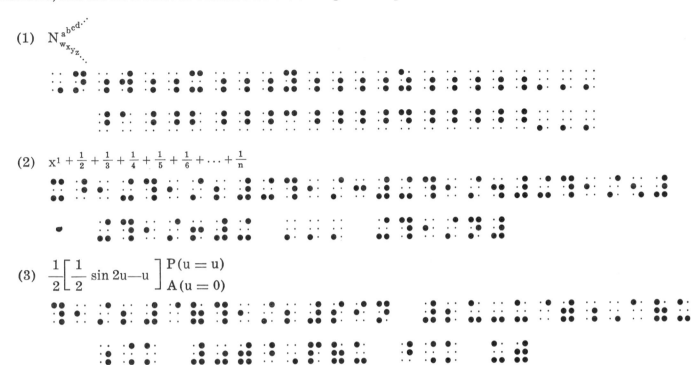 $N_{w_{x_{y_z}}}^{a^{b^{c^{d\cdots}}}}$

(2) $x^1 + \frac{1}{2} + \frac{1}{3} + \frac{1}{4} + \frac{1}{5} + \frac{1}{6} + \ldots + \frac{1}{n}$

(3) $\dfrac{1}{2}\left[\dfrac{1}{2}\sin 2u - u\right] \begin{array}{l} P(u = u) \\ A(u = 0) \end{array}$

vii. A division may be made between factors enclosed in signs of grouping.

(1) $(3x^2y)(3x^2y)(3x^2y)(3x^2y) = 81x^4y^4$

viii. A division may be made after the termination indicator of a modified expression or a radical. The five components of a modified expression must not be separated from each other by transition to a new braille line unless the modified expression as a whole is so long that it cannot fit inside the margins in effect. In such cases, a division should be made in the order of preference listed above.

(1) $\displaystyle\sum_{i=1}^{m}\sum_{j=1}^{n}\sum_{k=1}^{p} X_{ijk} = \sum_{k=1}^{p}\sum_{j=1}^{n}\sum_{i=1}^{m} X_{ijk}$

(2) $\displaystyle\sum_{i=1}^{6} \overline{P_{i-1}P_i}$

⠀⠀(braille lines)

(3) $\sqrt[3]{x}\ \sqrt[6]{x^2}\ \sqrt[12]{x^3}\ \sqrt[24]{x^4}\ \sqrt[48]{x^5}\ \ldots$

⠀⠀(braille lines)

(4) $\sqrt[5]{32a^5b^5c^5d^5}\ \ \sqrt[5]{2abc^2d^3}$

⠀⠀(braille lines)

(5) $\sqrt[3]{216a^6b^{12}}\ \sqrt{64x^6}\ \sqrt{32x^9}$

⠀⠀(braille lines)

§153. Nondivision of Symbols and Expressions:

a. The components of the following signs must not be divided between braille lines:

   i. Plus or minus

   ii. Minus or plus

   iii. Plus followed by minus

   iv. Minus followed by plus

   v. Signs of comparison compounded vertically or horizontally

   vi. Superposed signs

   vii. Tally marks belonging to the same group

   viii. Signs of shape with structural or interior modification

b. The following expressions must not be divided between braille lines:

   i. A hyphenated expression containing one or more mathematical components

   ii. An abbreviation and its related preceding or following numeral or letter

   iii. A sign of shape and its identifying numeral, letter, or sequence of letters

   iv. A function name or its abbreviation and the sign following it

HOMEWORK

Prepare the following homework for submission to your teacher. Proofread carefully.

EXERCISE 13

Find the value of each of the following.

1. $\sin \dfrac{5\pi}{12}$

2. $\tan \dfrac{7\pi}{12}$

3. $\cot 75°$

4. $\csc 75°$

5. Sine $195°$

Prove each of the following reduction formulas.

6. $\tan (90° + \theta) = -\cot \theta$

7. $\sin \left(\dfrac{3\pi}{2} + x \right) = -\cos x$

Verify that each of the following statements is true.

8. $2 \cos^2 330° - 1 = \cos 660°$

9. $\cos 225° = -\sqrt{\dfrac{1 + \cos 450°}{2}}$

10. $2 \sin^2 \dfrac{4\pi}{3} = 1 - \cos \dfrac{2\pi}{3}$

Prove each of the following identities.

11. $\cot 2\,\theta = \dfrac{\cot^2 \theta - 1}{2 \cot \theta}$

12. $\csc 2\,\theta = \dfrac{\sec \theta \csc \theta}{2}$

13. $\tan 2\,\theta = \dfrac{2 \tan \theta}{1 - \tan^2 \theta}$

Give the value of each of the following numbers.

14. Arcsin $\dfrac{1}{2}$

15. Arc cot $\left(-\dfrac{1}{\sqrt{3}} \right)$

16. Arc csc $(-\sqrt{2})$

17. Evaluate $\sin \arccos \dfrac{3}{5}$ and $\tan \arcsin \left(-\dfrac{15}{17}\right)$.

Write each logarithmic statement in exponential form.

18. $\log_3 9 = 2$

19. $\log_{\frac{1}{2}} 8 = -3$

20. $\text{logarithm}_7 7 = 1$

21. Is the following statement true? If not, replace the right-hand member with a numeral that makes it true.

$$4^{2\log_4 3} + 3^{2\log_3 4} = 1.$$

Write each expression in simpler form.

22. $e^{\log_e e}$

23. $\exp_e (\log_{e^2} 3)$

24. $\exp_8 (\log_4 2)$

25. $16^{\log_4 2}$

26. Find $\lim\limits_{x \to 0.6} 2^{25x^2 - 10x - 1}$.

27. Formulate a precise definition for
$$\lim\limits_{x \downarrow -\infty} f(x) = L.$$

28. If $\overline{\lim\limits_{n \to \infty}} a_n = A$ and $\overline{\lim\limits_{n \to \infty}} b_n = B$, must it be true that
$$\overline{\lim\limits_{n \to \infty}} (a_n + b_n) = A + B?$$

29. Find $\overline{\lim\limits_{n \to \infty}} a_n$ and $\underline{\lim\limits_{n \to \infty}} a_n$ when $a_n = (-1)_n$.

If θ is the angle from the first of the given vectors to the second, determine $\sin \theta$ and $\cos \theta$.

30. $(\cos 200°, \sin 200°)$; $(3\cos 100°, 3\sin 100°)$.

31. $(3\cos 20°, 3\sin 20°)$; $(6\cos 350°, 6\sin 350°)$.

32. State the general rules for determining a sine, a cosine, and a tangent. Of a cot, a csc, and a sec.

33. State the name of the following numeral in exponential form.
750,000,000,000,000,000,000,000,000,000.

34. Divide the following numeral by the use of the comma. Does this help you read it?
75692874205963429185208911576 2017215762.

35. Copy and complete so that the set is a set of equivalent fractions.
$$\left\{ \frac{6}{9}, \frac{?}{18}, \frac{?}{27}, \frac{?}{36}, \frac{?}{63}, \frac{?}{90}, \cdots \right\}.$$

36. Does $\left\{-4, -\pi, -3, -\dfrac{7}{3}, -\sqrt{2}, -2, -1, -0.5, 0, 0.5, 1, \sqrt{2}, 2, \dfrac{7}{3}, 3, \pi, 4\right\}$ represent a set of real numbers?

Determine which of the following statements is true. Give a reason for each answer.

37. $\{[(4\times3)-4]\div3\}\times6 \geq (4\times3)-[(4\div3)\times6]$

38. $9\left[\left(\dfrac{11-4}{3\cdot15}-\dfrac{1}{45}\right)-\dfrac{1}{45}\right]=4\div4$

39. To factor the expression $-2ab+a^2+b^2$,

   Gail wrote: $-2ab+a^2+b^2 = b^2-2ab+a^2 = (b-a)^2$
   Karen wrote: $-2ab+a^2+b^2 = a^2-2ab+b^2 = (a-b)^2$

   The teacher called both answers correct. Explain.

40. Find a single numeral to replace N.

   $$(9\times10^3)+(7\times10)+(8\times\dfrac{1}{10})+(5\times\dfrac{1}{10^2}) = N$$

   Prove each statement. Let $f = \{(x, y): y = a_0x^n+a_1x^{n-1}+\ldots+a_{n-2}x^2+a_{n-1}x+a_n\}$.

41. $f''(x) = n(n-1)a_0x^{n-2}+(n-1)(n-2)a_1x^{n-3}+\ldots+2\cdot1a_{n-2}$.

42. $\dfrac{f''(c)}{2!}$ is the coefficient of $(x-c)^2$ in the expansion of $f(x)$ in powers of $x-c$.

   Compute.

43. $\dfrac{(3.00\times10^{15})(1.53\times10^{-11})}{2.50(10^6)}$

44. $\dfrac{(1.21\times10^4)(6.937\times10^8)}{3.75(10^2)}$

   Simplify.

45. $[3t^2+(^-5)t^3+2t+^-4]+[^-3+(^-2)t+5t^3+(^-7)t^2]$

46. $[(^-1)s^4+7s^3+(^-3)s^2+2s^1+^-10]+[(^-3)s^4+5s^2+11]$

47. What is the sum of the exponential values in

   $s^{1+(-1)+\frac{1}{2}+(-\frac{1}{2})+\frac{1}{4}+(-\frac{1}{4})+\frac{1}{8}+(-\frac{1}{8})}$?

48. Multiply the factors: $(4x^9y)(7x^8y^2)(5x^7y^3)(6x^6y^4)$
   $(2x^5y^5)(x^4y^6)(9x^3y^7)(3x^2y^8)(8xy^9)$.

49. $\displaystyle\lim_{\substack{n\to\infty \\ m\to\infty}} \sum_{i=0}^{i=n}\sum_{j=0}^{j=m} a_{ij} = \lim_{n\to\infty}\sum_0^n a_i \sum_0^n a_i \lim_{m\to\infty}\sum_0^m b_j = AB$

50. How do you add 7 ft 2 in and 9 ft 5 in?

51. If a piece of tape is measured with a 6-inch ruler, how many times must you use the ruler if the tape is 108 inches long?

LESSON 14

CONTRACTIONS AND SHORT-FORM WORDS

§154. Review of Contractions and Short-Form Words: In the absence of specific restrictions on the treatment of contractions and short-form words, English braille rules are applied.

The rules for contractions and short-form words have already been introduced in the following situations:

a. Contractions must be used in a word or part of a word joined to a numeral or to a letter by the hyphen or the dash (see **§7a** and **§32b**).

b. The contractions for "st" and "th" must not be used in an ordinal ending attached to a mathematical expression (see **§27**).

c. Contractions must not be used where contractible letter combinations occur in a mathematical sequence of letters in which each letter has a separate identity (see **§33c**).

d. Contractions must not be used for the abbreviations "in." or "in," which usually means "inches." The "st" contraction may only be used as the abbreviation for "street" or "saint" (see **§37**).

e. The following contractions, whether capitalized, uncapitalized, or italicized, must not be used when in direct contact with a sign of grouping or with transcriber's grouping symbols: the one-cell whole-word alphabet contractions for *but, can, do, . . . , as;* the whole-word lower-sign contractions for *be, enough, were, his, in, to, into, was, by;* the whole- or part-word contractions for *and, for, of, the, with.* Nor may these contractions be used when they are separated from a sign of grouping by a punctuation mark (see **§50** and **§57c**).

f. Contractions must not be used in a combination of letters selected to represent a sign of shape or shape modification (see **§114** and **§116**).

g. Contractions must not be used in a capitalized or uncapitalized word, part of a word, or abbreviation in direct contact with the symbol for the slash line. Contractions may be used if the word, part of a word, or abbreviation is separated from the slash by a sign of grouping which permits the use of the contraction, or by a punctuation mark (see **§137b**).

h. Contractions must not be used in abbreviated function names. An unabbreviated function name must not be contracted in a mathematical context. In particular, the word "arc" must not be contracted when immediately preceded or followed by mathematical symbols (see **§144**).

§155. Additional Rules for Contractions and Short-Form Words:

a. Contractions and short-form words must not be used in a capitalized or uncapitalized word, part of a word, or abbreviation in direct contact with any item listed below or separated from a sign of comparison by a space. This rule applies even when the word or abbreviation is separated from an item by transition to another braille line.

If an expression contains a hyphen or a dash, only the word, part of a word, or abbreviation in direct contact with one of the listed items is subject to this rule.

Contractions may be used in a word, part of a word, or abbreviation separated from any of the listed items by a punctuation mark or a sign of grouping, or in other situations which permit the use of contractions.

i. Contractions and short-form words must not be used in a capitalized or uncapitalized word, part word, or abbreviation in direct contact with any braille indicator other than the capitalization indicator or the italic sign used in English braille.

(1) seven^2

(2)　seven$_3$

(3)　$44_{\text{four}} - 35_{\text{four}} = ?_{\text{four}}$

(4)　Area$_{\square}$PQRS

(5)　$(\text{ten}^2) + 1$

(6)　$(\text{ten})^2 + 1$

(7)　$\dfrac{\text{The length of Side AB}}{\text{The length of Side CD}}$

(8)　$\overline{\text{velocity}}$

(9)　heat $\rightarrow$

(10)　$\textcircled{\text{ten}}$

(11)　

(a picture of a piece of cheese is shown)

(12)　Use a **5-ampere** *electric current.*

(13)　1 inch-pound^2

(14)　100 revolutions-min^2

ii. Contractions and short-form words must not be used in a capitalized or uncapitalized word, part of a word, or abbreviation in direct contact with a numeral.

    (1)   2 Arc AB cosecant — $\dfrac{7}{5}$

    (2)   2 sine x

iii. Contractions and short-form words must not be used in a capitalized or uncapitalized word, part of a word, or abbreviation in direct contact with a single letter or with a sequence of letters in which each letter has a separate identity.

    (1)   a arc sin x

    (2)   xy sine z

iv. Contractions and short-form words must not be used in a word, part of a word, or abbreviation in direct contact with a sign of operation, the radical sign, the general omission symbol, or any other mathematical symbol.

    (1)   rate $\times$ time

    (2)   (Rate $\times$ Time)

    (3)   (rate) $\times$ (time)

    (4)   1 + seven + 1 + seven

    (5)   nine — seven = two

    (6)   (4 $\times$ seven) + (5 $\times$ one)

    (7)   divisor $\times$ partial quotient + remainder

(8) (divisor) $\times$ (partial quotient) + (remainder)

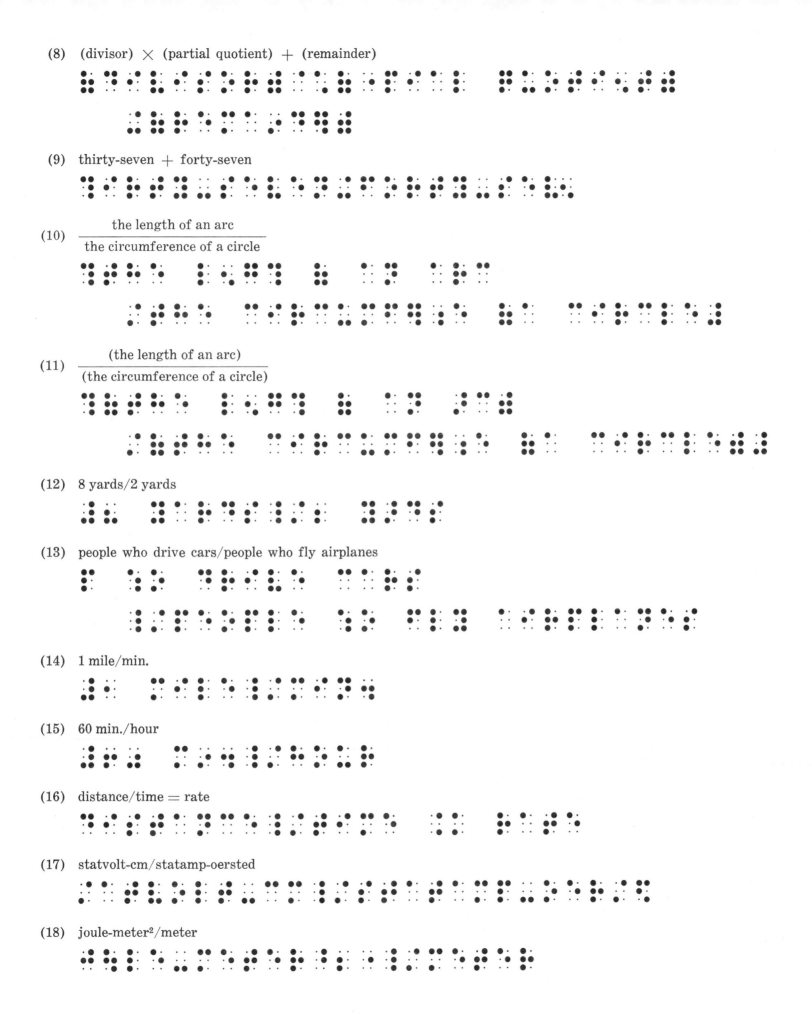

(9) thirty-seven + forty-seven

(10) $\dfrac{\text{the length of an arc}}{\text{the circumference of a circle}}$

(11) $\dfrac{\text{(the length of an arc)}}{\text{(the circumference of a circle)}}$

(12) 8 yards/2 yards

(13) people who drive cars/people who fly airplanes

(14) 1 mile/min.

(15) 60 min./hour

(16) distance/time = rate

(17) statvolt-cm/statamp-oersted

(18) joule-meter^2/meter

(19) 1 foot-pound/hour

(20) $\sqrt{\text{four}}$

(21) $\sqrt{\text{four}}$

(22) eight ? four = twelve

v. Contractions must not be used in a capitalized or uncapitalized word, part of a word, or abbreviation immediately preceding or following a sign of comparison, even when a space separates the sign of comparison from the word, part word, or abbreviation.

(1) 1 hour = 60 minutes

(2) 8 yards/2 yards = 4 yards

(3) 1 min = 60 sec

(4) 1 min. = 60 sec.

(5) (2000 pounds = 1 ton)

(6) 1 horsepower hour = 2.685 $\times$ 10^3 erg

(7) 1 light-year = 9.46 $\times$ 10^{12} km

(8) Let 5y = the smaller number

(9) seven + three = ten

(10) rate × time = distance

⠠⠗⠜⠞⠑ ⠦⠦ ⠞⠊⠍⠑ ⠐⠶ ⠙⠊⠎⠞⠁⠝⠉⠑

(11) (rate) × (time) = (distance)

⠷⠗⠜⠞⠑⠾ ⠦⠦ ⠷⠞⠊⠍⠑⠾ ⠐⠶ ⠷⠙⠊⠎⠞⠁⠝⠉⠑⠾

(12) Length × Width = Area

⠠⠇⠑⠝⠛⠹ ⠦⠦ ⠠⠺⠊⠙⠹ ⠐⠶ ⠠⠜⠑⠁

(13) {all x | each x < 8}

⠨⠷⠁⠇⠇ ⠭ ⠳ ⠑⠁⠡ ⠭ ⠐⠅ ⠼⠓⠨⠾

(14) What is the meaning of ≅?

⠠⠱⠁⠞ ⠊⠎ ⠮ ⠍⠑⠁⠝⠬ ⠷ ⠸⠐⠶⠶⠦

(15) Length of an arc = $\dfrac{n}{360}$ × 2πr

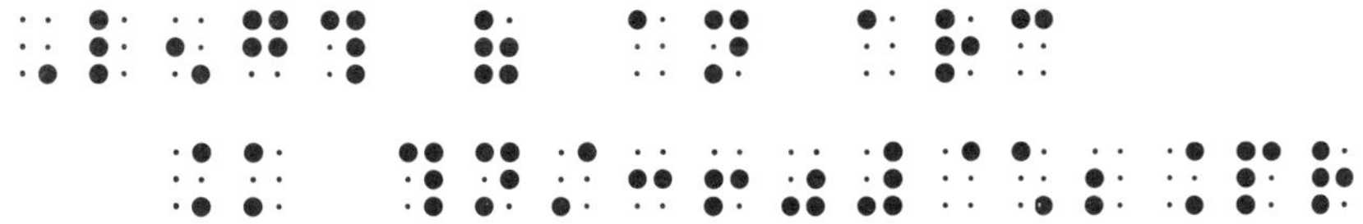

⠠⠇⠑⠝⠛⠹ ⠷ ⠁⠝ ⠜⠉

⠐⠶ ⠹⠝⠌⠼⠉⠋⠚⠼⠦⠦⠼⠃⠨⠏⠗

(16) It is a fundamental principle that ='s added with ='s are =.

⠠⠊⠞ ⠊⠎ ⠁ ⠋⠥⠝⠙⠁⠍⠑⠝⠞⠁⠇ ⠏⠗⠔⠉⠊⠏⠇⠑ ⠞�

⠞⠥⠞ ⠐⠶�⠎ ⠁⠙⠙⠫ ⠺⠊⠹ ⠐⠶�⠎ ⠜⠑ ⠐⠶⠲

(17) Use ">" and "<" in each sentence.

⠠⠥⠎⠑ ⠦⠐⠂⠴ ⠯ ⠦⠐⠅⠴ ⠔ ⠑⠁⠡ ⠎⠫⠞⠫⠉⠑⠲

b. The contractions for *to, into,* and *by* must not be used before any of the items listed below. When the contraction for the word "into" cannot be used, the contraction for "in" may be used in the word "into" unless prohibited by other rules of the code.

i. The contractions for *to, into,* and *by* must not be used before any braille indicator except capitalization indicators or the italic sign used according to the rules of English braille.

(1) Count to 100 by *two's.*

⠠⠉⠳⠝⠞ ⠖⠕ ⠼⠁⠚⠚ ⠃⠽ ⠨⠞⠺⠕�⠎⠲

(2) Ann divided the pie into 4 parts.

⠠⠁⠝⠝ ⠙⠊⠧⠊⠙⠫ ⠮ ⠏⠊⠑ ⠔⠖⠕ ⠼⠙ ⠏⠜⠞⠎⠲

(3) Join A to B and C to D.

⠠⠚⠕⠔ ⠠⠁ ⠖⠕ ⠠⠃ ⠯ ⠠⠉ ⠖⠕ ⠠⠙⠲

(4) ab is parallel to cd.

(5) Name the letters from α to ω.

(6) The vector is denoted by **i**.

(7) Divide $\frac{1}{2}$ by $\frac{1}{4}$.

(8) Add ⁻7 to ⁻4.

(9) ∠A is equal to ∠B.

(10) Is $\overline{AB}$ equal to $\overline{cd}$?

(11) In $.3434\overline{34}$, the recurring digits are shown by $\overline{34}$.

ii. The contractions for *to, into,* and *by* must not be used before a Roman numeral, a single letter, or a sequence of letters in which each letter has a separate identity, whether or not the Roman numeral, the single letter, or the sequence of letters requires the English letter indicator.

(1) The imaginary part is denoted by i = (0, 1).

(2) Is A : B equivalent to C : D?

(3) Draw a line to pq.

(4) AB is parallel to CD.

(5) Is a · b equal to b · a?

(6) Use numerals showing that 10 × 10 is equal to ab × ba.

(7) Explain the change from x̄ to y⃗.

(8) Read Chapters II to VI and IX to X.

(9) Solve examples i to iv.

(10) 17 is equivalent to VII + X.

(11) 17 is equivalent to vii + x.

iii. The contractions for *to*, *into*, and *by* must not be used before a dash, the ellipsis, or the general omission symbol.

(1) 50 divided by _____ equals 25.

(2) The pie is divided into _____ pieces.

(3) 31 added to ... equals 42.

(4) 6 × 4 divided by ... = 8.

(5) 63 divided by ? = 7.

(6) 14 × 4 is equal to ? × 28.

iv. The contractions for *to, into,* and *by* must not be used before any reference symbol or sign of grouping.

(1) Read §14 to §18, and ¶a to ¶d.

(2) Do exercises (1) to (5).

(3) Multiply (6 + 3) by (4 + 2).

v. The contractions for *to, into,* and *by* must not be used before any mathematical symbol of the code.

(1) What is denoted by $.a_1a_2a_3 \ldots$?

(2) Multiply +25 by —5.

(3) Add +4 to +7.

(4) Change > to < in all examples.

(5) If ='s are divided by ='s, the results are =.

(6) Divide by $\sqrt{5}$.

(7) Change the $100 into $5 bills.

(8) Convert each ratio to %.

252

(9) The empty set is denoted by ∅ or by { }.

(10) 1/x tends to ∞ as x → 0.

(11) The indefinite integral is to be denoted by ∫f(x) dx.

(12) The numeral 3 is represented by ///.

vi. The contractions for *to*, *into*, and *by* must not be used before any abbreviated function name or before an unabbreviated function name in mathematical context.

(1) y is proportional to log x.

(2) The ratio is expressed by cos A = .8000.

(3) The ratio is expressed by cosine A = .8000.

vii. The contractions for *to*, *into*, and *by* must not be used before an abbreviation.

(1) Turn to p. 46 to learn to convert 50 kg. into lbs.

(2) Convert mm to m.

(3) Convert 730 days into yrs. to obtain an answer.

viii. The contractions for *to, into,* and *by* must not be used before a word, part of a word, or abbreviation in a context in which contractions are not permitted by any of the other rules of the code.

(1) people who go by car + people who go by train

(2) the people who travel by car/the people who travel by train

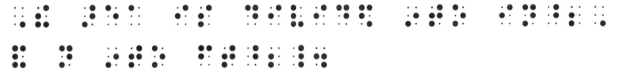

(3) The area is divided into in², and not into ft².

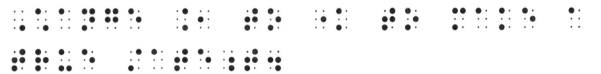

(4) Change > to < to make a true statement.

(5) Replace ? by = or ≠ to make a true sentence.

(6) Compare Seven₂ to Seven₃.

(7) Multiply ten⁵ by ten².

(8) The distance is equal to time × rate.

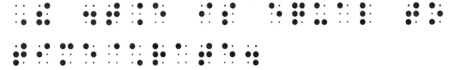

c. Contractions must not be used when they can be mistaken for mathematical expressions or symbols.

(1) Use the ∫ to find the volume.

(2) Can C = 100?

(3) a = b, but b ≠ c.

(4) We see that x = y.

(5) We know < means "is less than".

FORMAT (CONTINUED)

§156. **Special Format Requirements for Linked Expressions:** A linked expression must contain at least one sign of comparison. The part preceding the first sign of comparison is called the anchor. Each remaining part, beginning with a sign of comparison and ending before the next sign of comparison, is called a link.

A linked expression is subject to special braille format requirements if it appears in print in the following way:

a. The expression is displayed and not embedded in the text.

b. Its signs of comparison are vertically aligned, except possibly for the last few, which may occur on the last print line of the expression.

c. No sign of comparison is preceded by any expression on its left, excepting the anchor on the first line and any links on the last line.

$$33\frac{1}{3}\% = \frac{33\frac{1}{3}}{100}$$

$$= \frac{3 \times 33\frac{1}{3}}{3 \times 100}$$

$$= \frac{100}{300} = \frac{1}{3}$$

§157. **Braille Format for Special Linked Expressions:**

a. Under the special format requirements, when a linked expression occurs in unitemized explanatory portions of the text, the anchor must begin in cell 3, and its runovers must begin in cell 7. Each link must begin in cell 5, and its runovers must begin in cell 7.

(1) To factor ab + c² + ac + bc, the terms can be grouped in pairs with a common factor.

$$ab + c^2 + ac + bc = (ab + ac) + (bc + c^2)$$

$$= a(b + c) + c(b + c)$$

$$= (a + c)(b + c).$$

(2) We can reduce $12\frac{1}{2}\%$ to lowest terms in the following way:

$$12\tfrac{1}{2}\% = 12.5\%$$

$$= .125$$

$$= \frac{125}{1000} = \frac{1}{8}$$

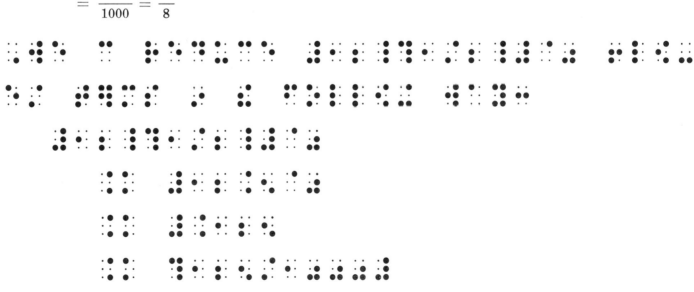

(3) We solve $45\left(\dfrac{1}{18}\right) + 45\left(\dfrac{1}{30}\right) + 45\left(\dfrac{1}{15}\right) - 45\left(\dfrac{1}{5}\right)$ in the following way:

$$45\left(\frac{1}{18}\right) + 45\left(\frac{1}{30}\right) + 45\left(\frac{1}{15}\right) - 45\left(\frac{1}{5}\right)$$

$$= \frac{45}{18} + \frac{45}{30} + \frac{45}{15} - \frac{45}{5}$$

$$= \frac{5}{2} + \frac{3}{2} + 3 - 9$$

$$= \frac{8}{2} + 3 - 9 = 4 + 3 - 9 = -2$$

(In print, the last three links appear on the same line).

b. In an itemized text containing no subdivisions, the anchor must begin in cell 5, and its runovers must begin in cell 9. Each link must begin in cell 7, and its runovers must begin in cell 9.

(1) 1. The example below shows a way of finding 6 × 245.

$$6 \times 245 = (6 \times 200) + (6 \times 40) + (6 \times 5)$$
$$= 1200 + 240 + 30$$
$$= 1470$$

Is there another way to find 6 × 245?

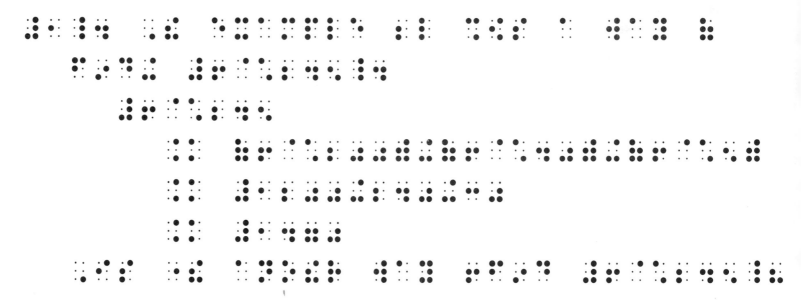

(2) 2. What is the function of the parentheses in the following:

$$(4 \times 10{,}000) + (4 \times 1000) + (4 \times 100) + (4 \times 10) + (4 \times 1)$$
$$= 40{,}000 + 4{,}000 + 400 + 40 + 4$$
$$= 44{,}444$$

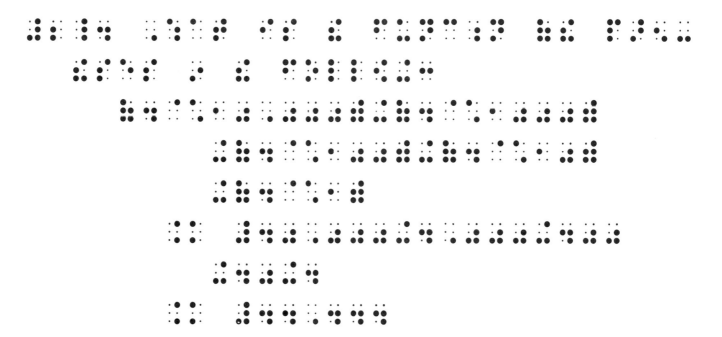

(3) 3. We can find the product of 6 and 44,444 by the distributive principle:

$$6 \times 44{,}444 = 6 \times (40{,}000 + 4{,}000 + 400 + 40 + 4)$$
$$= (6 \times 40{,}000) + (6 \times 4{,}000) + (6 \times 400) + (6 \times 40) + (6 \times 4)$$
$$= 240{,}000 + 24{,}000 + 2{,}400 + 240 + 24$$
$$= 266{,}664$$

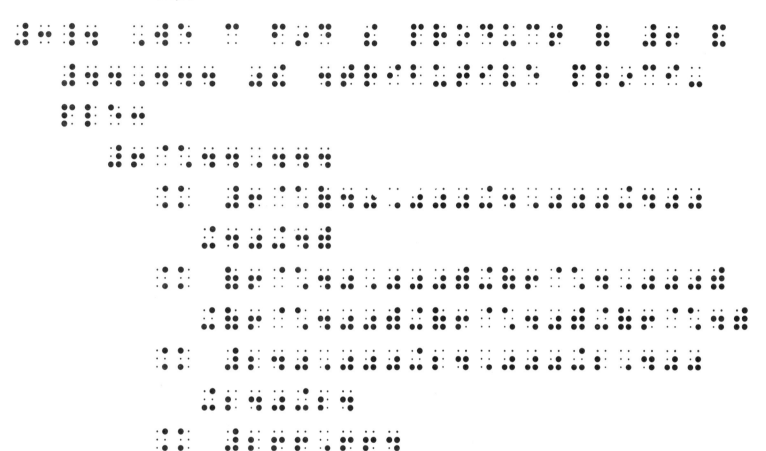

(4)   4. Using the binomial theorem to find 1.1⁵ to three decimal places, we see that

$$1.1^5 = (1 + 0.1)^5$$

$$= 1^5 + 5(1^4)(0.1) + 10(1^3)(0.1)^2 +$$
$$10(1^2)(0.1)^3 + 5(1)(0.1)^4 + (0.1)^5$$

$$= 1 + 0.5 + 0.1 + 0.01 + 0.0005 + 0.00001$$

$$= 1.61051 \approx 1.611.$$

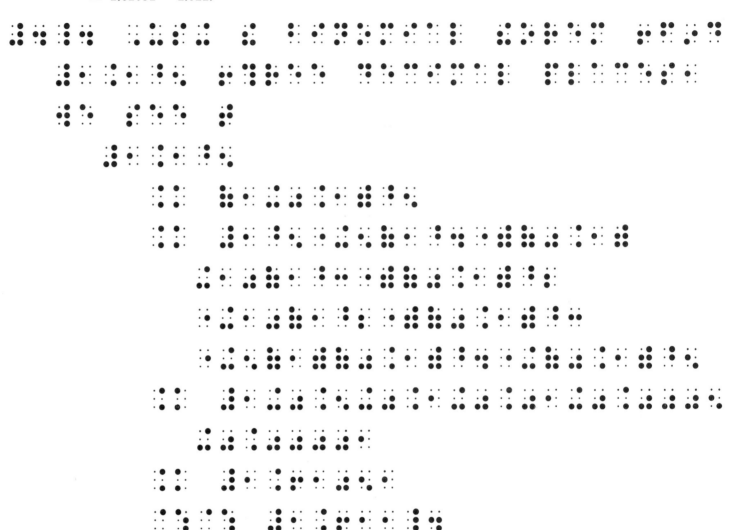

c. In an itemized text containing subdivisions, the anchor must begin in cell 7, and its runovers must begin in cell 11. Each link must begin in cell 9, and its runovers must begin in cell 11.

(1)   1. Study the following work.

(a)   Add the percents to find the sum:

$$75\% + 50\% + 37\frac{1}{2}\% + 33\frac{1}{3}\% + 12\frac{1}{2}\% + 6\frac{1}{4}\%$$

$$= 75 + 50 + 37\frac{6}{12} + 33\frac{4}{12} + 12\frac{6}{12} + 6\frac{3}{12}$$

$$= 214\frac{7}{8} = 214.875$$

(b)   Why is it necessary to use a common denominator?

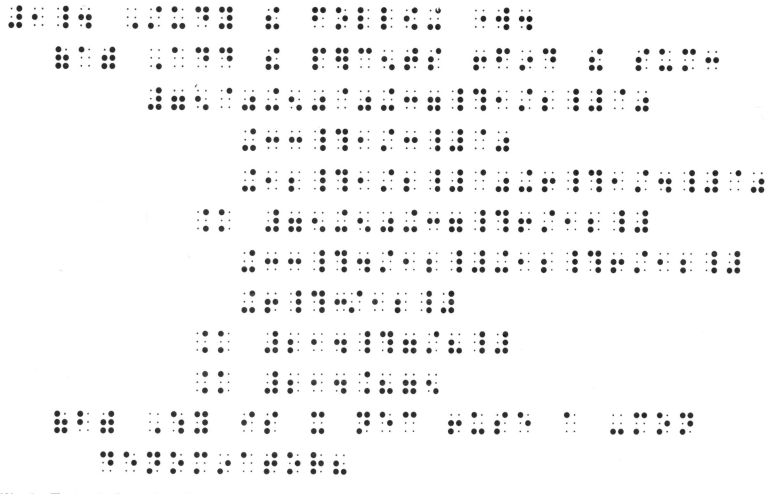

(2) 2. Factor 2a(b — c) — 3x (c — b).

(a) The factors b — c and c — b are divisible by (b — c) since
c — b = (—1)(b — c).

(b) Thus we see
2a(b — c) — 3x(c — b) = 2a(b — c) + 3x(b — c)
= (2a + 3x)(b — c).

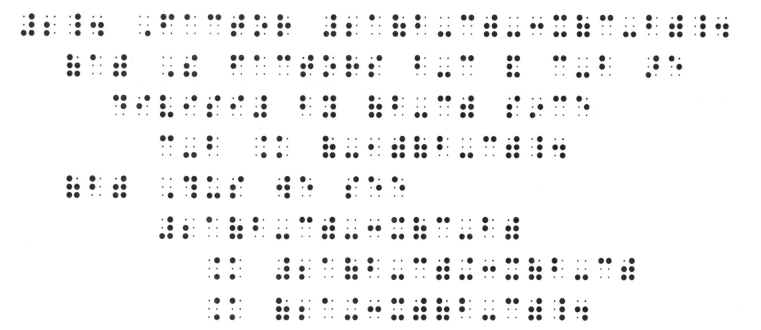

(3) 3. Study the following for given $\triangle$ ABC.

     a. The formula derived below is called the *law of cosines*.

$$b^2 = (a \cos B - c)^2 + (a \sin B - 0)^2$$
$$= a^2 \cos^2 B - 2ac \cos B + c^2 + a^2 \sin^2 B$$
$$= a^2(\sin^2 B + \cos^2 B) - 2ac \cos B + c^2$$
$$= a^2 - 2ac \cos B + c^2$$

     b. The formula is usually written in the form

$$b^2 = a^2 + c^2 - 2ac \cos B.$$

     Explain its use.

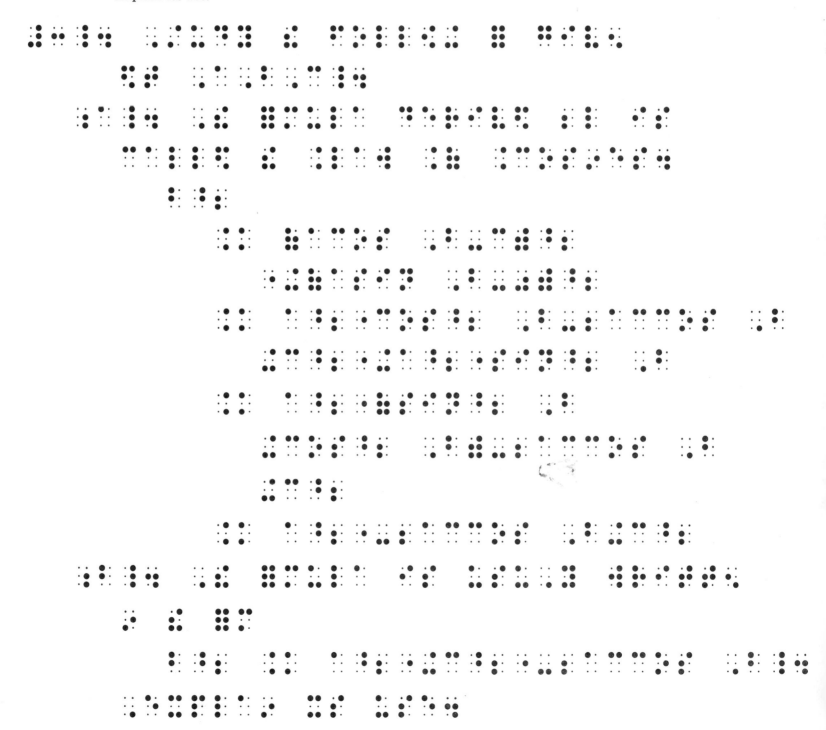

(4)   4. To express $\dfrac{4-2x}{(x^2+1)\,(x-1)^2}$ as a sum of partial fractions, we begin by letting

$$\frac{-2x+4}{(x^2+1)\,(x-1)^2} = \frac{Ax+B}{x^2+1} + \frac{C}{x-1} + \frac{D}{(x-1)^2}.$$

a. Then we have

$$-2x+4 = (Ax+B)\,(x-1)^2 + C\,(x-1)\,(x^2+1) + D\,(x^2+1)$$
$$= (A+C)x^3 + (-2A+B-C+D)x^2 + (A-2B+C)x + (B-C+D).$$

b. Assign a coefficient to each power of x, and complete the solution.

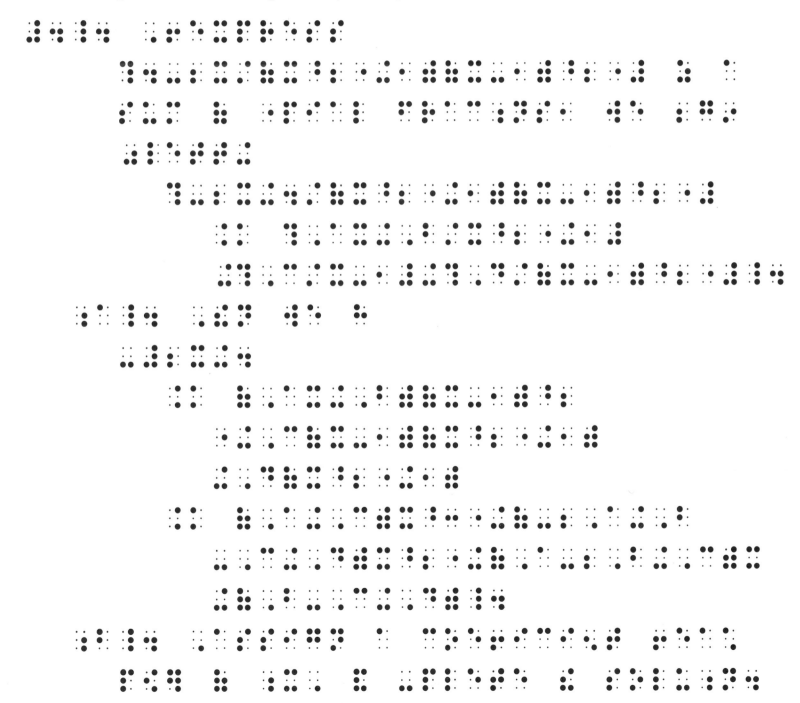

HOMEWORK

Prepare the following homework for submission to your teacher. Proofread carefully.

EXERCISE 14

1. If eight^2 $\times$ eight^3 = eight^5, what is the product of nine^{18} $\times$ nine^7?

2. What is the meaning of the phrase "inches-hour^2"?

3. $\boxed{\text{twenty}}$ $+$ $\boxed{\text{four}}$ $=$ $\bigcirc$

4. Is the following true: In a right triangle
$$(\text{leg})^2 + (\text{leg})^2 = (\text{hypotenuse})^2?$$

5. Solve:

   a. $1 \times \text{seven}^3 + 181$

   b. $(2 \times \text{seven} \times \text{seven}) + (4 \times \text{seven}) + (6 \times \text{one})$

   c. $30_{\text{seven}} + 1_{\text{seven}}$

   d. $(64)_{\text{eight}} + (42)_{\text{eight}}$

6. Find the frequency of the wave whose equation is given.
$$v = 5 \text{ sine } 120\pi t$$

7. Prove the identity.
$$\text{tangent } x \text{ sine } x = \text{secant } x -\text{-cosine } x$$

8. length $\times$ width $= \dfrac{\text{volume}}{\text{height}}$

9. If 2 is the multiplier, 3 is the multiplicand, and 6 is the product, their relationship may be stated as follows:
$$\text{mulitplier} \times \text{multiplicand} = \text{product}.$$

   Do you see that the relationship in a division example is:
$$\text{product} \div \text{multiplier} = \text{multiplicand}?$$

10. The volume of a right circular cone is denoted by the formula
$$\text{Volume} = \frac{(\text{area})(\text{height})}{3}.$$

11. You can find the rate of climb of an airplane by using the formula $r = \dfrac{33,000p}{w}$. In this formula, if r = the rate of climb in feet per second and p = the power of the engine, will w = the weight of the airplane in pounds? (33,000 is exact.) Find r if p = 1500 and w = 20,000 (to two significant digits).

12. The 2 boys can count to 1,000 and the 3 girls can count to 10,000.

13. Multiply 6 by 2, by 3, by 4, and so on until you find a number that is a multiple of 3 and 5.

14. Use the number line to add $+4$ to $+7$.

15. Instead of dividing 6 by $\dfrac{1}{2}$, can you multiply 6 by $\dfrac{2}{1}$?

16. If 1 kg. is about 2.2 lb., then 1 lb. is approximately equal to .454 kg. Then a pound is equivalent to how many grams?

17. Is line AB equal to CD? Is line ab equal to cd?

18. Use numerals and the symbols $>$, $<$ to write two true statements about the cardinal numbers in the pair of sets below:

   R = {Roger, Robert, Richard, Rufus}

   S = {Sally, Sandra, Sylvia, Sarah}

19. a. Add $^-119$ to $^-67$.

   b. Add $^-.38$ to $^-.42$.

20. What is the value assigned to π in section 15-3 of the text?

21. Find the answer in sections VI to X.

22. Find the quotients and remainders.

   a. 405 into 815,245 is equal to _____ with remainder _____.

   b. 588 into 2,755,000 is equal to __?__ with remainder __?__.

   c. 118,422 divided by 6025 is equal to ... with remainder ....

23. In §1 to §5 we studied fractions.

24. $(7 + 3)$ to $(7 + 5)$ are names for certain numerals. Find the three names and then multiply each by (-7).

25. Divide $\sqrt{4}$ by $\sqrt{9}$.

26. The function of x is denoted by cos x.

27. Turn 657 mins. into hrs. and then turn these hrs. into parts of days.

   To express $(-1 + i)^{-4}$ in the form a + bi, we first express $-1 + i$ in polar form:

   $$-1 + i = \sqrt{2}\ (\cos 135° + i \sin 135°).$$

We then apply the extended DeMoivre's theorem to obtain

   $$(-1 + i)^{-4} = (\sqrt{2})^{-4}\ [\cos(-4 \cdot 135°) + i \sin(-4 \cdot 135°)]$$

   $$= \frac{1}{4}\ [\cos(-540°) + i \sin(-540°)]$$

   $$= \frac{1}{4}\ (\cos 180° + i \sin 180°) = -\frac{1}{4} + 0i.$$

$\therefore (-1 + i)^{-4} = -\dfrac{1}{4} + 0i$ is the answer.

28. The distributive axiom enables you to simplify products of radical expressions.

   $$3\sqrt{2}\ (5\sqrt{3} + 2\sqrt{5})$$

   $$= (3\sqrt{2})\ (5\sqrt{3}) + (3\sqrt{2})\ (2\sqrt{5})$$

   $$= 15\sqrt{6} + 6\sqrt{10}$$

29. Find the distance between A(—1, 3) and B(4, —6).

    a. The distance between A and B is

$$d(A, B) = \sqrt{[4 - (-1)]^2 + [(-6) - 3]^2}$$
$$= \sqrt{(5)^2 + (-9)^2}$$
$$= \sqrt{106}.$$

    b. Similarly, the distance between B and A is shown to be

$$d(B, A) = \sqrt{[(-1) - 4]^2 + [3 - (-6)]^2}$$
$$= \sqrt{(-5)^2 + (9)^2}$$
$$= \sqrt{106}.$$

LESSON 15

INTRODUCTION TO SPATIAL ARRANGEMENTS

§158. Spatial Arrangements: Spatial arrangement is required with material arrayed on more than one line in print, as in addition, subtraction, multiplication, division, and determinants and matrices.

§159. Blank Lines With Spatial Arrangements: One blank line must be left above and below a spatial arrangement, even when it directly precedes or follows the line indicating a new ink-print page. If a running head is used, a blank line must be left between it and the spatial arrangement. However, no blank line is required if the spatial arrangement begins at the top or ends at the bottom of the braille page.

§160. Nonuse of Numeric Indicator: The numeric indicator must not be used in aligned arrangements of columns for addition, subtraction, multiplication, division, or other material aligned for computation.

§161. Spatial Arrangements With Addition and Subtraction:

    a. The separation line is composed of a line of dots 2-5. The line must extend one cell to the left and to the right of the longest entry appearing above or below it.

$$
\begin{array}{r}
24 \\
35 \\
\hline
59
\end{array}
$$

(1)

⠀⠃⠙
⠀⠉⠑
⠒⠒⠒⠒
⠀⠑⠊

$$
\begin{array}{r}
900 \\
125 \\
\hline
1025
\end{array}
$$

(2)

⠀⠊⠚⠚
⠀⠁⠃⠑
⠒⠒⠒⠒⠒⠒
⠁⠚⠃⠑

b. In spatial arrangements for addition and subtraction, the corresponding digits, commas, decimal points, fractions, and interior signs of operation or comparison must be vertically aligned one below the other unless they have been intentionally misaligned as an exercise for the student.

(1)   .36
       7.02
       3.04
       ——

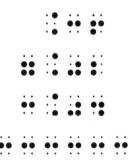

(2) 3,854
       602
     5,918
     ——

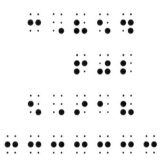

(3)   4x+20y+6z
    18x   —9z
         5y+4z
     ——————

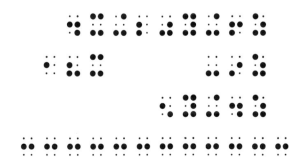

(4) Arrange the digits for proper place value.

25.92
10.4
3.796
‾‾‾‾

c. A plus, minus, or dollar sign must be placed in the same position as in ink-print. The dollar sign or sign of operation must be placed to the left, one cell beyond the largest numeric entry appearing *above* the separation line. If there is an answer, part of it may be shown beneath the plus, minus, or dollar sign.

(1)   4391
    +   81
    ‾‾‾‾‾‾

(2)   718
    —437
    ‾‾‾‾‾

(3)   900
    +100
    ─────
    1000

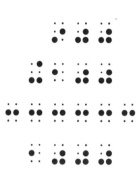

(4)   25.763
    — 4.239
    ───────
    21.524

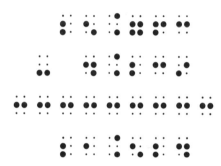

(5) $40
      3
     ───

(6) $ .36
     7.02
     3.04
     ────

270

(7) $ .36
     7.02
    +3.04
     ——————

⠀⠨⠼⠀⠀⠀⠨⠼⠒⠖
⠀⠶⠶⠀⠀⠼⠛⠲⠆⠂
⠀⠼⠒⠲⠲⠆⠲⠲

⠦⠦⠦⠦⠦⠦⠦⠦⠦

(the plus sign appears beneath the dollar sign in print)

(8) $1.45
     — 1.05
     ——————
     $ .40

(the minus sign appears to the left of the dollar sign in print)

(9) $1.45
     —1.05
     ——————
     $ .40

(the minus sign appears beneath the dollar sign in print)

(10) $5r+6s+17t$
        $-4r-3s$
        _____

⠀⠀⠀⠄⠄ ⠠⠄ ⠠⠂ ⠒⠒ ⠐⠂ ⠒⠂ ⠒⠄ ⠐⠂ ⠠⠂ ⠒⠒

⠀⠀⠀⠠⠂ ⠒⠒ ⠠⠄ ⠒⠄ ⠒⠒ ⠐⠂

⠀⠀⠀⠒⠒ ⠒⠒ ⠒⠒ ⠒⠒ ⠒⠒ ⠒⠒ ⠒⠒ ⠒⠒ ⠒⠒ ⠒⠒ ⠒⠒ ⠒⠒

d. When spatial arrangements contain omissions, only the general omission symbol may be used. The long dash and ellipsis must never be used. The same number of omission symbols as in ink-print should be used.

(1)   43
       2?
       7?
       109
       _____
       257

⠀⠀⠀⠒⠄ ⠒⠒

⠀⠀⠀⠂⠄ ⠒⠒

⠀⠀⠀⠒⠒ ⠒⠒

⠀⠀⠀⠐⠂ ⠒⠄ ⠐⠂

⠀⠀⠀⠒⠒ ⠒⠒ ⠒⠒ ⠒⠒ ⠒⠒

⠀⠀⠀⠒⠄ ⠐⠂ ⠒⠒

(2)   432
       +???
       _____
       1096

⠀⠀⠀⠒⠄ ⠒⠒ ⠂⠄

⠀⠀⠀⠠⠄ ⠒⠒ ⠒⠒ ⠒⠒

⠀⠀⠀⠒⠒ ⠒⠒ ⠒⠒ ⠒⠒ ⠒⠒ ⠒⠒

⠀⠀⠀⠂⠄ ⠒⠄ ⠒⠄ ⠒⠒

(3) $7.18
     — ...
     ─────
     $5.20

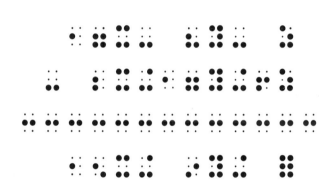

(the ellipsis is shown in print)

(4) 17x— 8y— z
     — 2x+17y+6z
     ─────────────
     15x+ 9y+____

(the long dash is shown in print)

e. When abbreviations occur in spatially arranged addition and subtraction, they are vertically aligned and transcribed according to the rules for abbreviations.

(1) 4 ft 7 in
     +3 ft 5 in
     ──────────

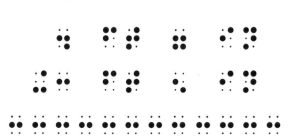

(2)

```
  4 ft.  7 in.
+ 3 ft.  5 in.
─────────────
  7 ft. 12 in.
```

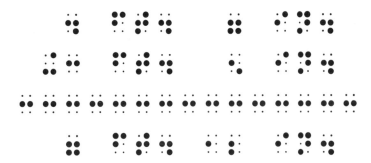

(3)

```
  9.5 m. 4 cm.
─ 6   m. 1 cm.
─────────────
```

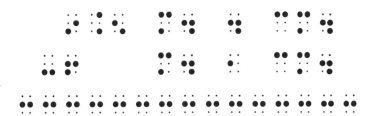

(4)
```
3.600 m
3.6    cm
───────
```

(5)
$$1\frac{2}{3} \text{ yr}$$

$$+5\frac{5}{6} \text{ yr}$$
───────

(6)   3 bu. 1 pk. $=$ 2 bu. 5 pk.
      $-$1 bu. 3 pk. $=$ 1 bu. 3 pk.
      _____
                      1 bu. 2 pk.

⠀⠒⠀⠀⠸⠑⠀⠊⠒⠀⠭⠀⠀⠒⠀⠀⠛⠛⠀⠊⠒⠀⠭⠀⠀⠒⠒⠀⠀⠑⠀⠛⠛⠀⠊⠒⠀⠭⠀⠀⠒⠀⠀⠛⠛⠀⠊⠒⠀⠭

⠠⠒⠀⠸⠑⠀⠊⠒⠀⠭⠀⠀⠒⠒⠀⠛⠛⠀⠊⠒⠀⠭⠀⠀⠒⠒⠀⠀⠑⠀⠛⠛⠀⠊⠒⠀⠭⠀⠀⠒⠒⠀⠛⠛⠀⠊⠒⠀⠭

⠒⠒⠒⠒⠒⠒⠒⠒⠒⠒⠒⠒⠒⠒⠒⠒⠒⠒⠒⠒⠒⠒⠒⠒⠒⠒

                    ⠒⠀⠛⠛⠀⠊⠒⠀⠭⠀⠀⠒⠀⠀⠛⠛⠀⠊⠒⠀⠭

f. In a spatial addition or subtraction arrangement containing fractions, the fraction lines must be vertically aligned. The numerator and denominator must be written unspaced from the fraction line. The corresponding parts of fraction indicators must be vertically aligned. The whole number parts of mixed numbers must also be vertically aligned.

(1) $\dfrac{3}{4}$

      $+\ \dfrac{1}{2}$
      _____

      ⠿⠀⠒⠒⠀⠄⠀⠒⠒⠀⠄

      ⠿⠿⠀⠒⠀⠒⠒⠀⠄⠀⠒⠒⠀⠄

      ⠿⠿⠀⠿⠿⠀⠿⠿⠀⠿⠿⠀⠿⠿⠀⠿⠿⠀⠿⠿⠀⠿⠿

(2)   1/2
      $+$ 3/4
      _____

      ⠄⠀⠀⠄⠒⠀⠄

      ⠿⠀⠿⠿⠀⠄⠒⠀⠿⠿

      ⠿⠀⠿⠿⠀⠿⠿⠀⠿⠿⠀⠿⠿⠀⠿⠿⠀⠿⠿

275

(3)

$$\frac{12}{16}$$

$$-\ \frac{3}{16}$$

_____

$$\frac{9}{16}$$

⠿ ⠒ ⠂ ⠇ ⠆ ⠣ ⠰
⠰ ⠿ ⠣ ⠂ ⠆ ⠣ ⠰
⠿ ⠿ ⠿ ⠿ ⠿ ⠿ ⠿ ⠿ ⠿ ⠿
⠿ ⠒ ⠇ ⠂ ⠣ ⠰

(4)

$$\frac{12}{16}$$

$$\frac{5}{6}$$

_____

⠿ ⠒ ⠂ ⠆ ⠂ ⠣ ⠰
⠿ ⠇ ⠂ ⠆ ⠰
⠿ ⠿ ⠿ ⠿ ⠿ ⠿ ⠿ ⠿ ⠿

(5)

$$\frac{1}{2}\ \text{lb.}$$

$$\frac{1}{2}\ \text{lb.}$$

_____

⠿ ⠒ ⠇ ⠆ ⠰ ⠿ ⠿ ⠒
⠿ ⠒ ⠇ ⠆ ⠰ ⠿ ⠿ ⠒
⠿ ⠿ ⠿ ⠿ ⠿ ⠿ ⠿ ⠿ ⠿ ⠿ ⠿

(6)   6 qt. $\dfrac{3}{4}$ pt.

      −1 qt. $\dfrac{2}{4}$ pt.
      _____

       5 qt. $\dfrac{1}{4}$ pt.

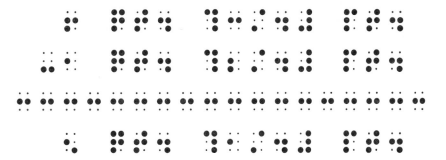

(7) 3/4 g
     3/4 g
     _____

(8) $2\dfrac{2}{4}$

      $+6\dfrac{1}{4}$
      _____

       $8\dfrac{3}{4}$

(9) $\qquad 2\dfrac{15}{16}$

$\qquad +10\dfrac{5}{8}$

(10) $\qquad 1\dfrac{5}{12}$

$\qquad +6\dfrac{5}{12}$

$\qquad 7\dfrac{10}{12} = 7\dfrac{5}{6}$

(11) $\qquad 4\dfrac{4}{8} = \quad 3\dfrac{12}{8}$

$\qquad -2\dfrac{5}{8} \ \div \ -2\dfrac{5}{8}$

$\qquad\qquad\qquad 1\dfrac{7}{8}$

(12)   8 min $6\frac{3}{10}$ sec

　　　$+1$ min $5\frac{2}{10}$ sec
　　　───────────

　　　9 min $11\frac{5}{10}$ sec

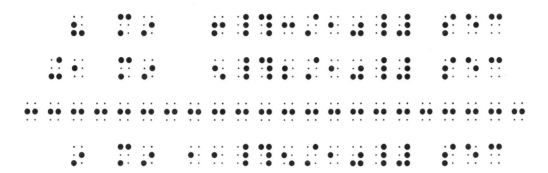

(13) $\frac{3}{8}$

　　$9\frac{1}{8}$
　　───

(14) $5\frac{1}{2}$

　　　$\frac{11}{12}$
　　　───

(15)   216

$$\frac{3}{4}$$

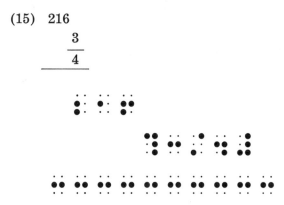

(16)   216

$$\frac{3}{4}$$

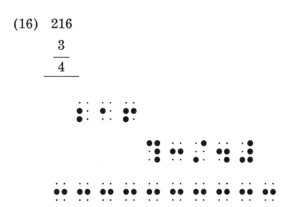

(the fraction is shown directly beneath the whole number in print)

(17)   216

$$\frac{3}{4}$$

$$216\frac{3}{4}$$

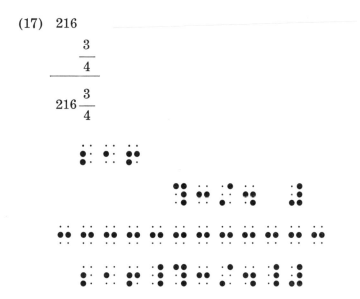

    g. In polynomials arranged spatially for addition or subtraction, each term, including its signs of operation, coefficients, letters, superscript, subscript, and baseline indicators, must be vertically aligned. When the baseline indicator is required, it must be placed in the first possible position consistent with this alignment. The corresponding symbols in each coefficient and superscript must be aligned vertically.

(1)
$$3a^2b^2-2ab-2b+1$$
$$-5a^2b^2-3ab+\ b+7$$
$$\overline{-2a^2b^2-5ab-\ b+8}$$

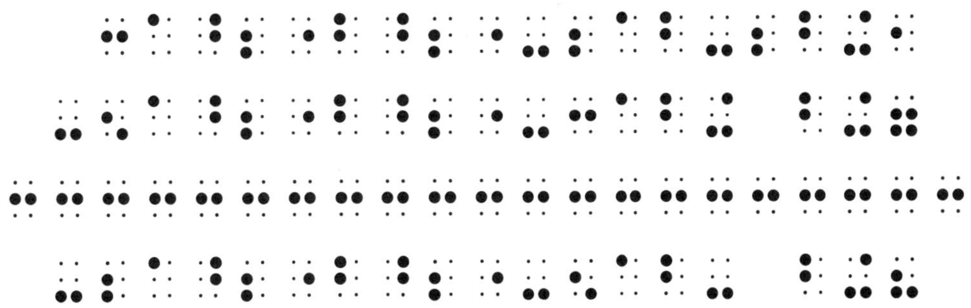

(2)
$$3x^2\qquad\ +2$$
$$x^2+4xy-5$$
$$\overline{4x^2+4xy-3}$$

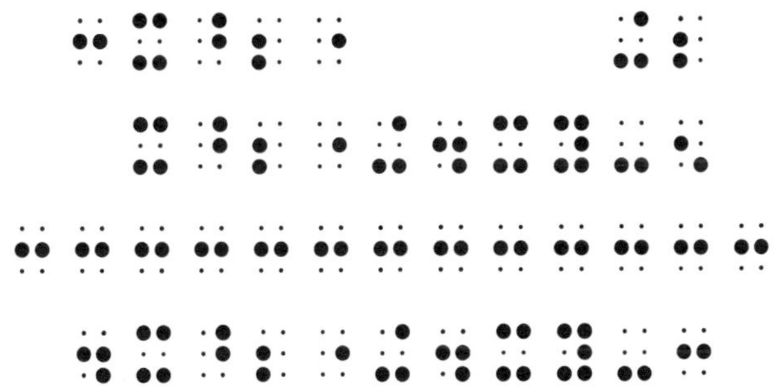

§162. Carried Numbers With Addition:

a. Carried Number Indicator for Addition
(varying in length)

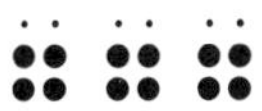

Carried numbers should appear in the same columnar position as in ink-print. A line of carried number indicators, the same length as the separation line, must be inserted between the carried numbers and the first line of the addition.

(1)
$$\overset{1\ 1}{213}$$
$$+\ 87$$
$$\overline{300}$$

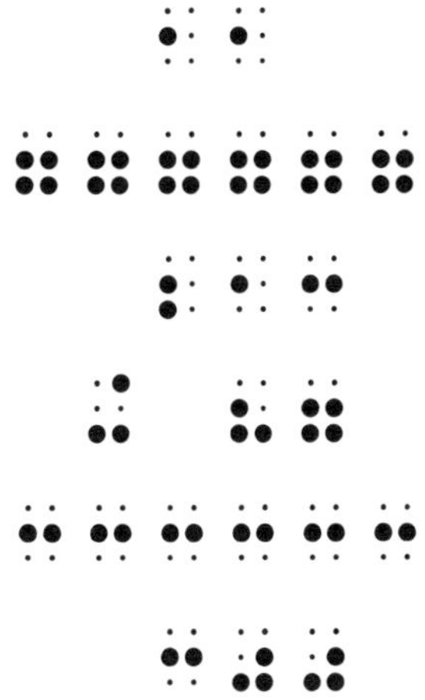

§163. Spatial Arrangement With Multiplication: In a spatial arrangement with multiplication, the multiplier and multiplicand must be aligned as in ink-print. In particular, dollar signs, commas, and decimal points should correspond to the ink-print placement. The multiplication sign, if shown in print, must immediately precede the multiplier. The separation line (dots 2-5) must extend one cell to the left and to the right of the longest line above or below it. If there is more than one separation line, each must be the same length. In multiplication, the general omission symbol, not the ellipsis or long dash, must be used in accordance with **§161d.**

(1)
```
  2704
 ×12
 ─────
  5408
 2704
 ─────
 32448
```

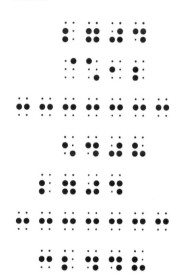

(2)
```
  132
 ×300
 ─────
 39600
```

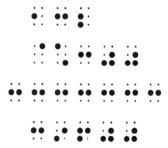

(3)
```
  $421
  ×6
 ─────
 $2526
```

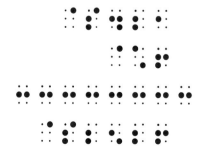

(4) $98
×100

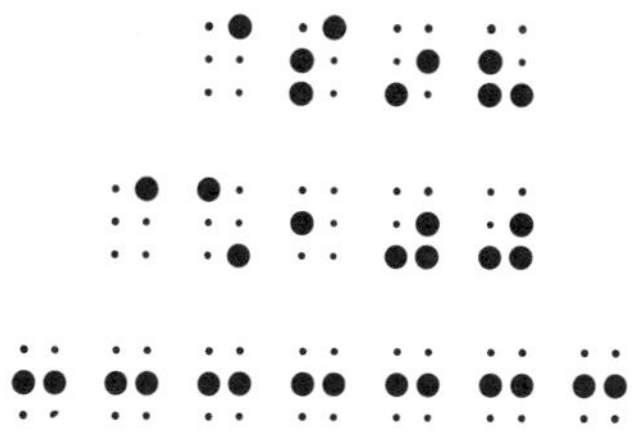

(5) 12.23
×15.3

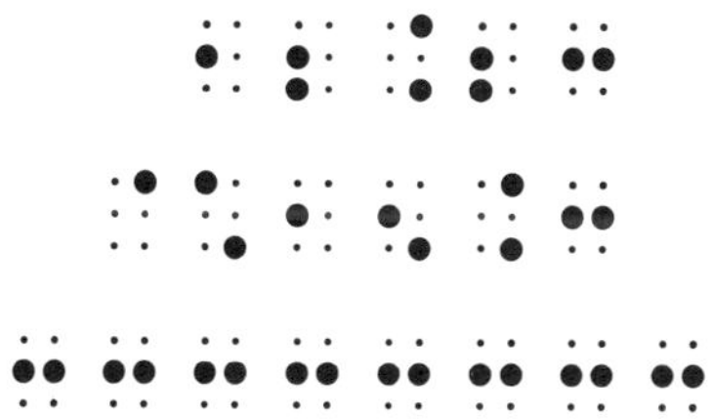

(6) 1,623
×5.27

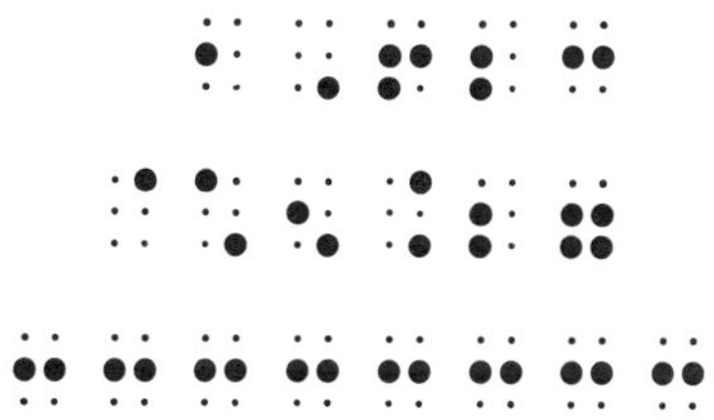

(7) 148
×15

7?0
?48

?2?0

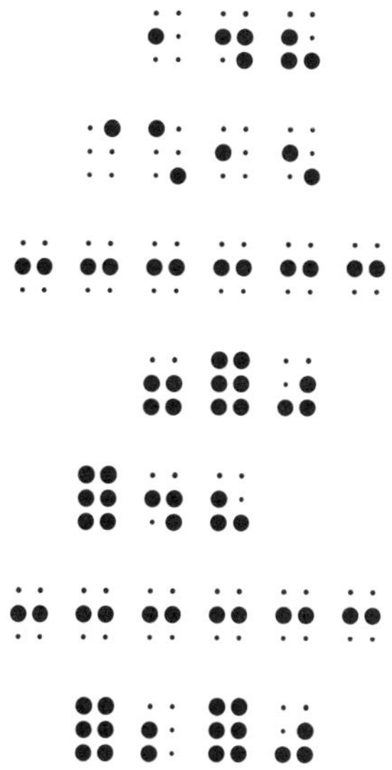

a. If the multiplication contains fractions, mixed numbers, or polynomials, its terms and indicators must be aligned vertically.

(1)
$$\frac{11}{12}$$
$$\times \frac{3}{4}$$

⠿⠿⠿⠿⠿⠿⠿⠿⠿⠿⠿ (braille)

(2)
$$1\frac{1}{2}$$
$$\times \frac{3}{8}$$

⠿⠿⠿⠿⠿⠿⠿⠿⠿⠿ (braille)

(3)
$$54$$
$$\times 2\frac{3}{4}$$
$$40\frac{1}{2}$$
$$108$$
$$148\frac{1}{2}$$

(braille)

(4) $8r +\ 9s$
  $5r -\ 6s$
  _____

  $40r^2 + 9rs$
  $\quad\ -48rs - 54s^2$
  _____

  $40r^2 - 39rs - 54s^2$

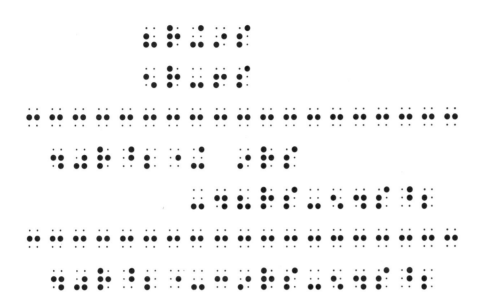

b. If a comma or a decimal point appears in the answer, the corresponding cells in the partial products above it should be left blank.

(1) $\quad$ 5,009
  $\quad \times .27$
  _____

  $\quad$ 35063
  $\quad$ 10018
  _____

  $\quad$ 1,352.43

c. In multiplication with subscripts denoting nondecimal bases, the partial products should be aligned for addition, and the subscript indicators should be vertically aligned immediately to the right of the addition arrangement.

(1)

$$54_{\text{eight}}$$
$$\times 23_{\text{eight}}$$
$$\overline{}$$
$$204_{\text{eight}}$$
$$130_{\text{eight}}$$
$$\overline{}$$
$$1504_{\text{eight}}$$

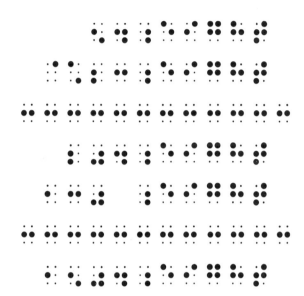

Division Signs

Curved Division Sign on Left, Separation Line Above	$\big)\overline{}$	⠿⠿⠿
Curved Division Sign on Right, Separation Line Above	$\overline{}\big($	⠿⠿⠿
Curved Division Signs on Left and Right, Separation Line Above	$\big)\overline{}\big($	⠿⠿⠿
Straight or Slant Division Sign on Left, Separation Line Above	$\big\lceil\overline{}$ or $\diagup\overline{}$	⠿⠿⠿

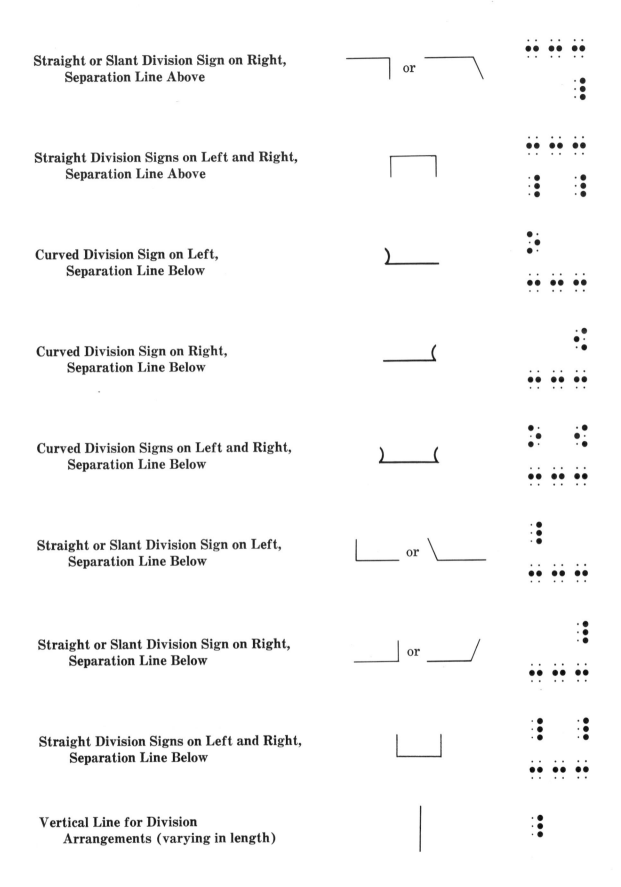

Straight or Slant Division Sign on Right, Separation Line Above	⌐ or ⌐
Straight Division Signs on Left and Right, Separation Line Above	⌐
Curved Division Sign on Left, Separation Line Below	)
Curved Division Sign on Right, Separation Line Below	(
Curved Division Signs on Left and Right, Separation Line Below	) (
Straight or Slant Division Sign on Left, Separation Line Below	⌐ or \
Straight or Slant Division Sign on Right, Separation Line Below	⌐ or /
Straight Division Signs on Left and Right, Separation Line Below	⌐
Vertical Line for Division Arrangements (varying in length)		

§164. Spatial Arrangement With Division: In spatial arrangements for division, the dividend and the partial products and differences must be aligned as in ink-print. The quotient must also be aligned with the dividend as in ink-print unless it has been intentionally misaligned as an exercise for the student.

a. The appropriate division symbol (⠊ , ⠱ , or ⠣) must be placed between the divisor and dividend as well as between the divisor and the quotient if they appear on the same line in ink-print. The horizontal line sometimes placed under the divisor as part of the ink-print sign should not be shown.

b. Each separation line (dots 2-5) must begin at the division sign and end at another division sign if it appears in ink-print. If the other division sign is not shown, each separation line must end one cell beyond the overall arrangement. All separation lines must be the same length.

(1)   7$\overline{)49}$

(2) $\dfrac{7}{49\,(7}$

(3)   7$\overline{)49}$(7

(4) $6\,\overline{\lceil 72}$ with quotient 12

(5) $\overline{72}\rceil 6$ with quotient 12

288

(6) 6 $\overline{|72|}$ 12

⠿ ⠿ ⠿ ⠿

⠿ ⠿ ⠿ ⠿ ⠿ ⠿ ⠿

(7) $10\overline{)110}$
          $\overline{11}$

(8) $\dfrac{110(10}{11}$

(9) $10\overline{)110}(11$

(10) $15\,\underline{|\,30}$
           $\overline{2}$

(11) $\dfrac{30 \mid 15}{2}$

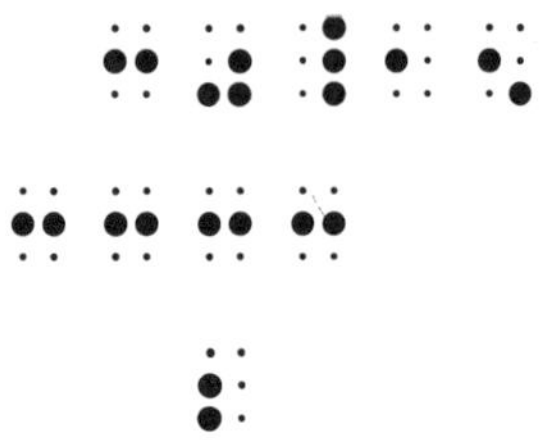

(12) $15 \mid 30 \mid 2$

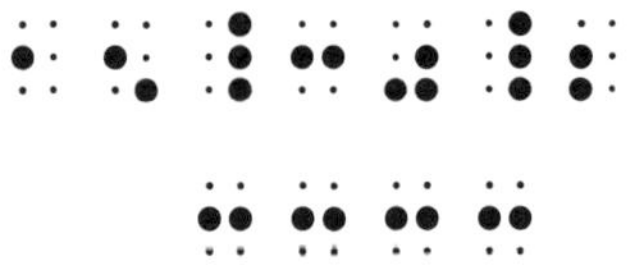

        $\begin{array}{r} 123 \\ 17\overline{)2091} \\ 17 \\ \hline 39 \\ 34 \\ \hline 51 \\ 51 \\ \hline \end{array}$

(13)

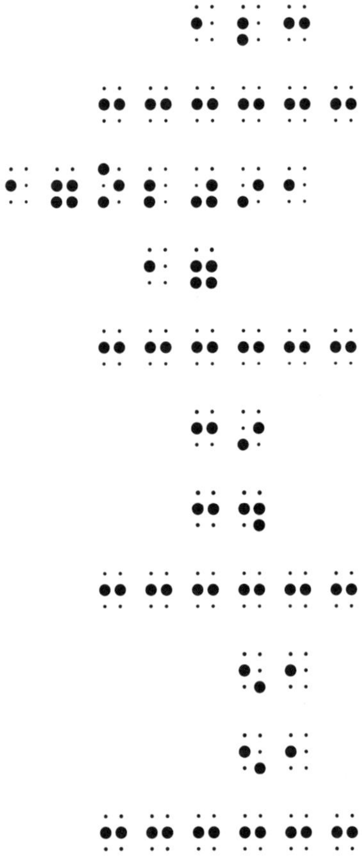

(14)

$$x-3 \overline{\smash{\big)}\ \begin{aligned}&x+\ 4\\ &x^2+\ x-12\end{aligned}}$$

$$\begin{array}{r} x+\ 4 \\ x-3\ \overline{\smash{\big)}\ x^2+\ x-12} \\ \underline{x^2-3x} \\ 4x-12 \\ \underline{4x-12} \\ 0 \end{array}$$

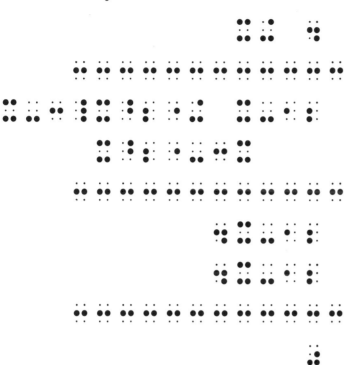

(15)

$$\begin{array}{r} 109 \\ 15\ \overline{\smash{\big)}\ 1635} \\ \underline{15} \\ 135 \\ \underline{135} \end{array}$$

(quotient unaligned in print)

291

c. When commas, decimal points, or carets occur in a dividend, corresponding blank cells should be left throughout the body of the division example, except in the separation lines. Since two cells are required for the caret, the decimal point replacing the caret in the quotient should be placed in the right-hand cell.

(1)

$$\begin{array}{r} \$\ 1.05 \\ 36\overline{)\$37.80} \\ 36 \\ \hline 1\ 80 \\ 1\ 80 \\ \hline \end{array}$$

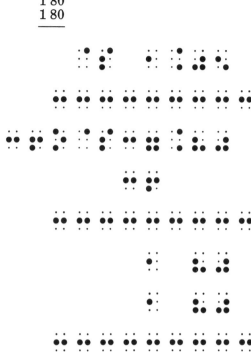

(2)

$$\begin{array}{r} 50.09 \\ 27\overline{)1{,}352.42} \\ 1{,}35 \\ \hline 2\ 42 \\ 2\ 42 \\ \hline \end{array}$$

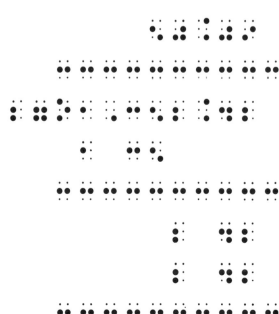

(3)
$$
\begin{array}{r}
11.4 \\
2.5_\wedge\overline{)28.7_\wedge0} \\
25 \\
\hline
37 \\
25 \\
\hline
120 \\
100 \\
\hline
20 \\
\end{array}
$$

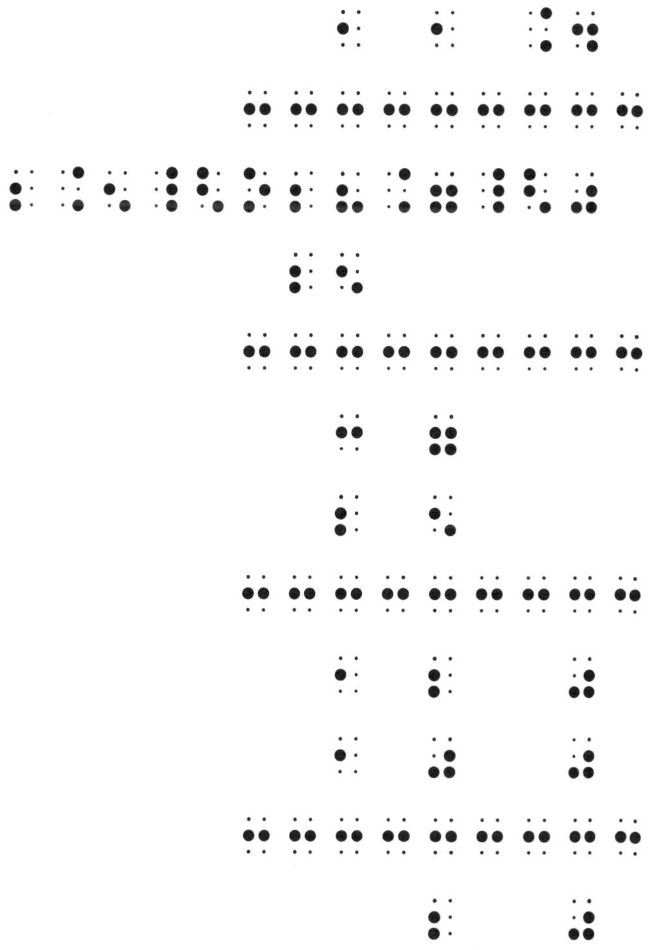

d. The capitalized or uncapitalized "r", indicating a remainder, should be preceded by a space and separated by the multi-purpose indicator (dot 5) from the numeral following it.

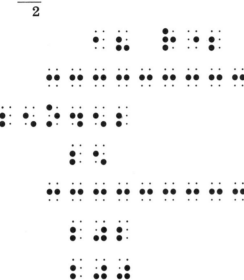

(1)
$$\begin{array}{r} 18\ \text{r2} \\ 25\overline{)452} \\ \underline{25} \\ 202 \\ \underline{200} \\ 2 \end{array}$$

(2)
$$\begin{array}{r} 25\ \text{R12} \\ 17\overline{)437} \\ \underline{34} \\ 97 \\ \underline{85} \\ 12 \end{array}$$

e. A vertical line in a division arrangement may be either drawn or represented by dots 4-5-6. One space must be left between the vertical line and any digit preceding or following it.

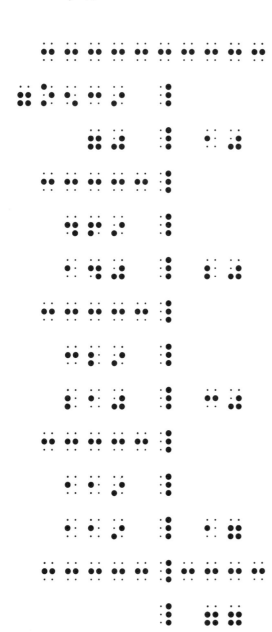

(1)   7)539

      70 | 10

    469

    140 | 20

    329

    210 | 30

    119

    119 | 17

         | 77

f. Carried Numbers in Division: When carried numbers appear in a division arrangement below their columns, the transcriber must insert the indicator for carried numbers between them and their related arrangement. The carried number indicator must have the same length as the separation line. Blank spaces must be left in the dividend to allow separate columns for the carried numbers.

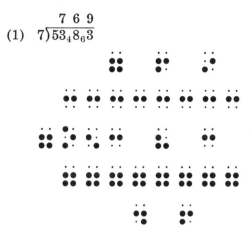

(1)   7)53₄8₆3 with 7 6 9 above

g. If the division arrangement shows only a divisor and a dividend, and the divisor and dividend are composed entirely of numerals, the arrangement must not be regarded as spatial. It is not necessary to show the separation line or to leave a blank line above or below the arrangement. The numeric indicator must be used where required according to other rules of the code.

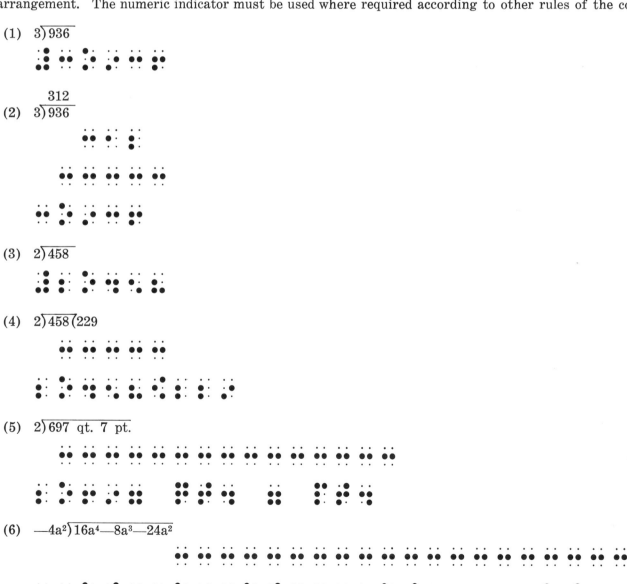

(1)   3)$\overline{936}$

(2)   3)$\overline{936}$ with 312 above

(3)   2)$\overline{458}$

(4)   2)$\overline{458}$(229

(5)   2)$\overline{697}$ qt. 7 pt.

(6) $-4a^2$)$\overline{16a^4-8a^3-24a^2}$

(7) You will notice a numeric relationship between the divisor and the dividend in

5)20

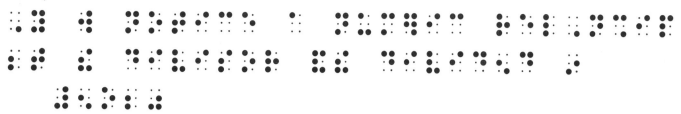

⠿⠿⠿⠿⠿⠿

Square Root Sign √‾‾‾ ⠩ ⠩ ⠩

⠩

§165. **Square Root Spatial Arrangements:** A square root spatial arrangement should conform to the ink-print format, and the procedures used with division arrangements should be applied. The termination indicator is not required in a spatial square root arrangement.

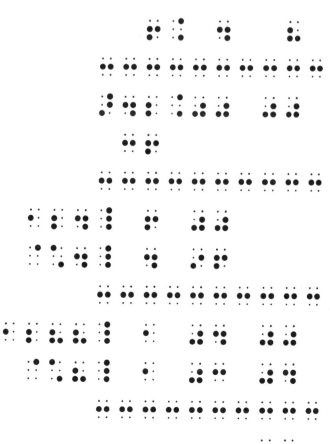

(1)

```
        6. 4 8
   √ 42.00 00
        36
   124 | 6 00
    ×4 | 4 96
  1288 | 1 04 00
    ×8 | 1 03 04
            96
```

§166. Spatial Arrangement for Synthetic Division:

$$\begin{array}{r}
\text{divisor} \quad +2 \enspace\Big|\enspace 1 \ -3 \ +4 \ +5 \quad \text{dividend} \\
+2 \ -2 \ +4 \quad \text{product} \\
\hline
\text{quotient} \qquad 1 \ -1 \ +2 \,\Big|\, +9 \quad \text{remainder}
\end{array}$$

In a synthetic division arrangement, the numerals in the dividend, product, and quotient must be aligned in vertical columns, as in ink-print. Signs of operation, if any, must also be vertically aligned. At least one blank cell must be left between adjacent columns.

A vertical line (dots 4-5-6) must be used between the synthetic divisor and the synthetic division arrangement in the position to the left or right as shown in ink-print. It must begin at the dividend and end at the product. No space should be left between the vertical line and the dividend or divisor. The separation line (dots 2-5) must extend from the vertical line to one cell beyond the synthetic arrangement. The vertical line should be used between the quotient and the remainder, as in ink-print. If the synthetic divisor appears boxed in on two sides, the boxing should be omitted.

(1)
$$\begin{array}{r}
+2 \enspace\Big|\enspace 1 \ -3 \ +4 \ +5 \\
+2 \ -2 \ +4 \\
\hline
1 \ -1 \ +2 \,\Big|\, +9
\end{array}$$

(2)
$$\begin{array}{r}
3 \ -7 \ -1 \ -23 \enspace\Big|\enspace 3 \\
+9 \ +6 \ +15 \\
\hline
3 \ +2 \ +5 \,\Big|\, -\,8
\end{array}$$

(3)
$$\begin{array}{r}
\Big|\,-1 \quad 1+2+2+4 \\
-1-1-1 \\
\hline
1+1+1\,\Big|\,+3
\end{array}$$

(In ink-print, the divisor is boxed in on two sides; there is no vertical line after the divisor.)

(4) $\quad 1 \;+2 \;+2 \;+4 \;\lfloor -2$

$\qquad\quad -2 \;+0 \;-4$

$\qquad \overline{1 \;+0 \;+2 \;+0}$

(In ink-print, the divisor is boxed in on two sides; there is no vertical line after the divisor.)

FORMAT (CONTINUED)

§167. Spatial Arrangements With Numeric or Alphabetic Identifiers: When spatially arranged exercises and the like are identified by numbers or letters, one blank space must be left between the last symbol in the identifier and the symbol furthest left in the overall arrangement including separation lines.

§168. Position of Identifiers: The numeric or alphabetic identifier associated with a spatial arrangement must be positioned as follows:

    a. Addition and Subtraction: The identifier must be placed on the first line of addition and subtraction.

(1) 1.   242
             372
        + 75

(2) (2)   7,562
            + 371

(3) A. $ 7.36
1.50
26.83

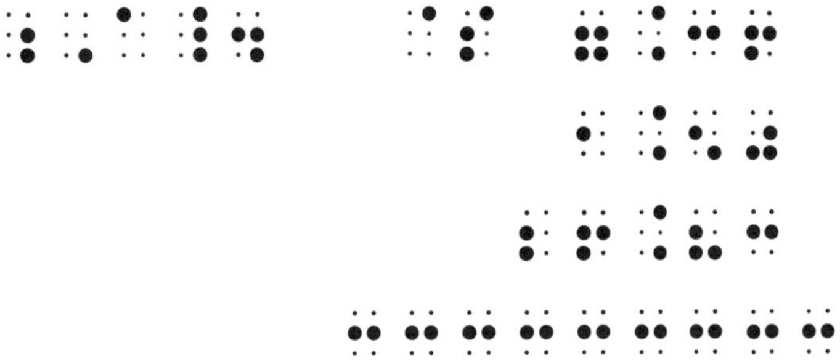

(4) iv. 879
— 63

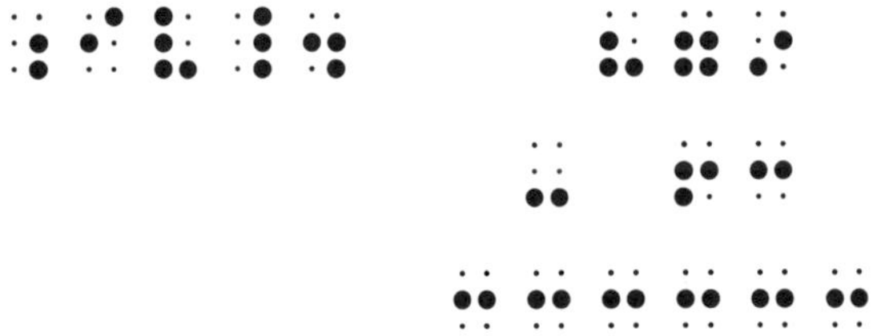

(5) b $9,672,103
— 43,914

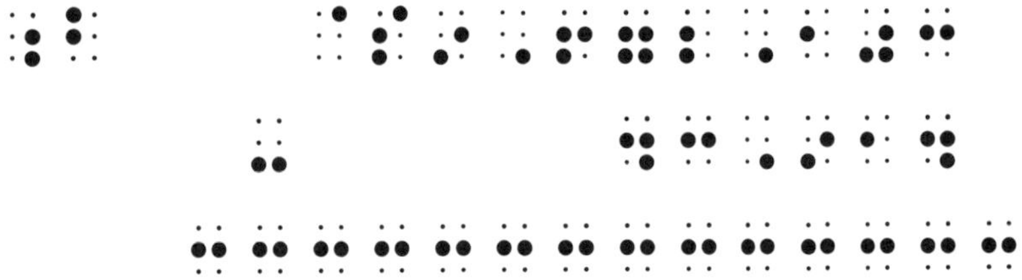

b. Addition With Carried Numbers: The identifier must be placed on the first line of the addition.

(1) A. $\overset{1\,2\,1}{662}$
1075
974

2711

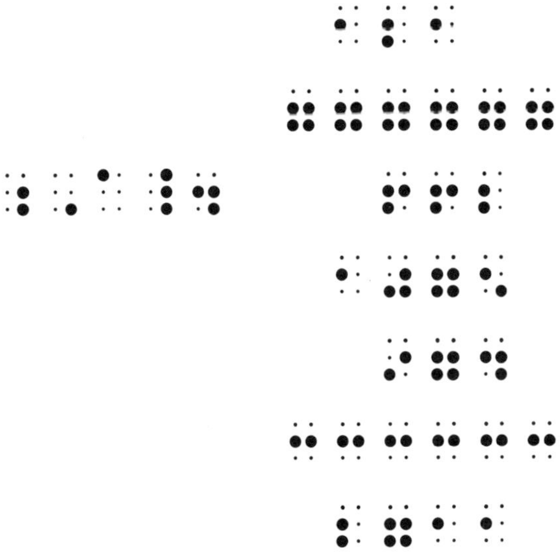

(2) 2. $12.\overset{1\ 1}{4}8$
        16.89
      ―――――
      $29.37

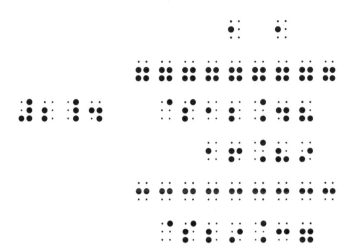

c. **Multiplication**: The identifier must be placed on the first line of the multiplication.

(1) A. 149
         ×700

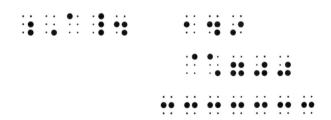

(2) *2 2,973
         ×5.7

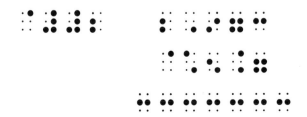

(3) (iii)   197
              ×76
             ‾‾‾‾
             11?2
             1?79
            ‾‾‾‾‾‾
            1?9?2

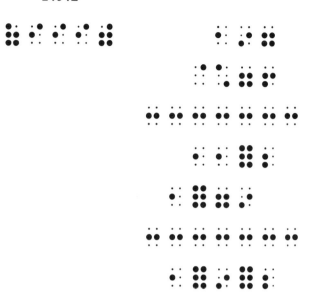

d. Division: The identifier must be placed on the line with the dividend.

```
          11 R44
         ‾‾‾‾‾‾‾
(1)  (a)  63)737
           63
          ‾‾‾‾
          107
           63
          ‾‾‾
           44
```

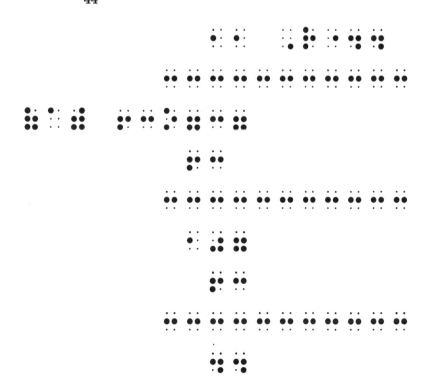

(2) B. 12$\overline{)144}$(12

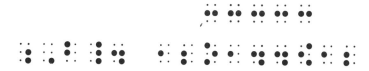

(3) 3. 72$\overline{)109185}$

e. **Radicals**: The identifier must be placed on the line with the radicand.

(1) ☆4. $\sqrt{\begin{array}{c} 7\ \ 4. \\ \hline 54\ 76. \end{array}}$

$\begin{array}{r} 49 \\ 144\overline{\smash{\big|}\ 5\ 76} \\ 5\ 76 \end{array}$

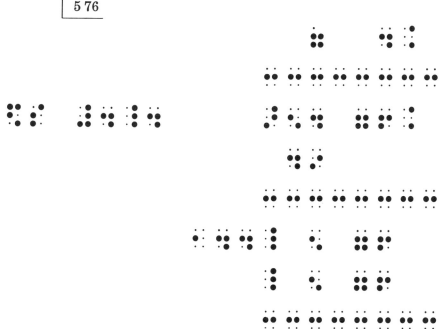

f. **Synthetic Division**: The identifier must be placed on the line with the synthetic dividend.

(1) C. $\begin{array}{rrr|l} 1 & -3 & 2 & 2 \\ & 2 & -2 & \\ \hline 1 & -1 & 0 & \end{array}$

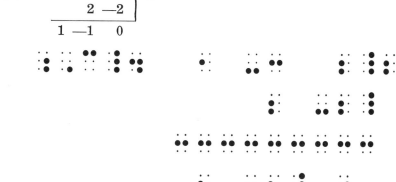

(2) 197. $\boxed{\begin{array}{l}+2\end{array}}$
$$
\begin{array}{rrrr}
1 & +6 & -\ 1 & -30 \\
 & +2 & +16 & +30
\end{array}
$$

§169. **Margins for Instructions Preceding Spatial Arrangements:** When spatially arranged material is preceded by instructions, the instructions must begin in cell 5, and runovers must begin in cell 3. One line must be left blank above such instructions unless they begin a braille page or follow a new page separation line. One blank line must be left between the instructions and the spatial arrangement below them. The last line of an instruction and the spatial arrangement below it must be on the same braille page.

§170. **Placement of Spatial Arrangements on Braille Pages:** When a spatial arrangement begins on the 1st or 2nd line or ends on the 24th or 25th line of a braille page, 3 blank spaces must be left between the symbol furthest to the right of the overall arrangement and the 1st symbol of the page number. The full width of the page may be used for spatial arrangements on lines 3 to 23 only.

(1)

$$
\begin{array}{rl}
S = & 0+1+2+3+4+5+6+7+8+9 \qquad\qquad 9 \\
S = & 9+8+7+6+5+4+3+2+1+0 \\
\hline
2S = & 9+9+9+9+9+9+9+9+9+9
\end{array}
$$

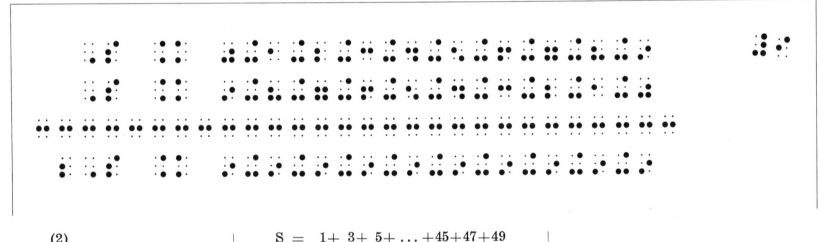

(2)

$$
\begin{array}{rl}
S = & 1+\ 3+\ 5+\ldots+45+47+49 \\
S = & 49+47+45+\ldots+\ 5+\ 3+\ 1 \\
\hline
& \qquad\qquad\qquad\qquad\qquad 62
\end{array}
$$

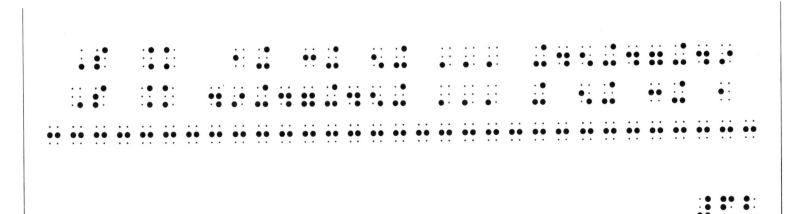

§171. Spatial Arrangements Having Main Divisions Only: When spatially arranged itemized material has main divisions only and no subdivisions, the item numbers with their associated spatial arrangements will follow one another sequentially across the page. Each item number which is to begin a new line must start in cell 1. The identifiers which follow across the line must begin to the right of the preceding spatial arrangements. One blank line must be left after the longest spatial arrangement before beginning the next spatial arrangement.

§172. Spatial Arrangements and Identifiers:

a. When spatial arrangements are placed side by side across a page without identifiers, at least one blank space must be left between the end of one separation line and the beginning of the next.

(1)   28   149   3,149
       +14   + 58   + 548

b. When spatial arrangements are identified by number or letter, no symbol of one spatial arrangement or its identifier may be less than three cells distant from any symbol on any line of a neighboring arrangement or its identifier, except at the ends of separation lines.

(1)

```
          Give the answers to these        4
        addition problems.

     1.     234        4.     2579
           +179             + 628
           ----             -----

     2.      49        5.    $ 17.45
             52             + 9.80
             82             -------
             97
             --

     3.      16
             17
             18
             19
             20
             --
                                       10
```

305

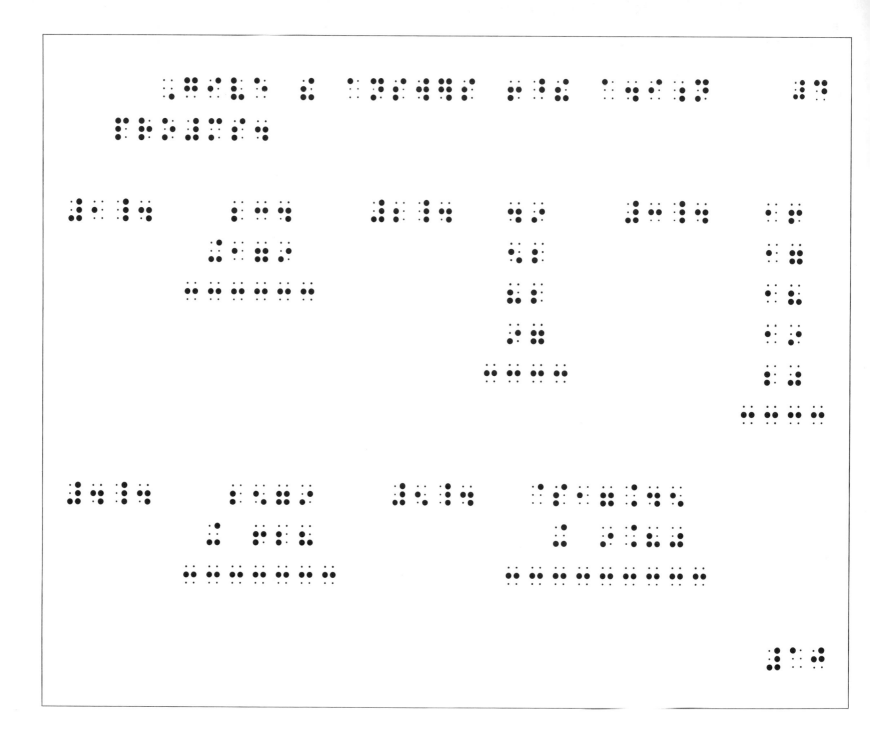

HOMEWORK

Prepare the following homework for submission to your teacher. Proofread carefully.

EXERCISE 15

1.	736	2.	9104	3.	$43.86	4.	$ .46
	850		6783		9.20		3.14
	792		8860		+ 4.00		+5.18
	+998		+ 569				

5.
```
   130
 −112
```

6.
```
  867
 − 46
```

7.
```
  12,134
 − 8,359
```

8.
```
  $602.09
 − 537.40
```

9.
```
  $156.24
 −  95.07
```

10.
```
  17x+2y+ 9z
 − 6x−5y+18z
```

11.
```
 4?1
 25?
 ?84
 900
```

12.
```
  ?01?
 −2?64
  62?6
```

13.
```
 3 ft. 12 in.
 4 ft.  7 in.
 +3 ft.  6 in.
```

14.
```
  1 lb 12 oz
 +2 lb  8 oz
  3 lb 20 oz = 4 lb 4 oz
```

15.
```
 14 hr. 12 min.
 − 2 hr. 11 min.
```

16.
```
 9 yr 1 mo = 8 yr 13 mo
 −2 yr 4 mo = 2 yr  4 mo
            6 yr  9 mo
```

17.
$$\frac{1}{5}$$
$$+\frac{3}{5}$$

18.
$$\frac{11}{12}$$
$$+\frac{5}{12}$$

19.
$$\frac{3}{10}$$
$$+\frac{1}{2}$$

20.
$$\frac{1}{2}\text{ oz.}$$
$$-\frac{3}{8}\text{ oz.}$$

21.
```
  7/8 in
 −5/8 in
```

22.
$$6\frac{5}{6}$$
$$+4\frac{5}{6}$$

23.
$$10\frac{3}{16}$$
$$-3\frac{1}{2}$$

24.
$$10\frac{2}{3}$$
$$-\frac{7}{8}$$

25.
$$16$$
$$-\frac{1}{2}$$
$$15\frac{?}{2}$$

26.
```
   7
 − 5/8
  6  ?/8
```

27.
$$9\text{ min }4\frac{1}{2}\text{ sec}$$
$$-2\text{ min }7\quad\text{ sec}$$

28.
```
 +5c²−4cd+3d²
 −4c²+3cd
 − c²     −2d²
    − cd+ d²
```

29.
```
  11
 760
 333
 +989
 2082
```

30.
```
  453
 ×?
  906
```

31.
```
 $8.56
 ×670
```

32.
```
 $6.50
 ×.07
```

33.
```
  74 .12
 × 8.3
  22236
  59296
  615.196
```

34.
```
   486
 × 34
  1944
  14580
  16,524
```

35.
$$1\frac{1}{3}$$
$$\times\frac{9}{10}$$

36.
$$\frac{1}{2}$$
$$\times\frac{5}{3}$$

37.
$$4\frac{1}{4}$$
$$\times 7$$
$$1\frac{3}{4}$$
$$28$$
$$29\frac{3}{4}$$

38.
```
 2x²−3x+1
    3x−1
 6x³− 9x²+3x
   − 2x²+3x−1
 6x³−11x²+6x−1
```

39.
```
  604_seven
 ×36_seven
  5133_seven
  2415_seven
  32313_seven
```

Complete the work, if necessary, and check the answers.

40.
$$
\begin{array}{r}
631 \; r3 \\
6\overline{)3\,?\,?9}
\end{array}
$$

41.
$$
\begin{array}{r}
5\,?4 \quad r1 \\
8\overline{)4033}
\end{array}
$$

42.
$$
\begin{array}{r}
41 \\
4\overline{)164} \\
16 \\
\hline
4 \\
4 \\
\hline
\end{array}
$$

43.
$$
\begin{array}{r}
.47 \\
15\overline{)7.09} \\
60 \\
\hline
109 \\
105 \\
\hline
4 \\
\end{array}
$$

44.
$$
\begin{array}{r}
30.4 \\
.04_\wedge\overline{)1.21_\wedge6} \\
12 \\
\hline
1\;6 \\
1\;6 \\
\hline
\end{array}
$$

45. $3\overline{)5 \text{ gal. } 1 \text{ qt.}}$

46. $19\overline{)437}(23$

47.
$$
\begin{array}{r}
x^2+3x-5 \\
4x-3\overline{)4x^3+\;9x^2+29x+17} \\
4x^3+\;3x^2 \\
\hline
12x^2-29x+17 \\
12x^2-\;9x \\
\hline
-20x+17 \\
-20x+15 \\
\hline
+\;2 \\
\end{array}
$$

48.
$$
\begin{array}{r}
\$\;.21 \\
15\overline{)\$3.25} \\
3\;0 \\
\hline
25 \\
15 \\
\hline
10 \\
\end{array}
$$

49.
$$
\begin{array}{r}
5\;5\;9 \\
5\overline{)2\;7^{\,2}9^{\,4}5}
\end{array}
$$

Divide.

50. $36\overline{)178}$

51. $45\overline{)9238}$

52. $44\overline{)42271}$

53. $15\overline{)14415}$

54.
$$
\begin{array}{r}
5.\;7\;\;4 \\
\sqrt{33.00\;00} \\
25 \\
\end{array}
$$
$$
\begin{array}{r|l}
107 & 8\;00 \\
\times 7 & 7\;49 \\
\hline
1144 & 51\;00 \\
\times 4 & 45\;76 \\
\hline
& 5\;24 \\
\end{array}
$$

55.
$$
\begin{array}{r|rrrrr}
-3 & 2 & 0 & -\;9 & 17 & 3 \\
& & -6 & 18 & -27 & 30 \\
\hline
& 2 & -6 & 9 & -10 & 33 \\
\end{array}
$$

56.
$$
\begin{array}{r|rrrr|r}
5 & -2 & -3 & 1 & 2 \\
& 10 & 16 & 26 & \\
\hline
5 & 8 & 13 & 27 \\
\end{array}
$$

57. Name the sums and missing addends.

$$
\begin{array}{ccccccc}
5 & 3 & 2 & 2 & 9 & 10 & 6 \\
+5 & +5 & +6 & +2 & -4 & -\;2 & +4 \\
\hline
\end{array}
$$

SPATIAL ARRANGEMENTS (CONTINUED)

Cancellation Indicators

Opening ⠨

Closing ⠶

§173. **Cancellation and Spatial Arrangements:** A spatial arrangement must be used whenever numbers and letters are canceled in print by any type of stroke through them. The opening and closing cancellation indicators must enclose the material being canceled.

§174. **Cancellation in Subtraction:** When cancellation is shown in subtraction, the material should be aligned for computation, and spaces should be left, where necessary, to achieve this. An identifying numeral or letter should be placed on the line with the minuend.

(1) A.
$$\begin{array}{r} \overset{7}{\not{8}}\,\overset{12}{\not{2}}\,\overset{4}{\not{5}}\,\overset{16}{\not{6}} \\ -2\;3\;4\;7 \\ \hline 5\;9\;0\;9 \end{array}$$

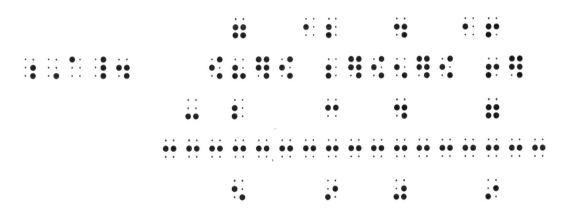

(2)
$$\begin{array}{r} \overset{7}{\not{8}}\,\overset{\overset{11}{\not{1}}}{\not{2}}\,\overset{13}{\not{3}} \\ -2\;5\;4 \\ \hline 5\;6\;9 \end{array}$$

(3)
$$9\frac{1}{2} = 9\frac{\cancel{4}^{\,8\frac{12}{8}}}{8}$$
$$-4\frac{7}{8} = 4\frac{7}{8}$$
$$\overline{ = 4\frac{5}{8}}$$

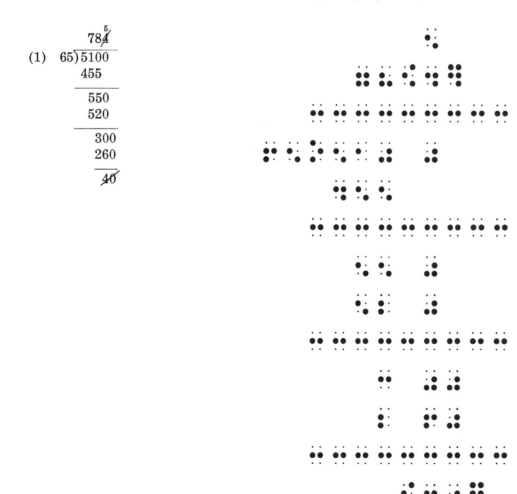

§175. **Cancellation in Long Division:** If cancellation is shown in long division, the canceled material must be enclosed in cancellation indicators, and blank cells must be left, where necessary, for proper alignment.

(1)
$$\begin{array}{r} 78\cancel{4}^{\,5} \\ 65\overline{)5100} \\ 455 \\ \hline 550 \\ 520 \\ \hline 300 \\ 260 \\ \hline \cancel{40} \end{array}$$

§176. Cancellation With Fractions: Where cancellation is shown within fractions, a spatial arrangement must be used. In a spatial fraction arrangement, the fraction line (dots 2-5) should be as long as the longest line of braille above or below it. The opening and closing fraction indicators should be placed at the ends of the fraction line. Items canceled individually in print should be enclosed in separate pairs of cancellation indicators. Since fractions do not contain material aligned for computation, the numeric indicator and English letter indicator must be used, where necessary. Fractions without canceled items should not be shown spatially. An identifying numeral or letter, if present, is placed on the line with the fraction line.

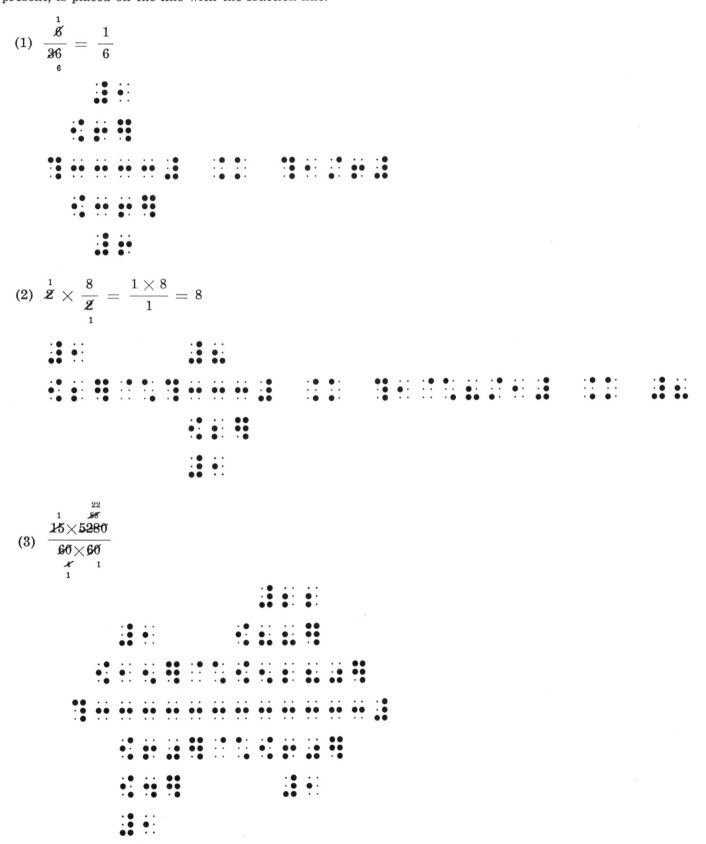

(4) d. $\dfrac{\cancel{x}\cancel{s}\cancel{v}}{\cancel{r}\cancel{s}\cancel{v}\text{v}}$

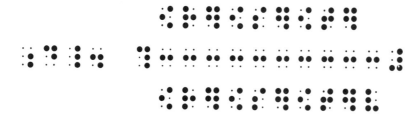

(5) $\dfrac{(rst)}{(rst)\,\text{v}}$

(6) $\dfrac{\overset{a}{\cancel{x}^{\ell}}}{\underset{1}{\cancel{a}}} = a$

§177. Simple Fractions Arranged Spatially for Illustration: It is often helpful to use a spatial arrangement if the parts of a simple fraction are explained or identified. The numeric and English letter indicator must be used, where necessary, within the arrangement.

(1) $\dfrac{2\ \text{numerator}}{3\ \text{denominator}}$

(2) $\dfrac{12}{4}$ number of cookies
number of children

⠰⠆ ⠒⠂ ⠲ ⠒⠒ ⠶⠂ ⠒⠒ ⠶ ⠶⠶ ⠶⠶ ⠶⠶ ⠒⠶ ⠒⠂ ⠶⠂ ⠒⠂ ⠒⠶ ⠶⠂

⠶⠶ ⠶⠶ ⠶⠶ ⠶⠶ ⠰⠆

⠰⠆ ⠶⠶ ⠶⠶ ⠶⠂ ⠒⠒ ⠒⠂ ⠶ ⠶⠶ ⠶⠶ ⠒⠶ ⠒⠂

§178. **Hypercomplex Fractions:**

Hypercomplex Fraction Indicators

    Opening   ⠂ ⠂ ⠶⠶

    Closing   ⠂ ⠂ ⠶⠆

    Horizontal Hypercomplex Fraction Line   ⠂ ⠂ ⠂⠂

a. A hypercomplex fraction is one whose numerator or denominator, or both, contain at least one complex fraction. A fraction is not a hypercomplex fraction if the only complex fractions it contains are at the superscript or subscript level.

(1) $\dfrac{1}{\dfrac{\frac{a}{b}}{2^{\frac{c}{d}}}}$

(this is not a hypercomplex fraction)

(2) $\dfrac{\dfrac{\frac{1}{2}}{\frac{3}{4}}}{5}$

(this is a hypercomplex fraction)

b. Hypercomplex fraction indicators must be used with hypercomplex fractions. Although it is permissible to use an entirely spatial arrangement or an entirely linear arrangement, it is preferable to use a linear arrangement within a spatial arrangement.

(1) $\dfrac{1}{\dfrac{\dfrac{mn}{m+n}(\overline{x}_1-\overline{x}_2)^2}{\Sigma(x_{1i}-\overline{x}_1)^2+\Sigma(x_{2j}-\overline{x}_2)^2}}$

(preferred method)

(2)
$$\cfrac{1}{\cfrac{\dfrac{mn}{m+n}\,(\bar{x}_1-\bar{x}_2)^2}{\Sigma(x_{1i}-\bar{x}_1)^2+\Sigma(x_{2j}-\bar{x}_2)^2}}$$

(complete linear arrangement)

(3)
$$\cfrac{1}{\cfrac{\dfrac{mn}{m+n}\,(\bar{x}_1-\bar{x}_2)^2}{(x_{1i}-\bar{x}_1)}}$$

(complete spatial arrangement)

Note: Hypercomplex fractions of higher order may be transcribed in the manner described above. Dot 6 should be added the appropriate number of times before the fraction indicators and the matching fraction lines.

§179. Continued Fractions: A continued fraction is one in which each denominator is the sum of a whole number and a fraction. Such a fraction must be transcribed entirely in a spatial arrangement. Each fraction line should be proportionately the same length shown in print. No fraction indicators may be used within a continued fraction.

(1) $n = 1 - \cfrac{7}{3+\cfrac{3}{2+\cfrac{2}{2-\cfrac{2}{3}}}}$

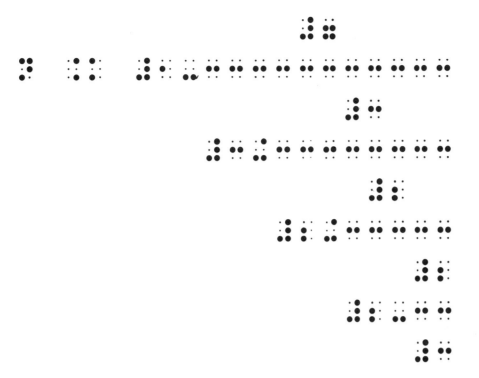

§180. **Enlarged Signs of Grouping:** Enlarged signs of grouping are used with determinants and matrices as well as with unified systems of equations.

Enlarged Parentheses

    Left   (

    Right   )

Enlarged Brackets

    Left   [

    Right   ]

Enlarged Braces

    Left   {

    Right   }

Enlarged Vertical Bar

    Single |

    Double ||

Enlarged Angle Brackets

    Left $\langle$ ⠈⠨⠪

    Right $\rangle$ ⠈⠨⠕

Enlarged Barred Brackets

    Left   ⟦   ⠈⠨⠷

    Right   ⟧   ⠈⠨⠾

Enlarged Barred Braces

    Left   ⦃   ⠈⠨⠣

    Right   ⦄   ⠈⠨⠜

Enlarged Half Brackets

    Upper Left   ⌈ or ⌈   ⠠⠈⠷

    Upper Right   ⌉ or ⌉   ⠈⠠⠾

    Lower Left   ⌊ or ⌊   ⠘⠈⠷

    Lower Right   ⌋ or ⌋   ⠈⠘⠾

§181. Unified Systems of Equations:

    a. When mathematical equations are arranged on two or more lines and joined by a sign of grouping, the arrangement is called a *unified system of equations*. Such an arrangement is considered to be spatial, and blank lines must be left above and below it. In braille, enlarged signs of grouping are used on each line of the unified system of equations and must be vertically aligned. The opening and the closing enlarged grouping symbol must be placed in the cells next to the items which extend furthest left and furthest right. If only the opening or closing sign of grouping is shown in print, only that sign should be shown in braille. Any material, such as punctuation, signs of comparison, signs of operation, or identifiers, should be shown on the top line in braille, even though it is centered in print.

(1)   A. $\begin{cases} x = y \\ 5x - y = 4 \end{cases}$

(2) $\begin{cases} \dfrac{1}{2}x + y = 7 \\ 3x - 2y = 9 \end{cases}$.

(3) $\begin{cases} 0.5(2x+y) = -3 \\ 5y+x = 6 \end{cases}$

(4) $\left.\begin{cases} \dfrac{x}{3} - \dfrac{y}{2} = 2 \\ 5x+3y = 51 \end{cases}\right\} = (?,\ ?)$

b. In a unified system of equations, the numeric indicator must be used or must not be used according to the rules of the code.

(1) $\begin{cases} x+2y = 6 \\ 2x - y = 7 \end{cases}$

(2) $\begin{cases} x+0y = 4 \\ 0x+y = 1 \end{cases}$

c. Ununified Systems of Equations: When mathematical equations are arranged on two or more lines and are *not* joined by any sign of grouping, the arrangement is not considered to be spatial, and no blank lines need be left above or below it.

(1) 13. Solve:

$$2x+3y = 2$$
$$8x - 4z = 3$$
$$3y - 8z = -1$$

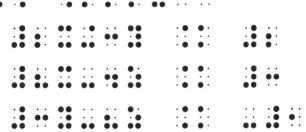

317

(2) 22. Solve:

$$2x - 5y + 6z = 11$$
$$3x - 2y + 3z = 9$$
$$2x + 4y - 9z = -3$$

§182. Enlarged Transcriber's Grouping Signs:

Left

Right

When an explanation or comment refers to more than one ink-print line and no print grouping symbol links these lines, the implied grouping is shown by a transcriber's enlarged grouping sign. The left- or right-enlarged transcriber's grouping sign must be used according to the position of the explanation in print. There must be a blank space between the grouping symbol and the explanation. All runovers of the explanation must be indented two cells from the beginning of the first line of the explanation.

(1) $3x - y = 7$

Transform the given sentence
into an equivalent sentence.

$3x - 7 = y$

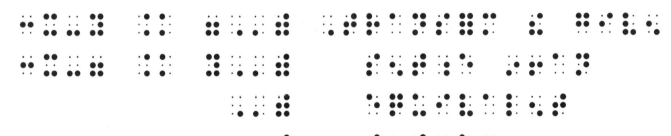

(2) $y > 2$

$x \; \varepsilon \; \Re$ and

$y \; \varepsilon \; \Re$

                    $x > 3$

§183. Determinants and Matrices:

a. Determinants and matrices are spatial arrangements. Thus, a line must be skipped above and below each determinant or matrix. At least one enlarged sign of grouping must appear on each line of the arrangement.

b. Each entry must be moved as far left as possible in its column, and one column of blank cells must be left between the columns of the arrangement.

c. Each opening sign of grouping must be in direct contact with an entry in the determinant or matrix. In the same way, at least one closing sign of grouping must appear in direct contact with an entry in the determinant or matrix.

d. The numeric indicator must be used with numeric entries in a determinant or matrix, even when such entries are in direct contact with an opening grouping sign.

(1)
$$\begin{vmatrix} 1 & 2 \\ 2 & -1 \end{vmatrix}$$

(2)
$$\begin{pmatrix} 1 & -\dfrac{4}{3} & \dfrac{5}{3} \\ 2 & 5 & 12 \end{pmatrix}$$

e. The English letter indicator must not be used with any letter or combination of letters in a determinant or matrix.

(1)
$$\begin{pmatrix} a & b & c \\ 0 & 0 & 0 \end{pmatrix}$$

(2)
$$\begin{vmatrix} ab & cd \\ ac & ce \end{vmatrix}$$

f. Material outside the determinant or matrix, such as identifiers, punctuation, signs of operation, or signs of comparison, should be placed on the top line of the arrangement, even though it is centered in print.

(1)

$$1. \quad \begin{vmatrix} 1 & -1 & 1 \\ 0 & 3 & 0 \\ 0 & 0 & 0 \end{vmatrix} \cdot \begin{vmatrix} x \\ y \\ z \end{vmatrix} = \begin{vmatrix} 4 \\ -5 \\ 0 \end{vmatrix} \cdot$$

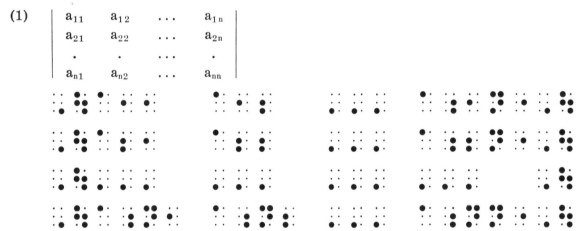

g. When dots are shown in a determinant or matrix to indicate omission of one or more rows, a series of dots 3 is used in braille.

i. If at least one dot appears in each column and no dots appear between columns, an ellipsis (...) is placed as far left as possible in each column.

(1)

$$\begin{vmatrix} a_{11} & a_{12} & \cdots & a_{1n} \\ a_{21} & a_{22} & \cdots & a_{2n} \\ \cdot & \cdot & \cdots & \cdot \\ a_{n1} & a_{n2} & \cdots & a_{nn} \end{vmatrix}$$

ii. When dots appear completely across a row and occupy space between the columns as well as in the columns, a sequence of dots 3 must be used, beginning in the first cell of the first column and extending to the end of the longest entry in the last column.

(1)

$$\begin{bmatrix} a_{11} & a_{12} & \cdots & a_{1n} \\ a_{21} & a_{22} & \cdots & a_{2n} \\ \cdot & \cdot & \cdot & \cdot & \cdot & \cdot & \cdot \\ a_{n1} & a_{n2} & \cdots & a_{nn} \end{bmatrix}$$

iii. If some of the columns contain no dots, a line of dots 3 must be used as in **ii** above.

$$(1) \quad \begin{vmatrix} a_{11} & a_{12} & \dots & a_{1n} \\ a_{21} & a_{22} & \dots & a_{2n} \\ \cdot & & & \cdot \\ \cdot & & & \cdot \\ \cdot & & & \cdot \\ a_{m1} & a_{m2} & \dots & a_{mn} \end{vmatrix}$$

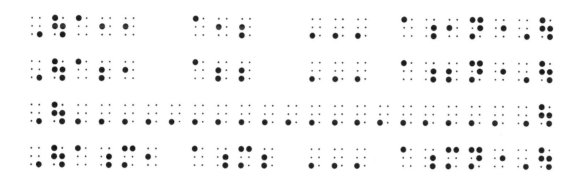

h. Sometimes space-saving techniques must be adopted to confine the arrangement to one braille page.

i. Entries may be run over to new lines. Each runover should be indented two cells from the first cell of the first line of the entry. No lines should be skipped between entries. If necessary, rules for preference in runovers can be ignored. No baseline indicator should be used before a closing grouping symbol unless it is the end of the item and touches the grouping symbol. This is the preferred space-saving technique.

$$(1) \quad \begin{pmatrix} a_{11}b_{11}+a_{12}b_{21} & a_{11}b_{12}+a_{12}b_{22} \\ a_{21}b_{11}+a_{22}b_{21} & b_{21}b_{12}+a_{22}b_{22} \end{pmatrix}$$

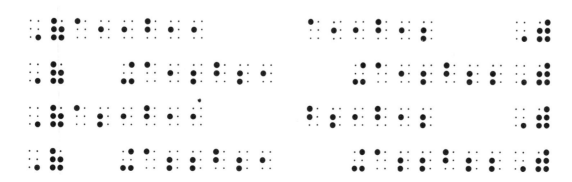

ii. Entries may be run over to new lines with no indentations. In this case, a line should be skipped between each row in the arrangement. Preference rules for runovers need not be observed if space would be saved.

$$(1) \quad \begin{bmatrix} -2te^t + e^{2t} & (3t+2)e^t - 2e^{2t} & -(t+1)e^t + e^{2t} \\ -2(t+1)e^t + 2e^{2t} & (3t+5)e^t - 4e^{2t} & -(t+2)e^t + 2e^{2t} \\ -2(t+2)e^t + 4e^{2t} & (3t+8)e^t - 8e^{2t} & -(t+4)e^t + 4e^{2t} \end{bmatrix}$$

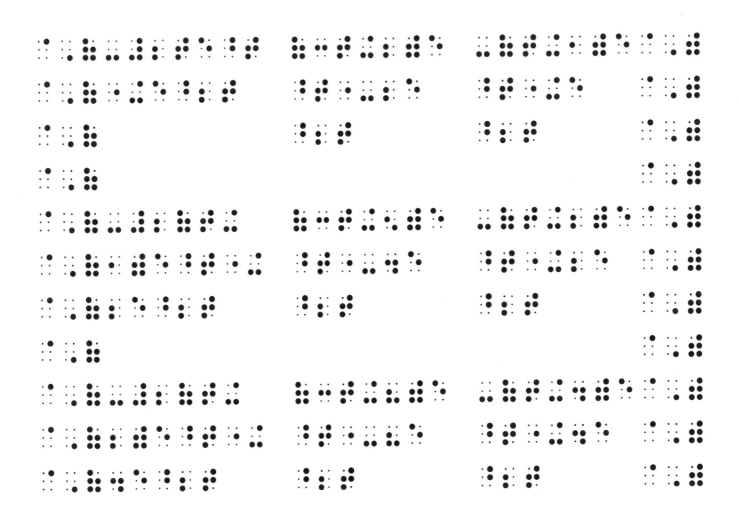

iii. Grouping symbols may be drawn in place of the braille equivalents.

iv. Fractions may be shown spatially. In this case, lines should be skipped above and below the rows containing the fraction.

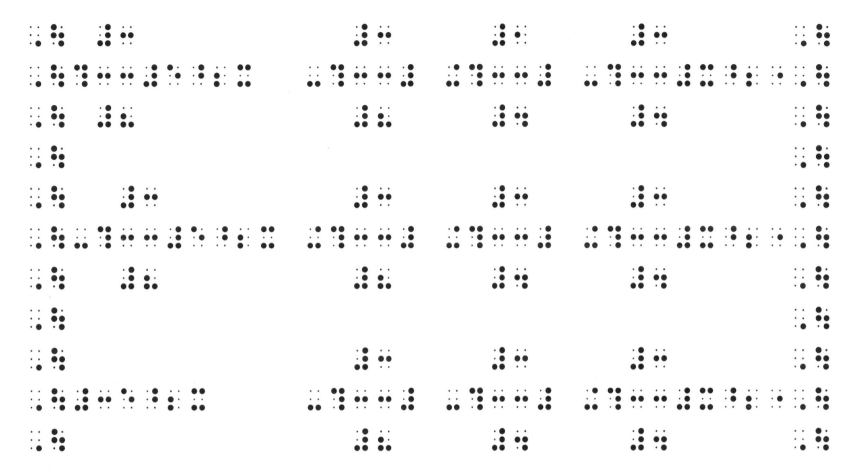

$$(1) \quad \left| \begin{array}{cccc} \dfrac{3}{8}e^{2x} & -\dfrac{3}{8} & +\dfrac{1}{4} & -\dfrac{3}{4}x^2 \\[2mm] -\dfrac{3}{8}e^{2x} & +\dfrac{3}{8} & {'}+\dfrac{3}{4} & +\dfrac{3}{4}x^2 \\[2mm] 3\ e^{2x} & -\dfrac{3}{8} & -\dfrac{3}{4} & +\dfrac{3}{4}x^2 \end{array} \right|$$

v. When no other method saves the required space, the technique of keying, discussed in §186, should be used.

TABLES

§184. **Tables:** In transcribing tables, the rules provided in the *Code of Braille Textbook Formats and Techniques* should be followed.

a. Letters in Tables: When letters appear in tables, whether as entries or headings, the English letter indicator must be used or must not be used as though the letters were not part of the table.

b. Numbers in Table Headings: When numerals appear in table headings, the rules for the use and nonuse of the numeric indicator must be followed.

c. Numbers in Table Entries: The numeric indicator must not be used when the entries in a table consist entirely of numerals, including interior commas and decimal points. If the entries in a table contain words, letters, signs of operation, signs of comparison, or any other mathematical signs, the numeric indicator must be used throughout the table.

(1)

e	e²	S
1	1	6
2	4	24
3	9	54
4	16	96

(2)

R	T	D
30	t+2	30(t+2)
45	t	45t

LABELS FOR FIGURES AND DIAGRAMS

§185. **Labels for Figures and Diagrams:** In labeling diagrams, the numeric indicator must be used with numerals. When a single English letter in regular type is used as a label in a diagram, the English letter indicator is required if the letter is in lower case, but omitted if the letter is capitalized.

324

(1)

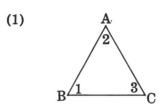

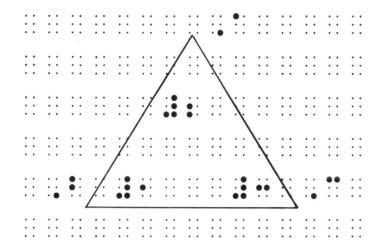

(2)

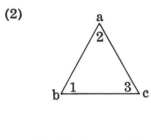

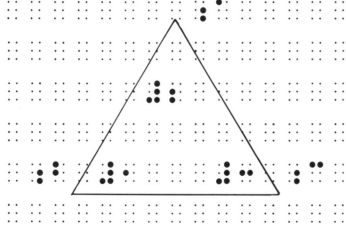

KEYING

§186. **Keying**: A numeric or alphabetic key may be substituted where there is not enough space for determinants, matrices, column headings, table entries, figure labels, etc.

    a. A numeric key should consist of consecutive numerals, beginning with number one, which should be written in the *upper* part of the cell and preceded by the numeric indicator but not punctuated. Identical items should be assigned the same key number.

    b. An alphabetic key should consist of two lower-case English letters suggestive of the item they represent, if possible. Identical items should be assigned the same key letters. The alphabetic key must not be used if the author uses two lower-case letters for entries in the table or for labels in the figure.

c. A key must be enclosed in transcriber's grouping symbols. It should begin in cell 3 with runovers at the margin. Key entries may begin at the margin with runovers in cell 3. Short entries may appear in columns. The closing transcriber's grouping symbol must follow the final entry. A blank line must precede and follow the key.

(1)

1	2	3	4	5	6	7
s	p	~ s	~ p	3→4	5∧1	6→2
T	T	F	F	T	T	T
F	T	T	F	F	F	T
T	F	F	T	T	T	F
F	F	T	T	T	F	T

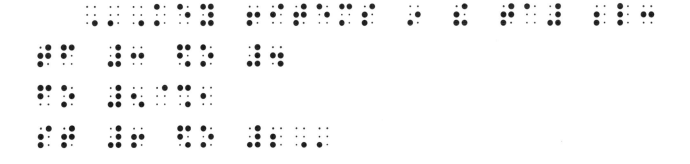

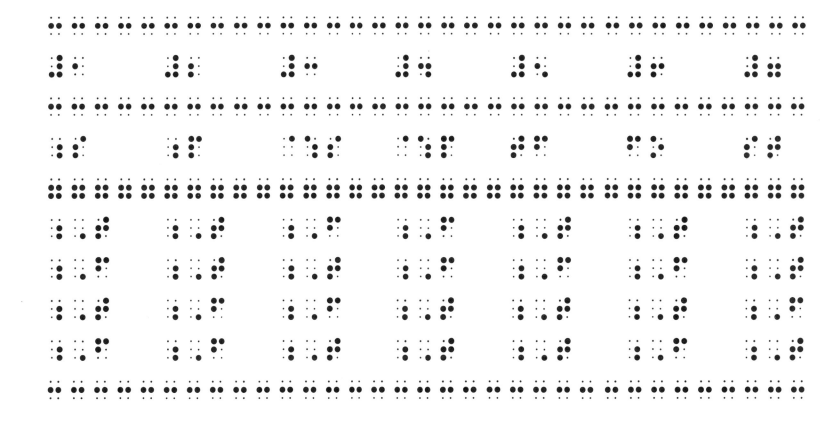

(2)

Eigenvalue	Eigenvectors	dim E (λ)
1, 1	$(a, b) \neq (0, 0)$	2
1, 1	$t(1, 0), t \neq 0$	1
1, 1	$t(0, 1), t \neq 0$	1
2	$t(1, 1)\ t \neq 0$	1
0	$t(1, -1), t \neq 0$	1

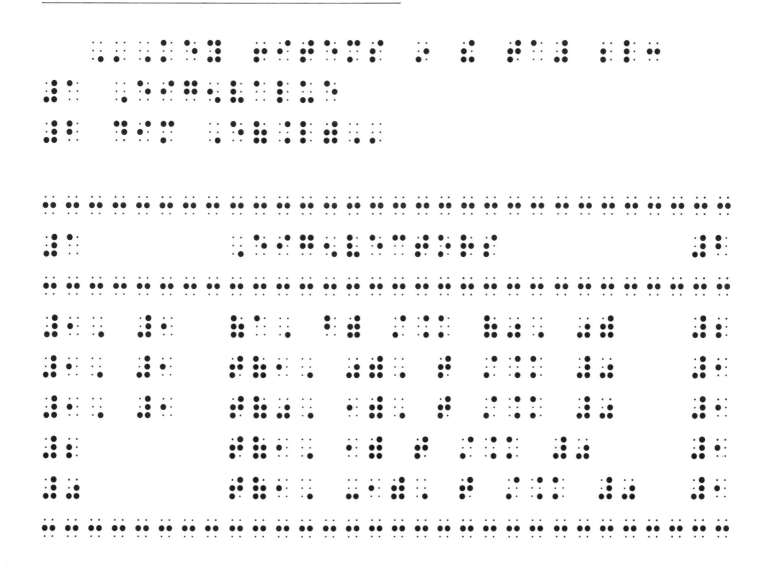

327

(3)

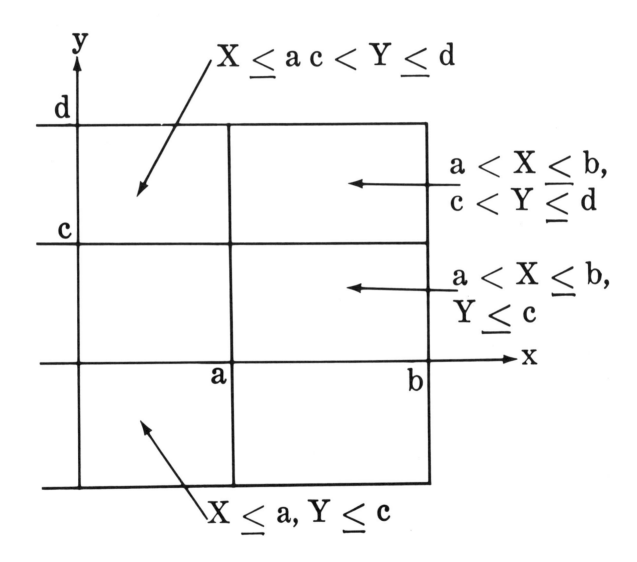

$X \leq a$ $c < Y \leq d$

$a < X \leq b,$
$c < Y \leq d$

$a < X \leq b,$
$Y \leq c$

$X \leq a, Y \leq c$

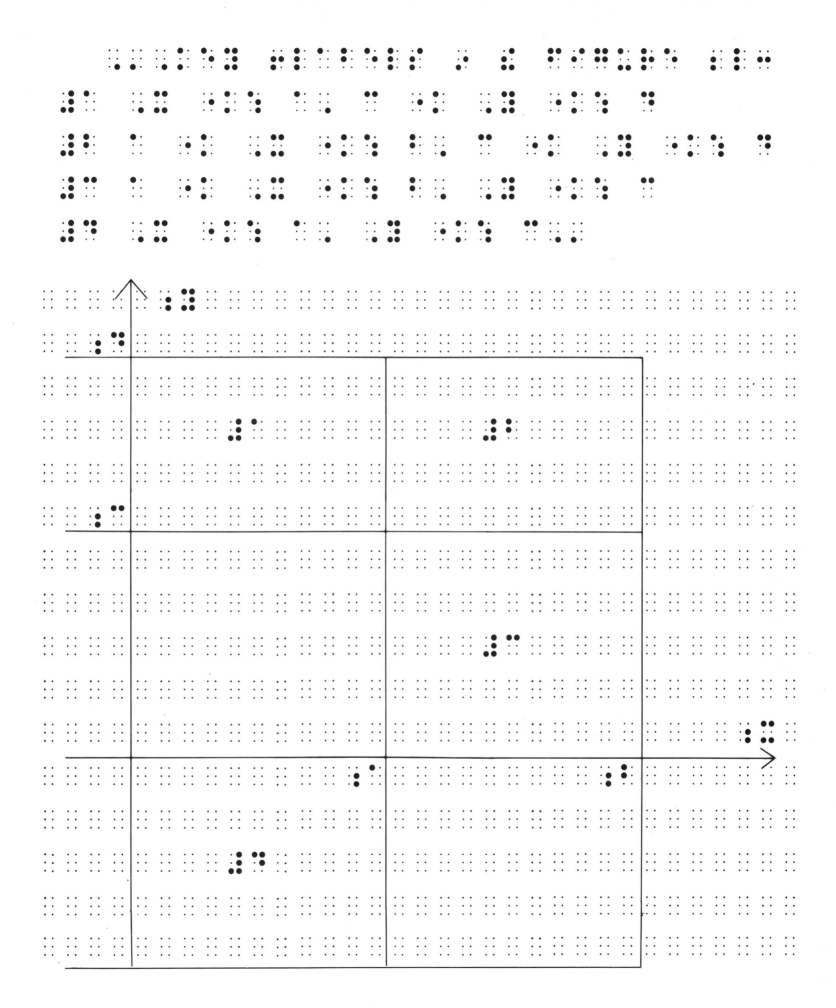

§187. Spatial Arrangements With Main Divisions and Subdivisions: When spatial arrangements contain both main divisions and subdivisions, the first main division should begin at the margin, and the first subdivision should follow on the same braille line if there is no material between the main division number and the first subdivision number. As many subdivisions as possible should be placed on one line. If additional subdivisions are left, they should be transcribed beginning in cell 3, after leaving a blank line below the longest arrangement above.

(1)

Solve   2

1. a.   27.5   b. a^2+b^2 c. $\dfrac{3}{4}$
       ×37.2   ×a+b

$\times\dfrac{1}{2}$

2. Perform the operations.

a.   97   b. .94   c.   37,120
   308   .58   −28,934
   536   .06
  2748   .75
    59

Prepare the following exercise for submission to your teacher. Proofread carefully.

EXERCISE 16

1. Check.

   a. $\overset{2}{\cancel{3}}\ \overset{11}{\cancel{1}}$
   $\underline{-\quad 5}$
   $\quad 2\ \ 6$

   b. $\overset{1}{\cancel{2}}\ \overset{12}{\cancel{2}}$
   $\underline{-\quad 8}$
   $\quad 1\ \ 4$

   c. $\overset{3}{\cancel{4}}\ \overset{14}{\cancel{4}}$
   $\underline{-\quad 6}$
   $\quad 3\ \ 8$

2.
$$3\tfrac{1}{5}$$
$$25\overline{)80}$$
$$\underline{75}$$
$$\ \ 5$$

3. $\left(2 + \dfrac{a}{b}\right) \div \left(4 - \dfrac{a^2}{b^2}\right) = \dfrac{2b+a}{b} \div \dfrac{4b^2-a^2}{b^2} = \dfrac{\overset{1}{\cancel{(2b+a)}}}{\cancel{b}} \times \dfrac{\overset{b}{\cancel{b^2}}}{\cancel{(2b+a)}\cdot(2b-a)} = \dfrac{b}{2b-a}$

4. $\dfrac{5x+15}{x^2-9} \div \dfrac{10x^2+10x}{4x-12}$

   $= \dfrac{5x+15}{x^2-9} \times \dfrac{4x-12}{10x^2+10x}$

   $= \dfrac{\overset{1}{\cancel{5}}\overset{1}{(x+3)}}{\underset{1}{(x+3)}\ \underset{1}{(x-3)}} \cdot \dfrac{\overset{2}{\cancel{4}}\overset{1}{(x-3)}}{\underset{1}{\cancel{10}x(x+1)}}$

   $= \dfrac{2}{x(x+1)}$

5. Suppose your mother made a little cake for you and your friends. Into how many equal parts would you divide it if there were four of you to share the cake? What would each part be called?

   $\dfrac{1}{4}$ the number of parts each child receives
   the total number of parts

6. $\dfrac{\dfrac{\dfrac{r^2-4s^2}{s^2}}{\dfrac{r+2s}{s}}}{\dfrac{\dfrac{4r-2s^2}{3s}}{\dfrac{2s^2-3r}{4r}}}$

7. Check for correctness.

$$\sqrt{3} = 1 + \cfrac{1}{3 + \cfrac{1}{3 + \cfrac{1}{3 + \ldots}}}$$

8. Solve and check.

$$\begin{cases} 3c = 4d + 17 \\ 2c + 3d = 0 \end{cases}$$

9. The system

$$\begin{pmatrix} x + 2y = 8 \\ 2x - 3y = 2 \end{pmatrix}$$

has the solution set $\{(4, 2)\}$.

10.
$$\begin{pmatrix} x + y - 5 = 0 \\ 4x - y - 10 = 0 \end{pmatrix}$$

11. Solve.

$$x + y + 3 = 0$$
$$x - y + 5 = 0$$

12. Solve and check.

$$x - 2y + 12 = 0$$
$$4x + y + 3 = 0$$

13. That $(0, 0)$ is the identity element for vector addition is shown below.

$$(v_1, v_2) + (0, 0) = (v_1 + 0, v_2 + 0) = (v_1, v_2)$$
$$(0, 0) + (v_1 + v_2) = (0 + v_1, 0 + v_2) = (v_1, v_2) \quad \text{For all real numbers } v_1 \text{ and } v_2.$$

14. If $A = \begin{bmatrix} x & 3 \\ 2 & y \end{bmatrix}$ and $B = \begin{bmatrix} 4 & 2 \\ 3 & 1 \end{bmatrix}$, find the values of x and y so that $A^T = B$.

15. $\begin{bmatrix} u_1 & v_1 \\ u_2 & v_2 \end{bmatrix} + \begin{bmatrix} 3 & 2 \\ -7 & 5 \end{bmatrix}$

16.
$$\begin{vmatrix} y_1 \\ y_2 \\ y_3 \\ . \\ y_r \end{vmatrix} = \begin{vmatrix} b_{11} & b_{12} & \ldots & b_{1n} \\ b_{21} & b_{22} & \ldots & b_{2n} \\ b_{31} & b_{32} & \ldots & b_{3n} \\ . & . & . & . \\ b_{r1} & b_{r2} & \ldots & b_{rn} \end{vmatrix} \begin{vmatrix} x_1 \\ x_2 \\ x_3 \\ . \\ x_n \end{vmatrix}$$

17. $dT = \begin{bmatrix} \dfrac{\partial y_1}{\partial x_1} & \dfrac{\partial y_1}{\partial x_2} & \ldots & \dfrac{\partial y_1}{\partial x_n} \\ . & . & . & . \\ \dfrac{\partial y_m}{\partial x_1} & \dfrac{\partial y_m}{\partial x_2} & \ldots & \dfrac{\partial y_m}{\partial x_n} \end{bmatrix}$

18. The Jacobian determinant of the mapping is

$$J(\rho, \theta, \phi) = \begin{vmatrix} \cos\theta \sin\phi & \sin\theta \sin\phi & \cos\phi \\ -\rho\sin\theta\sin\phi & \rho\cos\theta\sin\phi & 0 \\ \rho\cos\theta\cos\phi & \rho\sin\theta\cos\phi & -\rho\sin\phi \end{vmatrix} = -\rho^2 \sin\phi.$$

19. Can you make a vertical bar graph using the material given in this table?

City	Population	Telephones
New York	7,781,984	4,411,982
Chicago	3,550,404	1,894,012
Los Angeles	2,479,015	1,051,396
Philadelphia	2,002,512	1,083,041

20. Write the linear equations expressing the relations between x and y shown in the following tables:

a.

x	y
1	1
2	4
3	7
5	13

b.

x	y
-4	-1
-3	3
-1	11

c.

x	y
-8	-6
-12	-8
-14	-9

Use the following array to name all the equivalent fractions for: $\dfrac{1}{1}, \dfrac{1}{4}, \dfrac{2}{3}, \dfrac{3}{6}, \dfrac{1}{6}, \dfrac{0}{4}, \dfrac{5}{6}, \dfrac{1}{3}, \dfrac{3}{4}.$

$$\frac{0}{1} \qquad \frac{1}{1}$$

$$\frac{0}{2} \qquad \frac{1}{2} \qquad \frac{2}{2}$$

$$\frac{0}{3} \qquad \frac{1}{3} \qquad \frac{2}{3} \qquad \frac{3}{3}$$

$$\frac{0}{4} \qquad \frac{1}{4} \qquad \frac{2}{4} \qquad \frac{3}{4} \qquad \frac{4}{4}$$

$$\frac{0}{6} \quad \frac{1}{6} \quad \frac{2}{6} \quad \frac{3}{6} \quad \frac{4}{6} \quad \frac{5}{6} \quad \frac{6}{6}$$

$$\frac{0}{12}\ \frac{1}{12}\ \frac{2}{12}\ \frac{3}{12}\ \frac{4}{12}\ \frac{5}{12}\ \frac{6}{12}\ \frac{7}{12}\ \frac{8}{12}\ \frac{9}{12}\ \frac{10}{12}\ \frac{11}{12}\ \frac{12}{12}$$

Calculate the eigenvalues of each of the matrices.

21.(a) $\begin{vmatrix} 1 & 0 & 0 \\ -3 & 1 & 0 \\ 4 & -7 & 1 \end{vmatrix}$
(b) $\begin{vmatrix} 2 & 1 & 3 \\ 1 & 2 & 3 \\ 3 & 3 & 20 \end{vmatrix}$
(c) $\begin{vmatrix} 5 & -6 & -6 \\ -1 & 4 & 2 \\ 3 & -6 & -4 \end{vmatrix}$

22.(a) $\begin{vmatrix} 0 & 0 & 1 & 0 \\ 0 & 0 & 0 & 1 \\ 1 & 0 & 0 & 0 \\ 0 & 1 & 0 & 0 \end{vmatrix}$
(b) $\begin{vmatrix} 1 & 0 & 0 & 0 \\ 0 & 1 & 0 & 0 \\ 0 & 0 & -1 & 0 \\ 0 & 0 & 0 & -1 \end{vmatrix}$

334

338